PRE- & POST-
RETIREMENT
Tips for Librarians

PRE- & POST-
RETIREMENT
Tips for Librarians

EDITED BY CAROL SMALLWOOD

American Library Association | Chicago 2012

Printed in the United States of America

16 15 14 13 12   5 4 3 2 1

Extensive effort has gone into ensuring the reliability of the information in this book; however, the publisher makes no warranty, express or implied, with respect to the material contained herein.

ISBNs: 978-0-8389-1120-4 (paper); 978-0-8389-9369-9 (PDF); 978-0-8389-9370-5 (ePub); 978-0-8389-9371-2 (Mobipocket); 978-0-8389-9372-9 (Kindle). For more information on digital formats, visit the ALA Store at alastore.ala.org and select eEditions.

Library of Congress Cataloging-in-Publication Data
Pre- and post-retirement tips for librarians / edited by Carol Smallwood.
    p. cm.
  Includes bibliographical references and index.
  ISBN 978-0-8389-1120-4 (alk. paper)
  1. Librarians—Retirement—United States. 2. Retirement—United States—Planning. I. Smallwood, Carol, 1939–
  Z682.3.P69 2012
  646.7'9024002092—dc23

2011030071

Book design in Fanwood and Melbourne by Casey Bayer.
Cover illustration © prism68/Shutterstock, Inc.

♾ This paper meets the requirements of ANSI/NISO Z39.48–1992 (Permanence of Paper).

CONTENTS

PART I: BEFORE RETIRING

PART II: FINANCES IN RETIREMENT

FOREWORD

To BE WELL prepared is to be well armed. Financial planning and decisions made in early and mid-career can dramatically affect our opportunities in retirement. *Pre- and Post-Retirement Tips for Librarians* brings those issues into focus. For thousands of boomer librarians like me who are near to or eligible for retirement, the information contained in this volume is critical to the next phase of our life. Although broad in scope, this book contains detailed but easy-to-understand advice about key retirement concerns such as Social Security, developing a spending plan, and maintaining an active lifestyle on a budget.

Many of us have been in the workplace for three or more decades. Making a contribution to our communities and institutions is integral to how we view ourselves. Combined with the characteristics of librarianship—a commitment to advancing lifelong learning, the innovative use of new technologies, and expertise in effectively communicating with people—we are uniquely positioned to navigate the challenges of retirement. How to take advantage of what we have been doing every day is what this publication purports to provide, specifically, examples of our skill sets applied to retirement options that are personally and financially fulfilling.

Retired colleagues have often told me that they are busier than ever. Clearly, good health is fundamental to this positive outlook. But also important to them was the exploration of what they would do as retirees and the management of their time and money. Herein librarians will find guidance to chart their future with examples of post-retirement activities and ways to stretch retirement income.

Retiring from a library job does not mean retiring from librarianship. Recently, the American Library Association established the Retired Members Round Table to offer an avenue for sustained involvement with the profession. I urge each of you to join, share what you have learned over the years with newer librarians, and continue to participate in the ALA online and at conferences. Networking with others refreshes the spirit and keeps the mind nimble.

With planning, retirement can be an enormously creative and gratifying experience. I hope that you will find *Pre- and Post-Retirement Tips for Librarians* a useful tool in plotting a course for your retirement years.

ROBERTA STEVENS
2010–2011 President of the American Library Association

ACKNOWLEDGMENTS

VANDELLA BROWN, contributor, *Writing and Publishing: A Librarian's Handbook* (ALA 2010)

ANIKA FAJARDO, reference librarian, St. Catherine University, St. Paul, Minnesota; author of *The Dish on Food and Farming in Colonial America* (Capstone, 2012)

LISA FRASER, Adult Services Librarian, King County Library System, Bellevue, Washington; *The Frugal Librarian: Thriving in Tough Economic Times* (ALA Editions, 2011)

MICHAEL A. GERMANO, business librarian, California State University, Los Angeles; editorial board member, *The Bottom Line: Managing Library Finances*

KEROL HARROD, writer/coproducer of Library Larry's Big Day, Denton Public Library, Denton, Texas; first-place winner of 2010 TATOA Programming Awards

DR. ROBERT P. HOLLEY, Wayne State University, Detroit, Michigan; author of over one hundred articles

PROFESSOR DAVID V. LOERTSCHER, SLIS, San Jose State University, writer and publisher, and past president of AASL

WILL MANLEY, *American Libraries* columnist

NANCY KALIKOW MAXWELL, author, *Sacred Stacks: The Higher Purpose of Libraries and Librarianship* (ALA Editions, 2006)

ALINE SOULES, Library Faculty, California State University, East Bay

ROBERT G. WEINER, associate humanities librarian, Texas Tech University Libraries; editor, *Graphic Novels and Comics in Libraries and Archives* (McFarland, 2010)

INTRODUCTION

Pre- and Post-Retirement Tips for Librarians was compiled to provide insight from librarians as well as retirement specialists to fill a gap in the literature. It isn't intended as a source for investment advice. Retirement raises many questions as we enter uncharted waters: each librarian's situation is unique and yet similar to colleagues. Our skills give us an edge in planning as well as managing our lives after library employment that deserve to be shared.

I sought chapters on health, relocating, volunteering, going back to work full-time or part-time, financial planning, handling property, oral histories, Social Security, credit, using mediation, psychological adjustment, insurance, and related topics that librarians deal with before and after retiring.

Librarians and retirement planners each contributed 2,500 to 3,500 words; the foreword, which begins "To be well prepared is to be well armed," is by the president of the American Library Association, Roberta Stevens, when she was in office.

The book comprises 24 chapters divided into eight parts that deal with how to prepare for retiring, finances in retirement, ways to explore new roads, whether to continue working after retiring, volunteering, health concerns, financial planning, and where to live in retirement.

I ordered and received many materials about retirement through the U.S. Postal Service, my senators and representatives, and the Internet, and wish to mention just a few here:

- USA.gov, the U.S. government's official web portal as an excellent online source for retirement planning.
- Seniors Care Package, a collection of free brochures for seniors can be ordered (help@sec.gov) from the U.S. Securities and Exchange Commission.
- The *National Institute on Aging Publications Catalog* includes many titles of free materials: their toll-free number is 800-222–2225.
- The Federal Citizen Information Center offers a wide variety of free/inexpensive information on retirement: 800-FED-INFO.

It was a pleasure working with librarians as they contemplated retirement or with those who were already retired and willing to share experiences in what can be a daunting step, no matter your profession. With early retirement and longer life spans, retirement now can last another lifetime of years—years that deserve to be well planned, productive, and as worry free as possible.

My special thanks for the contributors for making this anthology such a relevant new resource for librarians. As Nancy Kalikow Maxwell, author of *Sacred Stacks: The Higher Purpose of Libraries and Librarianship* (ALA Editions), noted: "At last, a retirement guide exclusively for librarians."

CAROL SMALLWOOD
Editor

PART I

BEFORE RETIRING

1

EXPLORING YOUR RETIREMENT OPTIONS

Linda Burkey Wade

STOP SAYING RETIREMENT

If you hate the R-word, you are not alone. There used to be only three phases in a person's life: play, work, and retirement. Retirement meant a time of winding down and taking on a life of leisure golfing or knitting all day. In his book *The Third Act,* Edgar Bronfman (2002) refers to retirement as the third act or new phase. Bronfman does not like to use the word *retirement* and believes it is time to redefine and rename retirement as a new phase for those over 50. Regardless whether retirement is fast approaching, already here, or a decade away for you, it's time to plan for the next phase of your life. Whether you are thinking about continuing to work, taking on a new career, going back to school, spending time as a volunteer, or running for political office, you likely have begun to think about a plan for what to do when you start *your* new phase. This time almost certainly opens the way to discover new adventures you choose to explore or those that present new scenarios in your life. If you are already retired or retirement is a decade away, you are not alone: 78 million baby boomers are approaching the age of retirement and are planning to balance work and leisure and not settle for "boredom and isolation" (Franklin and Frick 2008, 95). The new retirement is an opportunity to choose the balance of activities in your life that offers an active lifestyle that might last thirty to forty years.

STEPS TO YOUR PLAN

You may be thinking, "What do I do now or what am I going to do? How do I get these thoughts organized?" Whether you have to supplement your retirement income or just want something to do, your life is not winding down; it has just begun. Start by asking the following questions:

- How would you like to invest in yourself?
- What are your interests, hobbies, politics, values, financial situation, and relaxing desires?
- Do you volunteer, go back to school, start your own business, continue at the current job, or begin a new career?

Personally, I have asked these questions only to be overwhelmed with numerous ideas to consider, which has led to the need to organize and decide on priorities.

There are seven steps to get a plan ready for the next phase of your life. You may have completed step one already or maybe you are looking for ideas. I have been working through the process that follows; however, each individual may approach these steps in a different order, just as some people read the newspaper from front to back while others begin reading in the middle or the end. The following steps are based on Joan Strewler-Carter's and Stephen T. Carter's (2008) book, *What's Next in Your Life: How to Find Meaning Beyond the Money,* and Sharon O'Brien's article, "10 Tips for Happy Retirement Living."

1. BRAINSTORMING AND DREAMING

First begin by brainstorming about this phase of your life, and here the sky is the limit. Think about your passions, hobbies, education, and interests. List those things you desire to pursue; for example, going back to school to become a doctor, learning flower arranging, running for a state office, starting your own business, volunteering, crocheting, and so on (see figure 1.1). Also include relaxation activities and time spent with those you love. Categorize the list by those items that are pastimes, educational interests, and part-time and full-time jobs. Some items may go in more than one category and can be listed for the amount of time you would like to spend on that option. While starting a business may be a difficult job, you may want to pursue it part-time. Another example would be going back to school to become a medical coder, which might offer the flexibility of working from anywhere you choose.

FIGURE 1.1 POSSIBLE RETIREMENT OPTIONS

Continuing education	Travel
Retraining	Volunteering
New career	Working from home
Getting involved in politics	Starting a business
Library consulting	Continuing with the same employer

Occasionally, you might be able to combine a job and travel, such as becoming a librarian on a cruise ship. Some interests such as learning to make flower arrangements and cake decoration may only consist of a few classes and could become a part-time hobby or a new business. The website www.whatsnextinyourlife.com will help you ask questions to target your personal interests for remaining on the job, learning a new skill, or going into business on your own. Don't get hung up on categorizing the list—it is just to help you think about the possibilities and how much time will be spent working, volunteering, and enjoying a balanced life. If you need help in this assignment, Strewler-Carter and Carter (2008) have a workbook that accompanies their book, *What's Next in Your Life?* In addition, Bronfman's book includes more questions to get your thinking focused on choices.

2. EVALUATE AND PRIORITIZE YOUR LIST

What do you have a passion to do? Think about your skills and qualifications. What are your strengths? What are your weaknesses? Ask what kind of time it would take to accomplish the individual entries on the list. What resources are needed: monetary, education/skill, and time? Will relocating be necessary? If you are already knowledgeable in an area, then you may not need to spend time and money on retraining or learning new skills. If you are not a self-starter, perhaps running an office out of your home will not work. Is there someone who might keep you on task or support you in a new business? Assessing the amount of time you want to spend on an option is just as important as being honest with yourself about what is possible.

Do what you like and are passionate about. Prioritize each opportunity based on your level of commitment and your level of passion for every entry on your list. Think about your values and what is most important to you. Likes and dislikes will surface doing this step. For example, I would like to become an endocrinologist, but I no longer have the level of commitment needed to invest the time and financial resources it would take to become a doctor and start a practice. However, it's still on my list even though it is the last thing (see figure 1.2). Another idea on my list is running for secretary of state in my state because I have always wanted to be the state librarian. This option will require a major commitment of time and money and support from various groups, in addition to the advice of an expert who could help increase my chances of getting my name on the ballot. Running for state office is a possibility and a long-time dream, so this option remains rather high on my list. Dead last on my list is forensic scientist, simply because I have little interest in studying chemistry. Becoming a real criminologist will not be the same as it is on television, nor will crimes be solved in an hour; therefore, becoming a forensic scientist goes to the bottom.

FIGURE 1.2 MY LIST

Library consultant	Cake decorator
Medical coder	Floral designer
Volunteer	Working from home
Running for state office	Endocrinologist
Crocheting	Forensic scientist

3. RESEARCH

This step should be simple to execute because you have the skills and already know about the tools for step three. Research your dreams and desires by obtaining all the specifics about the choices on your list. Calculate the costs and time investment you will need to make in order to meet various objectives on your list. Questions to help you get started include the following:

- How long will it take to complete a new degree?
- How long will it take to master a new skill such as cake decorating or flower arrangement?
- How long will it take you to become certified?
- Will the activity require a part-time or full-time commitment?
- Will your family support you?
- How much will it cost? Can you afford it?

If an option includes relocating, do not forget to research the area. When studying the climate and geography think about what you enjoy or what terrain you wish you lived in. Also, consider educational opportunities and health care systems available in the region. Check out the local cost of housing including property taxes and utilities. Look for economic growth and check crime reports for the area at www .fbi.gov. When moving to another state learn about local and state budgets to see how they are funding communities and libraries.

Discover all the details about the opportunities on your list by reading books, searching the Internet, talking to professionals, and utilizing your network contacts (Strewler-Carter and Carter 2008, 47). Questioning an expert in a field in which you are interested can further round out the research. It is perfectly fine to reorganize your list based on findings and interest changes. During this step do not forget about the contacts you have established. Networks could yield valuable information by tapping into colleagues' knowledge about a potential career, new contacts, and other resources.

Research should help meet your own objectives and fulfill your goals. Once you have sufficient information on each opportunity, your research should reveal the options you are passionate about pursuing and those that hold little interest for you. Although starting a new career might provide you with flexible work hours and a new learning experience, you may need to consider the easier choice of working longer with your current employer or in a similar position instead of struggling with a new job. Career consultants, life coaches, and family can help you evaluate all the information located in this step and help you to make decisions for the next phase of your life.

4. PROS AND CONS

Step four is perhaps one you have heard about time and time again: list the pros and cons for each choice. I have found this step to work very well over the years. List everything good or bad about an idea. Rank the time spent and the level of commitment for choices in this step. Relocation in particular can impact the time invested in an option. Weigh self-employment versus full-time or part-time employment and rank according to your situation. Add your strengths as pros and your weaknesses as cons. Put social gain as a positive and list monetary gains based on how much an option will cover bills and expenses. Add family support as a positive unless it is questionable; then it becomes a negative. Note resources as a positive as long as they will help in obtaining goals or support the opportunity.

Sometimes spiritual or social gain may outweigh the negative impact of a lower income. Will an option allow for vacation time? Will there be enough time for hobbies and family? Is it going to fit into the lifestyle you want? Consider the cost versus available finances. Take a good hard look at your weaknesses and how you might overcome them. If you are a procrastinator thinking of working from home or beginning your own business, do you know someone who can help keep you on task? For instance, the negatives to becoming a doctor may outweigh becoming a medical coder. The cons of becoming a doctor are the years of school and the financial drain to retirement finances and would have to be balanced against family support and social opportunities. Becoming a certified medical coder would involve less time in school and taking online courses from home with perhaps more family commitment, but it would provide only online socializing with classmates and the teacher. For me, the negatives of running for state office would include fundraising, speeches, public appearances, and being in the public eye. The positives would be campaigning, obtaining signatures, finding group support, and designing signs. If you find yourself listing more negatives than positives, then perhaps it is time to move that choice down or off the list. Likewise, if a prospective idea has more pros than cons, then perhaps that option becomes a priority. This is one of the simpler steps to help make a decision and will aid in determining which choices are worth pursuing.

5. CONSIDERING YOUR HEALTH

Consider your health in whatever you attempt next. Health benefits and making sure that coverage is available in later years will be a huge concern. The necessity of taking care of your body, mind, and spiritual needs should not be overlooked. Be aware of your physical and mental limitations but do not let that hold you back. Keep active during stressful times and maintain a healthy attitude. You have a new opportunity to grow in these new experiences.

Exercising and staying active help to preserve your physical, cognitive, and mental well-being. Regular physical activity improves your mood, combats chronic diseases, helps you manage weight, boosts energy levels, promotes sleep, positively affects sex life, and is fun (Mayo Clinic 2009). Older adults need to build flexibility, strength, and balance to reduce the risk of fractures and maintain an independent lifestyle. To aid you in staying active try exercises that focus on strength training, flexibility, and balance (such as walking, gardening, yoga, or Pilates). Always consult with a doctor before beginning new physical activity.

Good health is not all physical; it is psychological as well. Ways to preserve your mental health are to maintain social contacts and cognitive activities as well as keep a positive attitude. According to a 2010 report from the Centers for Disease Control and Prevention, exercise can reduce anxiety and depression while nurturing a feeling of well-being and improve your mood. Additionally, manage your stress by getting enough sleep, changing your attitude, locating support, and practicing relaxation techniques. Retain a healthy attitude by keeping a good sense of humor, and take time to enjoy those things that make you laugh. Focus on the positives and the things you are thankful for in your life. Put energy into the things you enjoy. Optimism and positive thinking go a long way toward embracing the challenges of aging. Look for the humor in life, for attitude is the one thing that an individual can control and do positively (Strewler-Carter and Carter 2008, 89).

Fostering social contacts is equally important to your mental and physical health. Remaining socially connected impacts your "health and longevity" (Center for Health Communication 2004, 15). Volunteering your time by giving to others provides a sense of identity and purpose and builds social connections. When you are volunteering get involved in activities that bring you joy and provide a routine to help with the transition phase to life after retirement (O'Brien, [1]). The American Association of Retired Persons (AARP) website at www.aarp.org/games has various games to keep your mind sharp. In addition, the site contains many good resources for personal growth, volunteering, and money and health matters.

Prevention is the number one way to remain healthy. Practice good health habits that include eating right and scheduling regular visits to your dentist, optometrist, and general physician. Working to stay mentally and physically alert will help you transition to the next phase of your life.

6. TIME

Time is a precious commodity, and it is so important to the plan to know how you want to spend your time. You need to know how much time you want to spend on any activity in your life. How much time is to be spent learning a new career or going back to school? What balance do you want between work and play? What fits best in your life, and what do you want to get out of it? What do you want to be recognized for the most? Finding balance between work, volunteering, giving back, rest, and fun is the reason this is a separate section. Spending time balancing work and fun will be your priority during this phase. You need to know what motivates you, what makes you happy. Personal motivators are what make each of us tick and what provides us with "satisfaction and fulfillment" (Strewler-Carter and Carter 2008, 23).

7. EXPLORE

Obtain all the experience and information you can with little financial investment. Take an opportunity to volunteer nights or weekends at a local business to learn about the job to see if it is in fact something you really want to do. Enroll in a couple of classes and see how it goes before making a commitment to return to school for another degree. There are several programs that allow you to test-drive your dream job or business. Take a vacation for one to three days at your dream job. The website www.VocationVacation.com offers over one hundred vocation opportunities without giving up your day job or investing much more than the cost of a typical vacation, and it provides a chance to experience the job of your dreams. The details of each reasonably priced package can be viewed online before booking a vocation which takes some time to plan with the mentor. Many vocations include all aspects of a job—even how to start your own business. See if the dream is real or work you are not interested in at all. Other alternatives would be volunteering at the business that has your dream job or start out working nights and weekends to see if it is spectacular or a nightmare.

The website www.whatsnextinyourlife.com will take you through each of these steps in great detail by asking you questions. The site will produce a "trip" plan in your own personal free account, helping you with the next steps for each "road trip" of your own various plans. The Chicago Life Opportunities Initiative at www .cloi.org has reference sources and provides in-person workshops regularly and on demand starting at $95 per person with a minimum group of eight participants to help you make a "blueprint" for the next phase of your life.

Finally, do not be afraid to change your mind or be open to opportunities as they come along. Planning for your new phase can be a scary and emotional time, but it is also a time when you are in the driver's seat. Linda Edelstein perceptively stated: "Transitions are bridges—beginning here and ending there. No one lives on a bridge; we cross them, often with a combination of fear and exhilaration" (Edelstein 1999, 159). You have before you a new opportunity to experience life in an entirely different way. Start planning the next great adventure in your life today!

REFERENCES

Bronfman, Edgar M. 2002. *The third act: Reinventing yourself after retirement.* New York: Putnam.

Center for Health Communication. 2004. Reinventing aging: Baby boomers and civic engagement. Harvard School of Public Health. http://www.hsph.harvard.edu/chc/reinventingaging/Report.pdf (accessed January 4, 2011).

Centers for Disease Control and Prevention. 2010. Physical activity and health: The benefits of physical activity, May 10. http://www.cdc.gov/nccdphp/sgr/olderad.htm.

Edelstein, Linda N. 1999. *The art of midlife: Courage and creative living for women.* Westport: Bergin & Garvey.

Franklin, Mary B., and Robert Frick. 2008. A satisfying combo: Work, leisure, and extra income. *Kiplinger's Personal Finance* 62, 94–99.

Mayo Clinic. 2009. Exercise: 7 benefits of regular physical activity, July 25. http://www.mayoclinic.com/health/exercise/HQ01676/NSECTIONGROUP=2.

O'Brien, Sharon. 10 tips for happy retirement living: Make the most of the rest of your life. About.com. Senior Living. http://seniorliving.about.com/od/retirement/a/retirement_livi.htm.

Strewler-Carter, Joan, and Stephen T. Carter. 2008. *What's next in your life? How to find meaning beyond the money.* Kansas City: Rockhill Books.

2

FOUR STEPS TO A BETTER RETIREMENT

Brett Hammond

WHAT'S YOUR VISION of the perfect retirement? Do you see yourself spending more time with family, volunteering, traveling, or pursuing new hobbies? Or do you picture retirement as a "second act" professionally, during which you may go back to school, change careers, or continue to work in your current career? Whether you're getting closer to retirement or already retired, planning for—and managing—this life change can be daunting. Here are four steps that can help you organize and structure your finances to ensure you're well prepared.

- Set financial goals.
- Create a budget.
- Understand your investments.
- Create an income floor.

SET FINANCIAL GOALS

Whenever you're planning for your financial future, it's important to set goals for yourself and for your family. Begin by clearly defining what your goals actually are. Rather than using abstract definitions, try to specify your goals in clear, personal words. You might say, for example, "I want to retire in five years" or "I want to be able to buy a second home that I can escape to in the winter months" or "I want to help send my granddaughter to an Ivy League college."

If sorting out your goals becomes difficult, try to distinguish your wants from your needs. It also may be useful to differentiate your goals by investment time horizon—that is, when will you need the money and how long will you need the money to last? For example, you can place your goals in three broad time horizons: short-term (one to three years), intermediate (three to ten years), or long-term (ten-plus years).

You should regard retirement as a long-term goal, since you may live twenty to thirty years or even more after you stop working. Also, when thinking about your retirement goals, ask yourself these questions:

- What are your personal goals for retirement? After you stop working, what would you like to do: Travel the world? Garden? Take up a new hobby? How you plan on spending your time in retirement can help you determine how much you'll need to save.
- What is your action plan to reach your goal in the time you want?

Next, create an action plan for achieving your specific retirement saving goals. Even if you're close to retirement, your action plan can include the following:

- If you have a defined contribution plan, such as a 401(k) or 403(b) plan, it's never too late to sign up and contribute as much as possible to it. If you're 50 or older at the end of the calendar year, you might be eligible to make catch-up contributions as well. Take advantage of your employer's retirement plan and contribute as much as possible to it.
- In addition to your employer's retirement plan, think about contributing additional amounts for retirement through other investment vehicles, such as IRAs.
- Understand your investment risk tolerance—the degree to which you can withstand the ups and downs of the market. This will help you determine what types of investments should be in your retirement portfolio.
- Identify how much you will need to save to reach your goals. You can find a variety of retirement savings calculators on the Internet that can help you determine how much you need to invest for your future.
- Once you have a good idea of how much money you'll need to save, develop a plan to help you get your money working for you.

- Also, be realistic and flexible. Think about your goals carefully and make sure you have the resources to reach them. Also, regularly review your goals to ensure you're on track.

CREATE A BUDGET

Establishing a budget is a good way to manage your finances before and during retirement. To prepare and use a budget successfully, you'll need to plan for the expected and the unexpected—a process that involves monitoring, adjusting, and controlling future income and expenses.

First, create a cash flow analysis. Begin by itemizing your sources of income and total them for the month. Before retirement, income might include salary and dividend and interest payments. After retirement, pension benefits, Social Security, and redemptions from savings come into play.

Next, itemize all expenses, including mortgage or rent, utilities, insurance, food, medical, entertainment, and other costs. Then, subtract your expenses from your income. From this calculation, you can create a cash flow statement to track your spending and saving.

Remember, health care costs have increased significantly in recent years, a trend that's likely to continue. Future health costs could affect your available income or savings. One way to predict how much of an impact health care costs will have is to find out about your employer's health care benefits for retirees. You can also research what you'd expect to pay for private health insurance—if you need to go that route—and long-term care insurance. You also should look into what benefits Medicare will provide and what those costs are projected to be when you retire.

You may find that after creating your cash flow statement, you're spending more than you should be. While you're working, you can increase your savings by establishing an emergency fund to meet unexpected expenses arising from an extended illness, job loss, or other cause. Early in your career, this fund should equal at least three months' worth of expenses; if you're in midcareer or approaching retirement, try to save at least six months' worth of expenses. Your fund should be invested in a liquid asset, such as a short-term bond mutual fund or money market fund, so you can get the money quickly if you need it.

Once you've got an emergency fund in place, put additional money toward your retirement goals using your employer-sponsored retirement plan, an IRA, or other investment vehicles. If you're saving for shorter-term goals like the down payment on a house, a car, home repairs, or a vacation, mutual funds can be useful investments to have.

Next, whether you're working or already retired, review your expenditures closely. Analyze your spending patterns and look for ways to reduce expenses. For example, consider eating out less frequently, use coupons when food shopping, or take your lunch to work more often. Other cost-saving strategies include shopping for cheaper homeowners' or car insurance, turning your furnace or air conditioner down when you're not at home, or taking advantage of free Internet access at public libraries or cafés instead of paying for monthly in-home service. Simple measures such as these—and many others besides—can go a long way toward increasing your nest egg or slowing down how quickly it gets spent.

It's also important to control debt. If you have consumer debt, such as multiple credit card balances, devise a strategy for reducing it. For example, first pay off credit cards with the highest interest rates. Or consolidate your bills with a card that offers the lowest rate you can find. If you're a homeowner, consider using a home equity loan to consolidate your debts, since the interest may be tax deductible. If you receive a tax refund or a windfall (such as an inheritance, a royalty check, etc.), use the funds to trim or eliminate your debt.

Finally, try to forecast your income and expenses for the upcoming year to help make your planning easier. For your income, don't forget to include your expected salary increases, conservative estimates for projected growth in investment income, and any sale of assets you're planning. For expenses, include any quarterly or semi-annual payments you might have, such as state tax bills or life insurance premiums. Since you probably make these types of payments in large lump sums, working them into your budgeting plan now can help you more accurately prepare to meet the next year's expenses.

UNDERSTAND YOUR INVESTMENTS

As has been evident over the past few years, the financial markets can be very volatile, with sharp and unpredictable ups and downs in performance. When investing for retirement, expect such volatility to be the norm and establish an investment strategy with which you're comfortable and that can help you pursue your long-term savings goals. If you need assistance in developing an investment strategy that's appropriate for your needs, consider seeking assistance from an independent advisor.

In order to help develop an effective investment strategy on your own, follow these guidelines.

DIVERSIFY YOUR INVESTMENTS APPROPRIATELY

Diversifying involves spreading your investment dollars across different asset classes such as equity (stocks), fixed income (bonds), real estate, and guaranteed funds or accounts. Allocating your assets appropriately is critical. Research has found that asset allocation is a significant or dominant factor in explaining differences in portfolio returns. For example, the prominent 1986 study, *Determinants of Portfolio Performance,* by Brinson, Hood, and Beebower (*The Financial Analysts Journal,* July/August 1986) determined that, on average, asset allocation accounted for more than 90 percent of the difference in returns among large U.S. pension plan portfolios—far more than market timing or individual security selection. Other studies suggest asset allocation has a lesser but still significant effect on the variability of portfolio returns.

How you diversify your investments will depend on your individual goals, time horizon, and tolerance for risk. Your goal should be to diversify *across* asset classes (i.e., having equities and nonequities in your portfolio) as well as to diversify *within* asset classes (e.g., for equities, including both international and domestic stocks in your portfolio).

Keep in mind that your investment time horizon doesn't end when you retire. As a result, your portfolio will likely need at least some exposure to the growth potential of stocks throughout most of what will hopefully be a long, healthy retirement.

While diversifying your investments does not guarantee that your portfolio won't lose money, diversification can keep you from being overly exposed to a major downturn in one type of investment. And since different types of investments tend to perform well at different times, diversification can also help you offset the volatility of a single investment and take greater advantage of the strengths of several.

When investing, it's important to remember that all assets contain some degree of risk, although some assets are more volatile (riskier) than others. Even factoring in recent market events, the asset class with the greatest range of returns also tends to be the asset class with the highest compound returns: stocks. Generally speaking, the longer the time frame in which you plan to keep your money invested, the larger percentage of equities you can hold in your portfolio.

DON'T TRY TO "TIME" THE MARKET

"Timing the market" means attempting to take your money out of the market before a downturn and then reinvesting it before the market heads back up. However, because the direction of the market is extremely difficult to predict, most people end up selling during downturns and reinvesting well after the market recovers. While attempting to time the market is a natural impulse during periods of loss, in order to time the market successfully, you need to be right twice—both the right time to buy and the right time to sell. This is why it's extremely difficult to time the market consistently.

So instead of trying to time the market, consider other strategies. For example, you can invest your money by depositing a certain amount in your accounts in a lump sum. Or you can invest in your accounts systematically with a strategy that is referred to as "dollar cost averaging." While dollar cost averaging does not ensure a gain, it allows you to make purchases when the market is increasing in value as well as when its value decreases. This means you purchase more units or shares when prices are lower and vice versa. Thus, the use of systematic deposits can give you the opportunity to achieve a lower average cost per share or unit.

UNDERSTAND THE IMPACT OF EXPENSES

No matter how you invest, you'll have expenses such as fees, annual maintenance charges, and possibly commissions. Pay close attention to the costs of your investments, because expense charges can have a substantial impact on your investment returns.

Think of it this way: The higher your investment expenses, the less you have to invest. To find out how much you're paying in fees, do some homework. If you're investing in mutual funds, for example, look at the company's investment track record and the individual fund charges or loads. Morningstar, Inc. provides a wide range of information on mutual funds, including their expenses.

Generally, investors shouldn't meddle too much with their investments. Keep fund transfers to a minimum wherever possible. Periodic rebalancing is a good idea. But excessive transactions may generate capital gains taxes or transaction costs, or both, which can have a noticeable impact on your overall returns.

TAX-DEFER AS MUCH AS POSSIBLE

When investing for retirement, contribute as much as you can to your retirement accounts, and keep contributing through both good times and bad. Beyond your employer's plan, you can invest in products such as IRAs and tax-deferred annuities. When you invest in a tax-deferred product, you pay less in taxes now and therefore contribute more for your future with money that would otherwise go to taxes. Tax-deferred investment products have restrictions as to when you can access the money; generally, for example, a withdrawal from these products before age 59½ can result in a 10 percent IRS penalty. So factor this consideration into your investment planning.

As I mentioned earlier, contribution limits for salary deferrals into defined contribution plans such as 401(k)s vary by age and by length of service. Taking advantage of higher limits as you get closer to retirement can help reduce taxes. The laws change on occasion so, again, an independent advisor can help you navigate this often changing landscape.

CREATE AN INCOME FLOOR

Whether you're starting to prepare for retirement or are already retired, it's becoming increasingly important to ensure you have sufficient *income* in retirement—that each month, regardless of how the markets perform, you have enough cash flow to take care of basics such as housing, food, clothing, and health care.

You can ensure this basic income by using a guaranteed fixed annuity to augment other sources of retirement income such as Social Security or a monthly check from a traditional pension. A guaranteed fixed annuity protects your principal, typically pays a guaranteed minimum rate of interest while you're saving, and when you're ready to retire can offer guaranteed income for life, backed by the claims-paying ability of the annuity's issuer.

The market gyrations of the last two years have shown very clearly that today's nest egg may not have the same dollar value as tomorrow's. Of course, your savings can increase in value as well as decrease. But when you're retired and need to draw down a set lump sum each month—and hopefully for a good long while—it's important to be able to take care of life's necessities regardless of where the market is day to day, and regardless of how long your retirement may be.

WHERE EXACTLY IS THE INCOME FLOOR?

It's important to ask yourself how much income you'll need out of pocket each month to cover the basics of shelter, food, clothing, transportation, and health care for you and, if applicable, your spouse or partner.

Research shows that most people need, very roughly, between $30,000 and $50,000 annually in today's dollars to meet these basic expenses in retirement. Of course, each individual situation is different, and where you live also has an impact on the amount you'll need to live on.

But even if you have the income to cover these basic—or nondiscretionary—expenses, you may need money to pay for other items that you regard as important to maintaining a comfortable standard of living in retirement. For example, you may want to maintain a modest entertainment or travel budget. When times are good, you can pay for these needs from your retirement nest egg, but when times are bad, you'll want to ensure you have a plan in place to pay for these basic expenses.

So if you think your income floor is $50,000 a year and your Social Security benefits and your pension will pay you $40,000, then you can cover the gap of $10,000 by using a guaranteed fixed annuity that pays a guaranteed *minimum* rate of interest. The annuity will also offer you guaranteed income for life, backed by the claims-paying ability of the annuity's issuer when you're retired.

Therefore, by creating an appropriate *guaranteed* income floor, you'll be assured that the expenses you need to cover in retirement aren't dependent on how the market gyrates each month.

DISCLAIMER

your financial ability and willingness to continue purchases through periods of low price levels. Dollar cost averaging does not assure a profit or protect against a loss in declining markets.

TIAA-CREF or its affiliates do not provide tax advice. Taxpayers should seek advice based on their own particular circumstances from an independent tax advisor. TIAA-CREF products may be subject to market and other risk factors. See the applicable product literature, or visit tiaa-cref.org for details.

TIAA-CREF personnel in its investment management area provide investment advice and portfolio management services through the following entities: Teachers Advisors, Inc., TIAA-CREF Investment Management, LLC, and Teachers Insurance and Annuity Association. TIAA, TIAA-CREF, Teachers Insurance and Annuity Association, TIAA-CREF Asset Management and FINANCIAL SERVICES FOR THE GREATER GOOD are registered trademarks of Teachers Insurance and Annuity Association.

3

HOW TO RETIRE GRACIOUSLY

Susan Carol Curzon

Most of the literature on retirement focuses on the financial and emotional well-being of the retiree. There is good reason for this focus because these two elements are critical for a successful retirement. No one would willingly retire with financial instability, especially with the knowledge that as we get older, it can be almost impossible to recoup our former earning power. The emotional dimension is equally important—a person must be ready to leave the workplace and to take on a new and unstructured life.

This chapter has a very different focus—on retiring graciously. To be gracious means to act with propriety, courtesy, and tact. To retire graciously means that we retire in a manner that is respectful of our colleagues, our library, our profession, and ourselves. The process of retiring from the library is often our final professional act. Retiring graciously is a statement about how much we cared about our library and about our profession.

GETTING READY

Before taking any action, decide when you are going to retire. Usually this decision is made based on your retirement plan and how your benefits can be maximized. It may also be based on other things, such as the need to care for sick relatives or grandchildren or to finish a major project at work. Regardless of the reason, focus on a definite date and stay with it unless something very important comes up to change your mind. You can make yourself a subject of jokes if you continually give people a date for retirement and then don't retire. If you really are uncertain about a date for retirement, then you really aren't ready to retire.

Once the date is set, make a time line. Look through this chapter, select those tasks that are relevant to you, and put them on a time line. For example, when will you tell the boss that you are retiring? When will you let your colleagues know? A time line is important because there are many retirement tasks ahead. You don't want to realize that you have forgotten something important just days before you retire. Also, you will find that the date of your retirement, no matter how far in advance you have set it, comes faster than you may think.

Be sure to give yourself some slack in your retirement time line. Remember that you are still working and that you still have a job to do. You are still on payroll. In addition to your regular work, retirement preparations will place more demands on your time. For example, you may be wrapping up certain tasks, cleaning out your office area, sorting and discarding files and e-mail, possibly training and passing the baton to your successor, and so on. Also, you must take into consideration the process of retirement itself—working with the pension office and with Human Resources. The paperwork can be substantial as you must make many important benefit decisions.

Retiring can be hard work. If you have been in the library a long time, it can take almost as long to get out as it did to get into the library.

TELLING THE BOSS

The first person to tell that you are retiring of course is your boss. No boss wants to hear from anyone other than you that you are going to retire. That means you need to keep your own counsel when you decide to retire. A person's retirement, no matter where he or she is in an organization, is big news and few can keep that secret. Of course, you cannot just walk into the boss's office and say you are retiring. To prepare for that day ask yourself the following questions:

- "How much notice will I need to give?" This depends on your level in the library. The higher you are in the library, the longer the amount of notice you need to give. There are two reasons for this: first, your leaving will have substantial impact on the library, and second, it often takes longer to replace you. There is a certain art to this exit strategy—too long and you run the risk of being a lame duck, and too short and it looks like you are leaving because you are angry or you have been asked to leave.

- "How will I give notice?" Most organizations require a letter, but a letter sent to the boss's office is cold and impersonal and implies alienation. It is always better to inform the boss in person. Not only is it more professional but it also gives you and the boss a chance to talk about the job a bit. However, do not mistake this for the exit interview—if you have one.

- "What do I plan on saying to my boss?" This is not an off-the-cuff meeting. State your intent to retire, say when, talk about any pending issues that may be of concern, and be prepared to receive and give gracious comments in return. Do discuss timing the public announcement because there will be people you will want to tell personally before the announcement goes out.

- "When should I formally deliver my retirement letter?" You can give the boss your retirement letter at the meeting, but it is better to send the letter as a follow-up. Every once in a while information comes up at such a meeting that may shape how you write the letter. Remember that the letter is not an occasion to air grievances but simply to state the date of your retirement and express appreciation for the opportunities you have received. These letters become part of your permanent file with the organization.

TELLING THE PEOPLE MOST AFFECTED FIRST

The next important step is to tell the people most affected by your retirement. They should hear directly from you first. The people most affected would be those who directly report to you, close colleagues, major donors, and significant supporters. Since news of your retirement may leak fast from the boss's office because of actions that need to take place, you should let these individuals know as soon as possible. In your time line, make a list of the individuals you want to inform so you don't miss anyone.

You do have to plan the timing of your discussions. Best of all is to let people know in back-to-back meetings or phone calls. That way, the news won't travel ahead of you too much. You can ask people to keep it confidential until you reach everyone, but give them a certain time. For example, you might say, "I hope to reach everyone by tomorrow, so could you keep it confidential until then?" This will work most of the time. Do plan on telling the people who are the most confidential first and leaving the ones who gossip until last. That way you have some chance of being the first to tell people of your plans.

Allow yourself plenty of time for the process of telling people. Discussions, meetings, and phone calls all take time depending on the number of people you need to contact directly. However, everyone will be appreciative because of the respect that he or she received from you.

The individual conversations also take time. People may have expected your retirement because they know you are approaching that age, but the exact date and the certainty of it can still come as a surprise. Be prepared for your direct reports and colleagues to express a sense of loss. Retirement is bittersweet. People will be happy for you, but also sad to not see and work with you anymore.

If you are involved in fundraising or nurturing friends of the library, you will want to let major donors and supporters know personally. At the least a personal call should occur, but going to lunch would be a good strategy. A direct conversation with you can assure donors and supporters of the continuity of the library's direction because many will be worried about the future of their endowments, funds, or projects.

If you are a director or supervisor, be sensitive to the impact that your retirement will have. A director or a supervisor telling staff about a retirement date is different from two colleagues sharing. The director's or supervisor's leaving means change and uncertainty. It brings a level of concern and possibly fear as to what will happen next.

MAKING YOUR RETIREMENT PUBLIC

Once the boss, your direct reports, close colleagues, and supporters know the date, you are ready for a public announcement. Usually, your boss will let people know formally. Be prepared for your boss or his or her assistant to ask you for some input on the announcement. For example, you might be asked to list your major achievements.

If you are the boss, then it may fall to you to do your own announcement. This is an announcement that you can prepare in advance when you are working on your time line. That way, you have time to think about it and revise your statement.

However you do it, it is still better for the announcement to go out quickly because the information will move very fast once you have told people personally.

Once the announcement is ready to go out, it obviously will go to all of your colleagues in the library. However, if you are the head of a library, the announcement will also go to peers such as the college deans on campus or department heads in the city or the organization. If you are in a university, you should also let the officers of the student body know. Depending on your situation, you might also want to let frequent users of the library know. Librarians in small public libraries in particular can get very close to the users.

Don't forget about your professional associations. Announcements should go to the various library journals and listservs. If you want, you can be ready with a black-and-white photo to submit at the same time. If you are serving on any professional committees, it also will be courteous to let fellow committee members know even if you intend to continue serving after retirement.

Still the most effective way to make a retirement announcement is an e-mail, which can also be posted to listservs. If you have a blog, you can do a second announcement there and add your thoughts about your career and some kind words about your colleagues.

If you are a director or have another high-profile position, be prepared for the press to call. The local press or the student newspaper will be interested. Have a few remarks prepared. They are sure to ask you what you consider to be your legacy, your favorite memories, and your plans in retirement. Be ready to answer these questions.

The amount of interest in your retirement may be directly proportional to your level in the organization and to the amount of time you have served in the organization. If you have been serving at a high level for years, the impact will be greater. Remember to prepare your announcement appropriately.

PLANNING THE TRANSITION

One of the best gifts you can leave your colleagues is a job in order and a trained successor. You usually don't have control over the latter, but you certainly do over the former.

Start by taking a look at your job. Think about your various tasks and responsibilities. Make a plan on what you can complete in the time remaining. Create a "desk manual" that will let your successor know how you accomplished your duties.

If a successor, either permanent or acting, has been appointed, create a training plan so that he or she will be up to speed as much as possible when you leave.

You can also help in other areas. For example, if they are starting a search for your position, you can help with the job description or at least by suggesting some new or changing dimensions to your work. In other words, be a part of the process.

If you are a director or hold a higher level job, create a transition plan. Rarely does a permanent successor come in right after your departure; usually an acting administrator is designated. Spend time showing your successor the ropes and let people know that you are doing so. Your colleagues need to know how the work will go on. This gives everyone the needed security in the uncertain time triggered by your announcement.

One question that often arises is how much the retiree-to-be should participate in the interview process for the successor. Generally speaking, you should not. The candidate wants to speak frankly about the job and potential changes. The interview panel wants to ask questions that may be delicate about your work or changes. Your presence can only hamper the interviewing process. You could offer to have coffee with the candidates so they can ask you questions about your job.

By now you might be asking yourself, "Why is any of this my responsibility?" Again, this process goes back to professionalism. Professionalism is not any easy concept to capture, but generally it is about maintaining standards and commitment to work.

It's important to keep your commitment to work hard. Sometimes people close to retirement come in late, miss attending meetings, or cut other corners. It is unfortunate because that is what your colleagues then remember about you. While you may get jokes about being a lame duck, you won't be one if you don't act like one. Work to the last minute. Keep up your professional standards.

Also be careful about your own jokes. Even while you prepare to exit, don't appear eager to leave. It just isn't nice to send a message that you can't wait to be done with everything and out of there. Have respect for the work you did and the people with whom you worked.

PREPARING FOR YOUR RETIREMENT PARTY

Retirement parties or events vary substantially from library to library. It depends on tradition and also funding. Many retirement parties also depend on the wishes of the retiree. If you really don't want a party, say so at the beginning. Many people don't want a party because they really don't want to be the subject of attention and are uncomfortable speaking in public. Be aware that people will want to do something for you, so be prepared to compromise.

The higher you are in the organization, the more likely there will be a retirement event. Remember, if you are a director, the event is as much about the library as it is about you. The success of the event, the number of attendees, and what is said are all a reflection on the library too. Be mindful of the political dimensions of such an event.

Make your invitation list early and review it carefully several times. You don't want to forget anyone at this important time!

Also work on your retirement remarks. Your remarks aren't about you and your achievements; others will talk about that. You will spend time thanking people and appreciating them. *Graciousness* is the keyword here.

At the actual event, there will be jokes and general ribbing. Some might not resonate well with you, but again be gracious, laugh at everything, and be in the best spirits. People mean well.

Don't be surprised if there are a variety of individual events such as luncheons. Surprise gifts can also come. Buy a box of thank-you notes ahead of time. Write a thank-you note for everything no matter how busy you are.

PREPARING FOR THE LAST WEEK

The closer you get to retirement, the more you should prepare for an emotional impact. Not only are you leaving the library and all your colleagues, but you also are leaving the profession. Your emotions will vary in accordance with your attachment to people and place and also to their attachment to you. You may feel nostalgia as you do things for the last time. You may review your career and wish there were things you had done differently. You will be aware of the many colleagues that you may never see again. You will miss having a place to go every day. There are myriad emotions and reactions that will come with the retirement process. Just let yourself experience them.

A day or two before you leave, consider sending an e-mail to everyone to say fare-well. Again express your appreciation and respect. Also prepare your workspace for your successor. Leave it immaculate. Yes, others may come in to clean and paint after you leave, but again it is a way of showing respect.

Don't leave your packing until the last minute. If you have been in your office for a while, there is more there than you might think. Slowly move things out so that the final clean-out is not too overwhelming for you or for your colleagues. Clear out files and other things that are normally unseen so your office still has a presence and so you are still sending the message that you are there to work. I recommend removing major items on the weekend or after work hours so it isn't so obvious. Be prepared with cartons and bubble wrap.

It is possible that you might be invited by your boss for an exit interview. Be thoughtful and respectful. It really isn't a time to tell it like it is—if it was inappropriate before, it will be now.

SOME FINAL THOUGHTS

Remember that you have never retired before, so if you make a few mistakes or wish you had done some things differently, just mentally note your thoughts and move on.

Be sure not to hang around afterward. We all have stories about people who retired but kept coming back. Plan on being gone for a while but keep in touch with people with whom you were close. It's common for many friendships to not transcend the workplace, but you can always cherish the memory of collegiality with your coworkers.

Think back on the good times but move on. Your work is completed. It is time for a new and exciting phase of your life.

4

SOCIAL SECURITY FOR PRE-RETIREES
BASIC ELEMENTS AND HELPFUL TIPS

Donald G. Frank

IN A RECENT article titled "The Anatomy of Social Security and Medicare," the author asserts that "Social Security in the United States is the largest government expenditure program in the world. . . . Despite its vast size and its effects on almost all Americans each year of their lives, the Social Security system is probably the most poorly understood government policy of all. The jargon alone is incomprehensible. . . . Probably no policy, however, is more important to understand because its consequences for the way we live and for how well we live are monumental."[1]

FOCUS GROUPS: INTERESTING COMMENTS

Seventy-five librarians from academic, public, special, and school libraries participated in conference calls and e-mails that I conducted in December 2010. Participants were randomly selected from ages 25 to 68.

The responses indicated that a significant number of librarians in their 50s and 60s were essentially unaware of the scope of Social Security's programs and services. Confidence in the potential sustainability of Social Security was somewhat limited for the professionals in their 20s, 30s, and 40s. A significant number of the librarians in their 50s and 60s indicate that they had not saved money on a regular basis. These librarians view Social Security as critically important. Some of the professionals in their 20s, 30s, and 40s were interested in the option of investing in the various equity markets. Librarians in their 50s and 60s were interested in the process of determining the ideal age to start taking retirement benefits. Retirement benefits dominated the discussions.

SOCIAL SECURITY: SOME BASIC ELEMENTS

In general, people view Social Security as a retirement program in which they receive monthly payments beginning at a specific age. Social Security's programs and services are relatively expansive. As of 2010, approximately 160 million people pay Social Security taxes, and approximately 52 million people receive monthly benefits from Social Security. These numbers were 164 million and 50 million in 2009, probably reflecting the consequences of the recession that officially commenced in December 2007. Social Security benefits are paid to citizens who have retired, to citizens who are disabled, to survivors of workers who have died, and to dependents of beneficiaries.[2]

Social Security taxes are deducted from wages up to a specified amount. In 2010, the amount was $106,800. Medicare taxes are applied to all of a worker's wages. If one works for a company or organization, the Social Security tax is 6.2 percent and the Medicare tax is 1.45 percent. The company or organization also contributes 6.2 percent and 1.45 percent for the employee. For those librarians who are self-employed, the Social Security tax is 12.4 percent and the Medicare tax is 2.9 percent. So, if a librarian works at a college or at a public library, for example, and earns $50,000 annually, then 6.2 percent of $50,000 will go to the individual's Social Security and 1.45 percent of $50,000 will go to Medicare. And if the same librarian earns $150,000 annually, then 6.2 percent of $106,800 will go to the individual's Social Security and 1.45 percent of $150,000 will go to the individual's Medicare. For 2011, the Social Security tax will be 4.2 percent as a result of legislation passed in December 2010.[3]

Social Security's retirement benefits are based on the totality of the annual salaries earned in one's lifetime. The Social Security Administration (SSA) uses a formula to calculate the retirement benefits. Calculations are generally based on the librarian's thirty-five highest years of earnings. In particular: "Retirement benefit calculations are based on your average earnings during a lifetime of work under the Social Security system. For most current and future retirees, we will average your 35 highest years of earnings. Years in which you have low earnings or no earnings may be counted to bring the total years of earnings up to 35."[4]

Disability benefits are distributed to qualified individuals who have a physical or mental disability that is expected to last, or has lasted, at least one year and also prevents the individual from doing substantial work in a job in which he or she earns at least $1,000 a month. This statement is obviously subject to a variety of interpretations in relation to the individual, the SSA, and the judicial system. One important guideline associated with disability benefits is that the individual's condition must be "medical," or be discovered and verified by doctors. A list of conditions is available on the SSA website. Additionally, a specified number of "work credits" is required to qualify for these benefits. This number depends on the age at which one becomes disabled.[5]

Survivors benefits are paid to a worker's spouse and children after the worker dies, assuming the worker earned a sufficient number of work credits. In general, a widow or widower can collect benefits if he or she is 60+ years of age; 50+ years of age and disabled; or any age if responsible for the deceased's child who is less than 16 years of age or disabled and entitled to Social Security benefits based on the widow or widower's record. In general, children can collect benefits if less than 16 years of age; between the ages of 18 and 19 as well as enrolled in an elementary or secondary school as full-time students; or 18+ years of age and severely disabled.[6]

Supplemental Security Income (SSI) is available to citizens with low incomes who are 65+ years of age as well as blind or disabled. It is also possible for children who are blind or disabled to obtain SSI.[7]

Medicare is the nation's health insurance program for people 65+ years of age. Specific individuals under the age of 65 can qualify for Medicare, however, "including those who have disabilities and those who have permanent kidney failure or amyotrophic lateral sclerosis." Medicare is operated by the Centers for Medicare and Medicaid Services (in the Department of Health and Human Services) in cooperation with the SSA. One applies for Medicare at the SSA. Part A of Medicare provides hospital insurance. Part B provides medical insurance (doctors' fees, for example). Part C includes the various Medicare Advantage plans. Part D provides prescription drug coverage. Medicaid is a state-operated program providing hospital and medical coverage for those with low incomes.[8]

The SSA administers other important programs and services. Examples include unemployment compensation, food and nutrition assistance (e.g., the food stamp program), and temporary assistance for needy families.[9]

IMPORTANT SOCIAL SECURITY ISSUES FOR WOMEN

Social Security is obviously neutral in relation to gender. Benefits are generally based on one's history of salaries in various jobs. Demographic data across all socioeconomic levels indicate that women are more likely to live alone at some point in time after the age of 65. As a result, Social Security is likely to be particularly important for these individuals. The following demographic points provide additional information or perspective:

- Average annual income from Social Security for all women 65+ years of age was $11,377 in 2008, compared to $14,822 for men.
- As of 2008, women who were 65 years of age were expected to live, on average, an additional 20.0 years, compared to 17.7 for men.
- In 2010, women represented 57 percent of all Social Security beneficiaries age 62+ and 69 percent of all beneficiaries age 85+.
- Statistically, women age 65+ are less likely to have significant income from pensions other than Social Security. In 2006, 23 percent of unmarried women aged 65+ received funds from private pensions, compared to 30 percent for unmarried men.
- Nearly 75 percent of all married women are eventually widowed.
- In 2008, the median salary for women who worked full-time was $35,000, compared to $45,000 for men.
- Women are more likely than men to miss several years of full-time work as a result of responsibilities associated with children or care for other members of the family. As a result, contributions to Social Security are affected.[10]

The above demographic data emphasize the importance of being informed in relation to Social Security, especially for women. A significant number of librarians have private or public pension plans and will not rely exclusively on Social Security. Nonetheless, some private pension plans have been affected by economic realities. And public pension plans in some cities and states have been affected.

As a significant number of women and some men miss several years of full-time work as a result of the time and efforts devoted to children, it is especially important for these people to be aware of the work credits needed to provide full benefits from Social Security. Additionally, a study conducted at the University of Pennsylvania's prestigious Wharton School indicates it is occasionally difficult for women to return to positions in the corporate world after taking some time off to care for children and/or other members of the family.[11]

Marital status, including divorce, is also a factor. For example, if a woman (or man) has been married for at least ten years and then becomes divorced, she will be eligible to receive retirement benefits from Social Security based on her husband's contributions. Generally, the woman or man is eligible to receive up to 50 percent of the ex's benefits, assuming she or he is 62+, unmarried, and divorced for two years. If either remarries, benefits from the ex are not an option.[12]

HOW TO CONTACT AND COMMUNICATE WITH THE SSA

The Social Security website (www.ssa.gov) is excellent. It provides comprehensive information on retirement benefits, disability benefits, survivors benefits, Supplemental Security Income (SSI), and Medicare. Contact information is provided, including communications via telephone (800-772-1213) and traditional mail. It is possible to ask questions, apply for benefits, create password-protected accounts, report changes in addresses or telephone numbers, obtain the addresses of local Social Security offices, listen to informational messages on a variety of topics, and order important publications associated with benefits (*Understanding the Benefits, Retirement Benefits, Disability Benefits, Survivors Benefits, How Work Affects Your Benefits, Benefits for Children with Disabilities,* and *What Every Woman Should Know*).

Two additional features on the SSA website are helpful. Some pages include a request to receive information as it changes: "Get e-mail updates when this information changes." These updates are particularly helpful. The second feature, "Find an Answer to Your Question," provides opportunities to do keyword searches on topics. If one is unable to obtain appropriate responses, the opportunity to ask specific questions via e-mail is provided.

Social Security's local offices are helpful. I made a 45-minute appointment at one of the offices to discuss several issues associated with Social Security. The representative was informed and willing to assist as needed. She responded directly to all my questions.

REVIEW YOUR ANNUAL SOCIAL SECURITY STATEMENT

The Social Security Statement is mailed to citizens annually and is an important document. An individual's estimated benefits are provided on the second page, including retirement benefits, disability benefits, family benefits, survivors benefits, and Medicare. If a librarian has earned a sufficient number of "credits" to qualify for retirement benefits, for example, the statement "You have earned enough credits to qualify for benefits" is at the top of the page. If the librarian needs additional credits to qualify for retirement benefits, the number needed to qualify is provided. It is important to remember that one's estimated benefits are only *estimates*. For example, if the estimated retirement benefit for the librarian's full retirement age is $2,000 per month, it is possible and likely that this estimate will be modified by the librarian's annual salaries in the future.[13]

The librarian's "Earnings Record" is provided on page 3. This includes the "Taxed Social Security Earnings" and "Taxed Medicare Earnings" for each year of employment. It is especially important to review these numbers for accuracy. Compare the numbers with the data on end-of-year tax and income statements from employers.[14]

WORK CREDITS AND POSSIBLE RETIREMENT AGES ARE IMPORTANT

A librarian's benefits depend on a variety of factors. One essential factor focuses on the "work credits" needed to qualify for benefits. For librarians born in or after 1929, 40 credits are needed to qualify for retirement benefits. This is equivalent to ten years of full-time work. In 2010, for example, an individual earned one credit for each $1,120 of income. So, after the individual earned $4,480 in 2010, he or she obtained four credits, or the maximum number of credits for one year.[15]

Full retirement age depends on one's date of birth. For those born from 1943 to 1954, the full retirement age is 66. Then the full retirement age gradually escalates. For those born in 1960 or later, the full retirement age is 67. It is not necessary to wait until one's full retirement age to collect benefits. It is also possible to work past the full retirement age, collecting increased retirement benefits at a later date. If a librarian was born in 1943 or later and decides to work past the full retirement age, his or her retirement benefits will increase 8 percent per year beyond the full retirement age (up to the age of 70). Some librarians decide to retire "early," or before the full retirement age. It is possible to retire as early as 62 years of age. If the individual retires prior to attaining the full retirement age, then the individual's retirement benefits are reduced *permanently,* based on the age of the individual. For example, if a librarian retires at the age of 62, his or her retirement benefits will be 25 percent lower than at the full retirement age.[16]

Determining the date of retirement or the date on which retirement benefits will be accessed depends on the librarian's personal situation. If a librarian decides to collect retirement benefits early but then lives past a specific age, referred to as the "break-even point," the librarian will collect less than if he or she had waited to collect these benefits at the full retirement age. Similarly, if the librarian waits until the full retirement age to collect retirement benefits but does not live past the break-even point, then the librarian will collect less than if he or she had decided to collect those benefits early. For example, the break-even point for librarians who collect retirement benefits at the age of 62 is between 75 and 76. The exact point between 75 and 76 depends on one's salary history and date of birth. This means that if a librarian decides to collect retirement benefits at the age of 62 and lives past the age of 75 or 76, then the librarian's lifetime retirement benefits will be less. This important decision depends on the librarian's personal conditions, including available financial resources (pensions, personal savings, or other financial resources), anticipated life expectancy, marital status, health, or other personal contingencies.[17]

Several online calculators are available on the SSA website. The Retirement Estimator provides an estimate of retirement benefits for desired retirement ages. The librarian inputs his or her historical annual salaries as well as estimates of future annual salaries. Estimates of annual retirement benefits are then calculated.[18]

Following are additional Social Security tips for librarians considering retirement:

- Examine the Social Security website at www.ssa.gov. The website is an effective portal to the programs and services provided by the SSA. Brochures and other publications are available to review or order. Call an SSA representative (800-772-1213). Locate responses to questions via keyword searches as well as the associated e-mail option (http://ssa-custhelp.ssa.gov). It is possible to apply for benefits on the website.
- Go to one of the local Social Security offices and confer with a representative. Locations of the offices are available via the SSA website.
- Become familiar with the Social Security Retirement Planner on the website. The "Near Retirement?" section is particularly helpful. Retirement benefits can be estimated for a particular age via the Retirement Estimator. Other calculators are available. Work credits are explained. It is the key point in the SSA website for someone considering retirement.
- Selected websites providing information for retirees and pre-retirees:
  » AARP (www.aarp.org)
  » 360 Degrees of Financial Literacy (www.360financialliteracy.org)

» Women's Institute for a Secure Retirement (http://wiserwomen
.org)
» "Planning to Retire" blog (http://money.usnews.com/money/
blogs/planning-to-retire)
» Retirement Living Information Center (http://retirementliving
.com)
» Top 10 Ways to Prepare for Retirement (www.dol.gov/ebsa/
publications/10_ways_to_prepare.html)

- Register for Medicare several months prior to one's 65th birthday.
- It is possible to work as well as collect retirement benefits. If a librarian
collects retirement benefits prior to the full retirement age and is still
working, his or her retirement benefits are reduced $1 for every $2 earned
that exceeds a specified annual limit ($14,160 in 2010). After the librar-
ian attains the full retirement age, it is possible to work and collect retirement benefits without any penalties.
- It is possible to appeal decisions made by the SSA.

NOTES

1. Edgar K. Browning, "The Anatomy of Social Security and Medicare," *Independent Review*
13, no. 1 (Summer 2008): 5–27.
2. U.S. Social Security Administration, "Retirement Benefits (2010)," http://www.ssa.gov/
pubs/10035.pdf (accessed December 8, 2010). U.S. Social Security Administration,
"Understanding the Benefits (2010)," http://www.ssa.gov/pubs/10024.pdf (accessed
December 8, 2010). U.S. Social Security Administration, "What You Need to Know When
You Get Retirement or Survivors Benefits (2010)," http://www.ssa.gov/pubs/10077.pdf
(accessed December 8, 2010).
3. Ibid.
4. Social Security Online, "Retirement Planner: Frequently Asked Retirement Questions,"
http://www.socialsecurity.gov/planners/faqs.htm (accessed December 10, 2010).
5. U.S. Social Security Administration, "Disability Benefits 2010," http://www.socialsecurity
.gov/pubs/10029.pdf (accessed December 12, 2010).
6. U.S. Social Security Administration, "Survivors Benefits 2010," http://www.socialsecurity
.gov/pubs/10084.pdf (accessed December 12, 2010).
7. U.S. Social Security Administration, "Supplemental Security Income 2010," http://www
.socialsecurity.gov/pubs/11000.pdf (accessed December 12, 2010).
8. U.S. Social Security Administration, "Medicare 2010," http://www.socialsecurity.gov/
pubs/10043.pdf (accessed December 15, 2010).
9. Social Security Online, "Social Security Programs in the United States," http://www.ssa
.gov/policy/docs/progdesc/sspus (accessed December 15, 2010).

10. U.S. Social Security Administration, "Social Security Is Important to Women," http://www.socialsecurity.gov/pressoffice/factsheets/women-alt.pdf (accessed December 16, 2010). Institute for Women's Policy Research, "Women and Social Security: Benefit Types and Eligibility," Briefing Paper (2005): 1–8.

11. KnowledgeWharton, "Women Who Step Out of the Corporate World Find It Hard to Step Back In," http://knowledge.wharton.upenn.edu/article.cfm?articleid=1257 (accessed December 16, 2010).

12. Melynda Dovel Wilcox, "How Divorce Affects Women's Social Security," *Kiplinger's Personal Finance* 48, no. 10 (1994): 132. Social Security Online, "Retirement Planner: If You Are Divorced," http://www.socialsecurity.gov/retire2/divspouse.htm (accessed December 18, 2010).

13. Social Security Online, "Social Security Statement," http://www.ssa.gov/mystatement (accessed December 18, 2010).

14. Ibid.

15. U.S. Social Security Administration, "Retirement Benefits 2010." http://www.ssa.gov/pubs/10035.pdf (accessed December 20, 2010). Social Security Online, "Electronic Leaflet: How You Earn Credits," http://www.socialsecurity.gov/pubs/10072.html (accessed December 20, 2010).

16. Social Security Online, "Retirement Planner: Plan Your Retirement," http://www.socialsecurity.gov/retire2 (accessed December 21, 2010).

17. Ibid.

18. Social Security Online, "Benefit Calculators: About the Retirement Estimator," http://www.socialsecurity.gov/estimator (accessed December 21, 2010).

PART II

FINANCES IN RETIREMENT

5

YOUR INCOME IN RETIREMENT
STEPS TO A SOLID SPENDING PLAN

Maria A. Bruno, CFP

IF YOU'RE READING this chapter, take a moment to congratulate yourself. This likely means that you've already retired or are close to reaching this milestone. While that's exciting, it can also be overwhelming to begin thinking about how to replace a steady paycheck with other sources of income, such as Social Security and investments you've accumulated over the years. Our goals for this chapter are to break down the process of setting up a retirement spending plan and provide you with guidelines you can apply to your personal financial situation.

We'll address the topic in four sections. First, we'll discuss the need for a budget in order to determine whether your fixed income sources are sufficient or whether you'll need to spend from your investments. Next, we'll review common spending strategies you can adapt. We'll follow that with information about safe spending rates that will help you balance your need for income while ensuring you don't prematurely run out of money. Finally, once we've established how much you can spend, we'll provide useful tips on how to actually implement a plan.

One last word before we begin: This is not a once-and-done decision. Your spending plan needs to be flexible because your retirement lifestyle can and will change over time.

PART 1: GETTING STARTED WITH A RETIREMENT BUDGET —

A general rule of thumb suggests that you may need to replace about 70 to 80 percent of your preretirement income. While this is a good start, realize that expenses will change along with ongoing life changes. For example, early in retirement you may want to spend more on leisure and travel, but later you might worry about the increasing cost of health care. The closer you get to retirement, the more important it becomes to prepare a realistic budget. There are two main steps to this process: estimating your expenses—the cost of your retirement—and determining your income sources.

ESTIMATE YOUR EXPENSES

Expenses will typically fall into two buckets:

- *Nondiscretionary spending.* This bucket includes your mortgage or rent payments, food, transportation, health care, taxes, insurance premiums, and utility bills. These expenses are somewhat fixed in nature.
- *Discretionary spending.* This bucket covers items such as vacations, hobbies, entertainment, gifts, and charitable donations. These expenses are more variable.

You'll also want to consider the following when you think about your spending:

- *Emergency funds.* Don't forget about unexpected events. Your emergency cushion should be enough so that you'll feel financially secure if you find yourself in need.
- *Inflation.* Although you may have a good idea of what your expenses are now, make sure to account for the likelihood of inflation—a general rise in the prices of goods and services—over the course of your retirement years.

DETERMINE YOUR RETIREMENT INCOME SOURCES

Now that you have a good idea of what your expenses will be, the next step is to identify all of your sources of retirement income. Keep in mind that there are two different kinds of income: fixed or guaranteed, which you can always count on, and variable, which can change in amount or duration.

Some possibilities for "guaranteed" income in retirement include:

- *Social Security.* Your Social Security benefits will provide a first level of reliable income. The exact amount will depend on how long you've worked, how much you've earned, and at what age you started receiving benefits. To get an estimate of your benefits at various ages, call the Social Security Administration at 800-772-1213 or go to its website: www.ssa.gov.
- *Pensions.* If you have a pension, remember that most offer several options for taking distributions. Check with your current or former employer for more information.
- *Fixed income annuities.* This guaranteed income stream can help minimize your risk of running out of money if you live longer than expected or if the financial markets perform poorly. (We'll discuss income annuities later in this chapter.)

Variable income may include:

- *Part-time employment.* Many of today's retirees plan to continue working part-time to supplement their income in the early years of retirement.
- *Investment income.* Depending on how your assets are invested, you may receive interest, dividends, and capital gains distributions from your taxable investments. You will also want to include required distributions from retirement accounts such as a 401(k) plan or IRA.

When estimating your retirement expenses, be careful not to overlook taxes. True, once you collect your last paycheck, you no longer owe Social Security or other payroll taxes. Also, your federal, state, and local income taxes may be lower, and if you are age 65 or older, you will have a higher standard deduction on your federal income tax. But even though some taxes will disappear when you retire, remember the following:

- Your taxes may actually go up. If you own your home, property taxes will likely rise.
- Your income taxes could rise when you start withdrawing money from your retirement accounts.
- You may owe taxes on Social Security. If your total income—whether from a part-time job, pension, annuity, or other source—exceeds certain levels, you may owe federal income tax on up to 85 percent of your Social Security benefits.

Once you've had the chance to evaluate your expenses and income, you should have a pretty good idea of your financial health. While some people will find that they have more than enough income to live comfortably, others will realize they won't be able to cover their expenses. Figure 5.1 shows you what you should consider if your retirement budget exercise yields a surplus (i.e., your income exceeds your spending) or a shortfall or deficit (i.e., your spending exceeds your income).

FIGURE 5.1 STEPS TO CONSIDER AFTER COMPLETING YOUR BUDGETING EXERCISE

IF YOU HAVE A SURPLUS

Make sure your emergency fund has sufficient reserves—enough cash to cover at least six to twelve months of anticipated spending needs.

Reinvest accrued excess cash to periodically rebalance your portfolio and restore your target asset allocation.

IF YOU HAVE A SHORTFALL

Spend from your portfolio (see Part 2 for a discussion on how much to spend and Part 3 for common withdrawal approaches).

Reduce your expenses. Look to trim your discretionary spending first.

Consider working part-time in retirement.

An increasing number of retirees today are leaving the workforce with lump sum retirement plan balances instead of traditional pension plans. This may mean that you will have to translate a lump sum into a source of income that will last through retirement. Next, we'll provide some guidelines on how to manage your spending plan.

PART 2: IF YOU NEED TO SPEND FROM YOUR INVESTMENTS, HOW DO YOU START?

There are essentially two methods of withdrawing funds from your portfolio in retirement: dollar inflation-adjusted withdrawals or percent of portfolio withdrawals. Each method has pros and cons to consider before you pick one or adapt one to fit your lifestyle.

DOLLAR INFLATION-ADJUSTED WITHDRAWALS

With this method, you start by withdrawing a base percentage amount of your investment portfolio in the first year. A common guideline, as we'll discuss in the next section, is 4 percent. In the second year, you adjust the dollar amount based on inflation, typically using the consumer price index (CPI) as a guideline. In each subsequent year, you adjust the previous year's spending level by the new inflation rate.

Example: Mary has a $500,000 portfolio and wants to spend 4 percent during her first year in retirement.

- Year 1: She withdraws $20,000—4 percent of the portfolio balance.
- Year 2: Inflation is 3 percent, so Mary withdraws $20,600—the previous year's withdrawal ($20,000) adjusted for inflation ($600).
- Year 3: Inflation is 1 percent, so Mary withdraws $20,806—the previous year's withdrawal ($20,600) adjusted for inflation ($206).

If you follow this approach, your withdrawals will be relatively predictable and generally keep pace with inflation. The downside is that if the market should undergo a prolonged or severe downturn (as we recently experienced in the late 2000s)—especially early in your retirement—your assets could be substantially depleted since you're essentially spending a larger percentage of your portfolio. In this situation, it's a good idea to adjust withdrawals based on the new balance.

PERCENT OF PORTFOLIO WITHDRAWALS

Using this method, you withdraw the same percentage of the portfolio balance annually.

Example: Mike starts out with $500,000 and wants to spend 4 percent during each year of his retirement.

- Year 1: Mike withdraws $20,000—4 percent of the portfolio balance.
- Year 2: Mike's portfolio is up 5 percent and the balance is $504,000, so he withdraws $20,160.
- Year 3: Mike's portfolio is down 6 percent and the balance is $454,810, so he withdraws $18,192.

In general, this method is easier to use. And while your portfolio may shrink over time, you are unlikely to run out of money. The tradeoff, however, is that your withdrawals will fluctuate annually, depending on market performance, and you will need to be comfortable with potentially wide swings in spending.

So, how do you choose? If you're looking for a fairly predictable income stream from year to year and are willing to regularly monitor your actual spending level, then dollar inflation-adjusted withdrawals may be a good approach. If, you're more comfortable knowing your portfolio is less likely to be depleted and are willing to accept swings in annual income, percent of portfolio may be a better fit. You may end up incorporating a hybrid of both methods. Regardless, remember that flexibility is key and will help you handle any unexpected expenses that life throws your way.

PART 3: SPENDING FROM YOUR INVESTMENTS: WHAT'S REALISTIC AND WHAT'S NOT?

If you're like most retirees, one of the first questions you will likely ask is, "How much can I safely spend from my portfolio without outliving my assets?" A well-known approach to addressing this question is the "4 percent spending rule." According to this guideline, a retiree with a diversified portfolio balanced between stocks and bonds can safely adopt a 4 percent dollar inflation-adjusted withdrawal approach without running out of money over a thirty-year time horizon.

To determine whether a 4 percent spending guideline is suitable for you, consider the following:

- What is your time horizon? While this is one of the most important factors, it depends on some guesswork. Given today's longer life expectan-

THE IMPORTANCE OF ASSET ALLOCATION

Regardless of what investing stage you're in, one of your first steps is to establish an asset allocation for your investments. Allocation is typically based on your goals and objectives, time horizon, and risk tolerance. These factors continue to be important when you retire. You should not base your asset allocation strictly on trying to maximize your current income. Doing so could jeopardize your portfolio's long-term growth potential and subject you to additional market risk as well. If you'd like help with determining your asset allocation, tools are available online, including Vanguard's Investor Questionnaire at www .vanguard.com/myassetallocation.

cies and improved health care, living to age 95 and beyond is entirely feasible. At the onset of retirement, you might adopt a 4 percent spending rule, or even less, as a safeguard. But as you advance through the years, you can spend more as your life expectancy shortens. It's reasonable to assume that you can spend 5 to 7 percent as you reach your 70s and 80s.

- What is your portfolio asset allocation? Is your allocation—or mix of stocks, bonds, and cash investments—considered conservative, moderate, or aggressive for your age? Although a more aggressive approach with greater allocation to stocks may allow for higher spending levels, you will need to be prepared for—and comfortable with—greater fluctuations in your portfolio's value. On the other hand, a more conservative portfolio allocated heavily toward bonds or cash would be able to support lower overall spending levels.

- What is your desired level of certainty? How important is it to you to be certain your assets will last as long as—or longer than—you live? You generally cannot plan with 100 percent certainty that you won't run out of money when you spend from your portfolio; therefore, if you desire greater certainty, you should expect to spend less overall.

FIGURE 5.2   LEVERS THAT INFLUENCE SPENDING RATES

	LOWER SPENDING RATE	HIGHER SPENDING RATE
Time horizon	Longer	Shorter
Asset allocation	More conservative	More aggressive
Degree of certainty	Higher	Lower

STEP 4: PUTTING YOUR SPENDING PLAN INTO ACTION

Once you've inventoried your income sources as discussed above, you'll want to designate a "spending account" as your cash management account. This is typically a money market or bank checking account. A good rule of thumb is to keep enough cash on hand to cover at least six to twelve months of anticipated spending needs. If you have a short-term goal, like a big vacation or home project, you might opt to keep a higher balance.

To facilitate cash flow, direct your primary income sources to your spending account. These include payments such as Social Security, pensions, and part-time income. You'll also want to direct to this account any investment cash flows such as required minimum distributions (RMDs) from tax-deferred accounts and dividends, interest, and capital gains distributions from taxable accounts. Since this money will be subject to income taxes anyway, it generally should be the first source tapped for spending, allowing the assets that remain invested the potential for continued tax-sheltered growth.

If these cash flows suffice, you don't likely need to make any withdrawals from your investments. Any significant surplus in the spending account may be reinvested in the portfolio to help with periodic rebalancing to maintain the target asset allocation.

But what if the cash flows are not sufficient? In this case, you'll need to take withdrawals from your investments. A systematic withdrawal plan (SWP) from your portfolio gives you the most flexibility. You maintain control over your investment strategy and have complete access to your money. But there are risks as well. If the market drops significantly early in your retirement, you may have to adjust your withdrawal amount so that you don't run the risk of running out of money. And again, you'll want to make sure you maintain the right asset allocation—an appropriate mix of stocks, bonds, and cash.

WHICH ASSETS TO DRAW DOWN FIRST

If you're like many investors, your portfolio may consist of different account types, including taxable, tax-deferred retirement, and Roth accounts (see figure 5.3). If

WHAT ARE RMDS?

When you reach age 70½, the IRS requires you to withdraw at least a minimum amount from all of your IRAs and retirement plans and pay ordinary income taxes on the taxable portion of your withdrawal. If you do not take your required minimum distribution (RMD), you'll owe the federal government a 50 percent penalty on the difference between the amount you withdrew and the amount you should have withdrawn. In addition, you'll still have to withdraw the required amount and pay any income taxes due. Generally, your RMD must be taken by December 31, either as a lump sum or in installments. However, for your first RMD when you turn 70½, you can delay taking the distribution until April 1 of the following year.

this is the case, a good strategy is to withdraw from your taxable accounts first. This approach generally has two benefits. First, your tax-deferred and Roth accounts can benefit from additional future growth potential. Second, this spending order most likely will produce a lower current tax bill. Withdrawals from taxable accounts are taxed at lower capital gains tax rates, while distributions from tax-deferred accounts are taxed at the higher ordinary income tax rates. When taking distributions from tax-deferred accounts, you generally have to pay income taxes on the entire withdrawal at the higher rate. To net the same amount as from a taxable account, you

A WORD ON INCOME ANNUITIES

When you purchase an income annuity, you're promised a stream of payments in exchange for the purchase price (i.e., a lump sum payment). This income can last for as long as you live, for as long as you or your spouse lives, or for a specific number of years. Income annuities are a form of insurance against longevity risk—the risk that you will outlive your assets. When shopping for an income annuity, you should seek a highly rated insurance company that is considered financially strong enough to honor its obligations.

There are many different types of income annuities, but the most common include the following:

- Single premium annuities are purchased with a single payment, typically at retirement.
- Immediate-income annuities begin to pay regular cash benefits right away.
- Single life annuities could provide benefits for as long as you live.
- Joint-and-survivor payments continue over your lifetime and that of another person, such as your spouse.
- Guaranteed number of years means that payments end after the guaranteed period, even if you live longer. If you die during the guarantee period, remaining payments go to your beneficiaries.

Most individuals are already getting an income annuity through Social Security benefits, and some also have employer pensions. In most cases, the question you want to answer is not whether you need an annuity but rather, "Do I need a higher guarantee as a floor for my base expenses?" If the answer is "yes," then you may want to consider an inflation-adjusted income annuity.

An income annuity purchase is typically irrevocable, so you give up flexibility in return for guaranteed payments. You're buying a stream of regular income, but it's not an asset that you can pass along to heirs or cash in for emergencies. You'll want to weigh the value of the insurance provided against the additional costs.

would have to take a higher withdrawal. Over time, the acceleration of income taxes and the resulting loss of tax-deferred growth could negatively affect the portfolio by causing lower balances or possibly a worst-case scenario of depletion.

FIGURE 5.3   GENERAL WITHDRAWAL ORDER BY ACCOUNT TYPE

BEFORE AGE 70½
1. Taxable accounts
2. Tax-deferred accounts (traditional IRAs and employer-sponsored retirement plans)
3. Roth accounts

AFTER AGE 70½
1. RMDs from tax-deferred accounts
2. Taxable accounts
3. Tax-deferred accounts
4. Roth accounts

Certainly, in some situations you may want to consider a different spending order. For example, if you expect to be in a much lower tax bracket in the future, you may want to think about spending from tax-deferred accounts first. The framework we've outlined above can serve as a prudent guideline for most investors. If you're considering a personalized spending program, you may benefit from consulting a tax-planning professional.

CONCLUSION

Generating income in retirement is not a new challenge; many generations have done so effectively using a variety of tried-and-true investment strategies. What is different today is that many retirees will receive their benefits in the form of a lump sum instead of the traditional lifetime pension. This, coupled with longer life expectancies, can create additional challenges.

In deciding how to allocate your resources, you'll want to incorporate the guidelines in this chapter into your specific retirement plan. Understand your options, recognize the relative tradeoffs, and implement the strategy you feel can best meet your goals. Remember to be realistic—a prudent plan is based on practical long-term spending levels, diversification of risk, and sensible expectations for future market returns. Most important, don't adopt a "set it and forget it" mentality. Your retirement years will bring changes to your personal life—both expected and unexpected—and your retirement income plan will need to be similarly flexible to meet those needs.

For more information about retirement planning topics, visit Vanguard's website: www.vanguard.com/retirementinsights. Vanguard offers additional insights for any stage of retirement, as well as tools to help you model simple "what-if" scenarios. Remember that all investments are subject to risk.

REFERENCES

Bruno, Maria A. 2010. *Income in retirement: Common investment strategies.* Valley Forge, PA: The Vanguard Group.

Jaconetti, Colleen. 2007. *Spending from a portfolio: Implications of a total return versus an income approach for taxable investors.* Valley Forge, PA: The Vanguard Group.

The Vanguard Group. 2009. *Live the life you imagined as you reach retirement.* Distributed by Vanguard Marketing Corporation.

———. 2010. Evaluate your retirement expenses and income. https://personal .vanguard.com/us/insights/retirement/nearing/evaluate-expenses-and-income -needs.

6

INVESTMENT STRATEGIES FOR FISCALLY CHALLENGED LIBRARIANS

James B. Casey

Abraham Lincoln was never reputed to be a "high earning" lawyer. In one famous story he is said to have returned $10 to a client out of the total of $25 that was paid for his services with the admission that the client had mistaken him for an "expensive lawyer." Nevertheless, Lincoln amassed a considerable amount of personal wealth during his years of modest earnings as a lawyer, even though it was noted that he was not considered to be as skillful at "getting" as he was at "keeping." Librarians have never been among the higher salaried professions. Nor do librarians generally possess elaborate pensions that allow for early retirement at nearly full salary. Nevertheless, librarians can use their research skills to identify small, but prudent investments over time that can gradually build for a more comfortable retirement.

Without attempting to present a full tutorial on investments, I will offer what I believe are the two best ways to use comparatively small amounts of money in gradual investments over time that could save or earn many thousands of dollars and help to build a more comfortable retirement. They involve dealing with two of the most serious threats to retirement planning— debt and inflation.

Debt cannot be avoided unless you are independently wealthy. Nevertheless, not all debt obligations pose the same level of threat. Some debt is clearly not manageable. However, the containment and elimination of high-interest consumer debt is a prerequisite for sensible retirement planning and investment. High-interest debt from credit cards is a serious trap into which many people fall when lured by the low minimum payments touted on credit card bills. With interest rates on credit cards in double digits and some over 20 percent, paying off the entire balance as soon as possible should be a priority but often is not because of other obligations. The prudent librarian/investor chooses to stop adding debt to credit cards and focuses full attention on liquidation of the debt. You may want to consider home equity loans or other lower interest debt to provide the cash to close out the higher interest credit card debt. Doing so also will allow you to move away from credit cards to debit cards as a way to avoid spending beyond your means and incurring high interest debt. If you must use credit cards, be sure that you are in a position to pay off the entire bill each month.

Sometimes incurring debt can be strategic and help to build wealth over the long term. School loans, for example, offer the opportunity to acquire higher credentials that can increase earnings potential dramatically. Mortgages for homes or condos represent significant debt, but they also allow you to build equity in a home rather than simply pay rent. In most instances, loans for education or homes or automobiles carry a small fraction of the interest that credit card debt requires. A wise strategy for dealing with the larger, but more manageable interest debt involves paying additional amounts toward the principal on mortgage and other long-term obligations. In the early years of most mortgages, very little if any of the money paid per month goes toward the principal on the loan. Paying any additional amount each month—even if it is only $25—is helpful especially at the beginning because it reduces the number of dollars against which the interest is calculated. If you can keep chipping away at the principal through additional payments, you will be shortening the duration of the time needed to pay off the mortgage and save many thousands of dollars of interest payments over time. When thinking about when to retire, owning your home free and clear is an important consideration and probably represents your single most important investment.

The other inevitable threat to retirement planning is inflation. Whatever money put aside that is not used to reduce high interest debt should be invested in ways that will enable it to grow and keep pace with or exceed the annual inflation rate. A bankroll of $10,000 kept "safe" under your bed almost certainly won't be worth that much in purchasing power in ten or twenty years. The wise librarian will find ways to invest those dollars for the future and turn it into $20,000 or $30,000. But, liquidating any high-interest consumer debt should always come before investing in any markets. Absolutely nothing is gained by making good investments earning an average of 10 percent per year in the stock market while carrying credit card debt charging you 15 percent or more. Liquidate the credit card debt before venturing into battle with inflation.

Buying bank CDs or putting money into passbook savings accounts has the advantage of being insured up to $250,000 per depositor in banks insured by the Federal Deposit Insurance Corporation (FDIC). While this is very helpful and offers peace of mind, during this era of bank failures, the 1 or 2 percent interest generally available for small deposits likely won't outrun the march of inflation. The wise librarian will invest at least a portion of savings in the riskier world of financial markets where gains of as much as 20 or 30 percent are possible in a good year (such as in 2009), but where inevitable losses are also possible.

With low salaries, mortgages and loans to repay, and family responsibilities, many librarians might feel that the tiny sums of money they might have available to invest would be totally inadequate to venture into the realms of the financial markets. The ups and downs of the markets might also provide a disincentive to "gamble" hard-earned money. Nevertheless, investment instruments such as mutual funds and investment strategies such as dollar cost averaging can enable you to purchase shares with modest investments of as little as $50 at a time. Diversified and professionally managed portfolios of stocks, bonds, and other instruments offer the advantage of risk controlled by diversification and with the opportunity for long-term growth over time.

I would recommend that the enterprising librarian who has eliminated credit card debt and accumulated a few thousand dollars to invest avoid going to a local broker for investment advice. Brokers earn sales commissions regardless of the performance of your investment dollars and charge fees for their services and advice, thereby diminishing your return. Your objective should be to put every one of your investment dollars in the hands of experts who will manage a portfolio of investment instruments while charging you as little money as possible—or nothing at all.

Although there are many kinds of investment instruments available within the financial markets, among the safest and most conservative choices for the investor of modest means are mutual funds. Mutual funds are "investment companies" where the investor buys shares of a professionally managed portfolio that may contain as many as several dozen or even hundreds of different stocks, bonds, and other investment vehicles. Each mutual fund will have a strategy or philosophy of investment and a prospectus that explains in detail the nature of that strategy and the levels of risk expected. Diversification controls risk by balancing the loss of investment of one company or bond against many others that perform well and can compensate for any loss.

Many outstanding mutual funds are also affiliated with larger "families" of funds to which investors can move their investments over time in the event that a given fund has a disappointing performance. Moving your investment from one fund to another within the same family could be accomplished as easily as making a phone call and often costs nothing. Many outstanding mutual funds are also "no load" and require absolutely no sales commission or percentage of the investment payable upon initial purchase. Just as investors must pay brokerage fees when buying stocks, loads can eat into the initial investment and put lower-income investors at a disadvantage. With no-load funds, every dollar of the investment goes toward the purchase of shares in the mutual fund. The fund managers of such no-load funds draw a percentage from the aggregate fund growth rather than out of the individual investor's money. In other words, they make their money based on the performance of the fund rather than as a sales commission such as those charged by brokers.

The next objective in retirement planning is to shelter the money invested and the gains on those investments from taxes for as long as possible in order to maximize the growth potential. Librarians should ask their employers about 403(b) and 401(k) opportunities available to them. A 403(b) plan enables employees to have a set amount removed from their paycheck before taxes are deducted to be invested with a mutual fund on a regular basis. The amount per paycheck can be as little as $50. In the case of a 401(k), the employer adds to the sum regularly contributed by the employee. In either case, the taxes are deferred and the investment grows over many years until the money is withdrawn—presumably after retirement when your income and tax obligations will be lower. In addition to the tax deferment benefits, steady investment of money into a diversified, professionally managed portfolio enables the wise librarian to avoid the risks associated with market volatility through dollar cost averaging. The steady investment over time of the same amount of money means that shares of the mutual fund purchased in a high market when the price is high are balanced by those purchased when the market is down and shares are less expensive. Hence, the risk of market timing is eliminated or greatly reduced.

Individual retirement accounts (IRAs) represent another excellent means by which the librarian of modest means can invest for the future while reducing tax obligations. The IRA investment is tax deductible up to $5,000 per year ($6,000 if you are over 50) for those with adjusted gross incomes of $56,000 or less ($89,000 for married filing jointly). Partial deductions can be made for those earning over the limits noted above. More important, the growth and dividends attained by your IRA investment are tax deferred. You may begin to withdraw funds from the IRA without penalty at age 59½, but you must have the IRA investments withdrawn and taxable by age 70½. At the time when IRA proceeds are no longer tax deferred and you finally make use of the money, most of you would be retired and reporting a much lower taxable income than when you were fully employed. The Roth IRA is an investment option that is even more advantageous than the regular IRA. Although you cannot deduct the initial investment from your taxable income, the money can be withdrawn tax-free after age 59½, which means your investment results will be actually tax free rather than tax deferred. A modest IRA investment of just $1,000 in a well-managed no-load mutual fund can not only achieve the kind of diversification and professional management once available only to affluent investors, but it also avoids brokerage and load fees as well as initial tax obligations.

Modest investments can accumulate handsomely over time and sometimes even surpass larger investments made with less prudence and reduced by brokerage fees. If a 35-year-old librarian was able to invest $1,000 in a no-load mutual fund and add $50 per month to that investment via a 403(b) plan at work with an average return of 9 percent, at the end of thirty years that investment would have grown to $102,412.81. On the other hand, $10,000 invested in bank instruments earning 3 percent over thirty years and with no additional investment would reach only $24,272.62. There are several "compound interest calculators" available on the Internet that can assist with such computations. This is one of my favorites: www .moneychimp.com/calculator/compound_interest_calculator.htm. Of course, the reality faced by most of us investing in the markets has been a mix of experiences. We have seen huge gains balanced with heavy losses in down markets. If the funds you select are sound choices, the long-term results of the market ups and downs should see substantial overall growth. Outside of insured accounts, however, there are no guarantees.

How then do you select the best mutual funds from among the thousands in the marketplace? It should be a comparatively easy job—especially for an enterprising librarian using the many books, periodicals, and websites available in your library. Publications such as *Forbes, Barron's, Business Week, Fortune, Kiplinger's Personal Finance, Smart Money,* and the *Wall Street Journal* often contain summary ratings and reports on the performance of mutual funds. *Forbes* has even published an "honor roll" of the best performing mutual funds in up and down markets. Morningstar.com is one of the largest and most comprehensive sites assessing all investment instruments with a one- to five-star rating scheme and detailed breakdowns of fund performance, fees, and loads, and biographical information about the fund managers. Checking out a book or two about mutual fund investing might also be worthwhile. One of the best investing titles of 2010 was the sixth edition of *Mutual Funds for Dummies* by Eric Tyson (Wiley).

After looking over some of the literature and sites reporting on mutual funds, you will want to visit the actual sites of the larger no-load fund families to look over their products and also to discuss your investment strategy with one of their account executives. Keep in mind that the fund families are inclined to promote and sell their products just as any broker might. However, they can provide valuable information and the prospectuses and charts for each and every fund under management and not charge you a load or fee for such information.

One of the best features of mutual funds is that you as the shareholder will not have to do much work or make any significant stock or bond purchasing decisions. The fund managers do the work, and if you have chosen your fund wisely the results should be highly gratifying in the long run. When mutual fund shareholders try to micromanage their fund managers by attempting to time the market, the results will likely be disappointing. I once pulled funds out of a highly successful stock mutual fund and put the money in a safe money market fund within the same fund family just before a large market drop. For a time, I felt like I had outsmarted the market. However, a few years later it was clear that those who had not pulled out before the drop were actually poised to take full advantage of the recovery, while I had delayed getting back into the stock fund. My own IRA was several thousand dollars below those investors who hadn't been as "clever" as I had tried to be in pulling out before the downturn.

Just as Lincoln proved to be especially good at accumulating personal assets despite a modest personal income from his work on the legal circuit as an "inexpensive lawyer," many librarians can use their knowledge and research skills to build financial security that could surpass that of other higher salaried persons who are less careful about managing the assets that they have. For Lincoln, the failure of a business venture in the early 1830s left him with a huge debt that he jokingly called "the national debt." After many years, he finally liquidated that debt and began to slowly, carefully accumulate wealth. Many librarians with modest incomes may have to do the same—liquidating high-interest consumer debt and then proceeding with confidence to use their research skills to seek out the best investments to put their hard-earned money to work in preparation for retirement.

7 —————————————————————————————————

LEARNING TO BE FRUGAL
FINDING THE BEST DEALS TO MAINTAIN AN ACTIVE LIFESTYLE

Rose Parkman Marshall

THE FIRST MONTH after retirement, I realized I would not be watching daytime television, which is chock full of home shopping, infomercials, tell-all DNA testing episodes, and too many shows with little or no redeeming social value! What's a retired librarian to do? Well, age has its benefits, and making the transition into retirement has not been difficult because I "practiced" for retirement. Practice you say? Yes, at age 55 I learned I was a "senior" and discovered that seniors get discounts on everything—movie tickets, hotel rooms, a daily cup of java, luxury spa packages, and even free desserts and appetizers at restaurants. Remaining active, entertained, and well-traveled in retirement are all important, so I still actively search for deals to help stretch my pension dollars. Let me share some of my tried-and-true tips with you in the next few pages.

Entertainment and recreation are areas I thought would be scaled back in retirement. However, with a bit of research I learned that botanical gardens, zoos, amusement parks, and sporting arenas often have discounts for seniors. Many museums, seasonal shows, libraries, and special collections charge no admission and are great places to while away an entire day. Harvard University alone boasts of having 90 libraries, including archives and special collections. When you travel, put a library tour on your itinerary. Just last week I spotted a sign on the interstate highway, detoured, and spent three hours touring the Billy Graham Library and family home place in Charlotte, North Carolina. You may also join a local city or county-run senior center in your community and take advantage of day trips for apple picking, wine tasting, autumn foliage tours, or even a visit to a casino—a few of the offerings in my hometown. If you are new in town, the chamber of commerce provides valuable information, including maps and brochures, for all kinds of recreational and cultural events. The chamber in the city where I retired even has a listing of "senior communities" and assisted-living facilities.

One of the best finds since retiring is the "America the Beautiful" senior pass from the National Park Service. Check out this $10 lifetime pass for citizens and permanent residents at www.nps.gov/fees_passes.htm. This pass admits the pass holder and passengers in a noncommercial vehicle at per vehicle fee areas or the pass holder and three adults. You can purchase the pass in person at any park, and it is free for people with permanent disabilities.

Retirement does not mean I'm "going to pot" and not going out! Librarians are naturally curious, and intellectual curiosity and a keen awareness of our environment are hallmarks of librarians. Therefore, living in or near a college town may be just the ticket for continuing access to top-notch cultural and artistic events. Many local colleges and universities offer classes as part of a "senior network," and retirees can audit classes free of charge if seats are available. This is a great opportunity to interact with people of all ages, maybe learn a new skill, and continue to exercise your brain cells. Get on a mailing list to receive notices about exhibitions, theater productions, special celebrations and guests speakers, and cultural activities that may be free or discounted. To get more information, look on a university website and be sure to check its continuing education department, senior academy, or life-long learning program for all kinds of programs and opportunities.

As we age, access to health care is critical, and enjoying good health is considered the "single most important factor impacting retiree happiness" (Lagier 2010). Many seniors choose a retirement community based on the reputation of the local hospital or for its proximity to a large regional trauma hospital. Additionally, some retirees may not be able to afford quality medical and dental care, but if there is a medical or dental school in your vicinity, free or affordable health care may be available. Note that dental schools are more likely to provide free or reduced fees than medical schools. The National Association of Free Clinics at www.freeclinics .us lists free stand-alone clinics for low-income individuals, including seniors. Finally, low-income retirees and those with excessive medical expenses may qualify for Medicaid assistance at their state's Department of Health and Human Services Medicaid Office. For more information, go to the website of the Centers for Medicare and Medicaid Services, the federal agency that administers the program at www.cms.gov.

One big question for me on retiring was whether I could continue to eat out and how often. Most sit-down restaurants now ask customers to complete cards in order to receive weekly discount coupons and notices of specials. One of the oldest ways to save money is to clip coupons or print them from websites for your favorite eateries; however, it is recommended that you bookmark only a few selected, reputable sites. A few of the more notable sites that proved helpful are the following:

- www.seniordiscounts.com
- www.coupons.com
- www.wow-coupons.com

Many restaurants offer seniors free or discounted appetizers, desserts, and beverages, and they highlight senior items or have a separate senior section on their menus. Do not be ashamed to ask for the senior discount, and do not be offended when the clerk automatically gives you the senior price! Regularly check out this website to see which national chains offer discounts to your favorite restaurant: http://frugalliving.about.com/od/frugalseniors/a/Senior_Discount.htm.

For the sports minded, living in or near a college town affords great benefits. In every university town that I have lived, there is no admission charge for most women's sporting events. (I do not know why this is a trend, but I suspect it has to do with low attendance at these events.) I have enjoyed basketball, soccer, tennis, disc golf, and softball without ever having to pay. As with cultural events, many colleges and universities allow retirees to participate in a senior wellness plan. Seniors may use the fitness facilities at off-peak times and enjoy all the amenities of a well-equipped gym without a contract or steep monthly fees. Often, there is a chance to participate in nutrition and exercise research studies, experiments, and programs to help seniors maintain active lifestyles. Another part of good health for retirees is good nutrition. Small towns and cities often boast cooperatives, farmers' markets, and pick-your-own fruit farms. During harvest time, seniors have plentiful options for fresh, local produce, and many businesses offer special senior discount days. Again, your local newspaper and chamber of commerce are good sources of information.

Before I move on from recreation, I want to pass on a tip for golfers. I attended the 2010 Masters Tournament in Augusta, Georgia, and the pass for the practice round was the best $38 I have ever spent. Last year's champion and the best golfers in the world practice "up close and personal." All the big names come early for two or three days of practice before the tourney begins. Soon after the tournament, go on the official Masters website, print an application for tickets to next year's practice round, and mail it and wait for the letter indicating whether you are eligible to purchase tickets. Remember, go to the official site, not the sites selling practice round tickets for $250! Check for similar deals wherever PGA tournaments are held across the country. Finally, green fees are generally 30 to 50 percent cheaper in the fall, but check your local course to learn if it has a discount day or time each week, or check when senior fees are offered. You can find great green fees at www .greatgreenfees.com.

Many large retail chains realize retirees have time to shop when others are at work. Therefore, merchants often provide a senior discount day—generally Tuesday, Wednesday, or Thursday—to encourage seniors to avoid weekend crowds. To learn when national retailers have discount days, go to the Frugal Living website for a selected list: http://frugalliving.about.com/od/frugalseniors/a/Senior_Discount .htm. This list includes retailers such as department stores, movie theaters, and stores that sell seconds or factory overruns. Goodwill Industries and Hancock's Fabrics have senior discount days, too Be sure to inquire if your favorite local or regional stores set aside discount days. Another great find sure to appeal to librarians is GoodSearch.com, a search engine that donates 50 percent of its sponsored search revenue to the charities and schools designated by its users. Is has a link for "GoodShop," and 30 percent of purchases from this site also go to charity. Be sure to click on "Coupons and Deals" to get deals at more than 1,500 stores.

Other selected categories that may appeal to retirees include style, transportation, and vacations. For fifteen years, I have had my hair cut at cosmetology and barber colleges. Students need someone to practice on, and I never mind them trimming my hair or giving me a perm. Nowadays, many colleges also offer manicure and pedicure services. If you live where there is no college, check to see if local beauty and barber salons offer a discount to seniors. Many national salons offer discounts that vary from 10 to 20 percent, but these will add up over time. Check out the senior age limits at these salons to see if you qualify for deals:

- Supercuts—www.supercuts.com
- Master Cuts—www.mastercuts.com
- Great Clips—www.greatclips.com

You may also want to call schools that train *estheticians and massage therapists. My baby boomer body needs their skills, and these students also need clients on which to practice.*

Most librarians have already bookmarked the best sites to search for deals on airline tickets. The following familiar sites are already in my Delicious database, and many of these travel services include hotel and car rental packages with their airfare deals:

- Travelocity—select the 65+ box: www.travelocity.com
- Cheap Air—select the 65+ box: www.cheapoair.com
- Expedia—select the 65+: www.expedia.com

A word of caution: Even though a senior price is offered, most travelers know the +65 fare may not be the cheapest fare. It is always wise to shop around, compare prices, and search a number of sites to get your best deals. Do not forget to search official company sites to see what kinds of specials are available. The sites below do not have a senior option, but check to see if they offer great deals:

- Orbitz—www.orbitz.com
- Priceline—www.priceline.com
- Hotwire—www.hotwire.com
- Cheap Tickets—www.cheaptickets.com
- Last Minute—for U.S. travel, http://us.lastminute.com

My first-ever train ride was last summer on Amtrak, and the agent automatically gave me a discount when he checked my ID. Amtrak's website states, "Amtrak travelers 62 years of age and over are eligible to receive a 15% discount on the lowest available rail fare on most Amtrak trains." At www.amtrak.com, select the "Deals" tab, then select "Passenger Discounts." If you wish to visit several destinations, you may want to examine Amtrak's USA Rail Pass. Not 62 yet? You can use your AAA card and receive a 10 percent discount. If a bus is more your speed, Greyhound gives a 5 percent discount on unrestricted passenger fares—www.greyhound.com. The bus is a good option if you are traveling 200–400 miles from home, would be driving alone, or if gas prices are prohibitive. Both carriers require appropriate identification to verify age; please check their websites for any restrictions.

Now that we no longer need to cut vacations short in order to return to work, retired librarians have time for longer vacations. One way to vacation longer is to get hotel and resort rooms at a "steal." First of all, American Association of Retired Persons (AARP) cards may be used to get discounts at hotels and resorts throughout the United States. Hotels.com boasts that it can find the best deals for over "120,000 hotels in more than 60 countries." Take advantage of its price match guarantee. There are hundreds of sites offering deals on vacations worldwide, but librarians know how to navigate through information to find the most reputable sites. Here are a few sites I have used with great success:

- Hotels.com—www.hotels.com
- Resort Vacations to Go—www.resortvacationstogo.com
- Resort Complete is part of Hotels.com and offers deals on cruises as well as resort destinations—www.resortcompete.com

A few hints and tips not addressed elsewhere:

- In the United States, "senior" may mean any age between 50 and 65.
- Get an AARP membership. The card often offers discounts in unexpected places.
- Identify yourself as a senior before placing an order.
- Also identify yourself as a senior when making reservations and be sure to ask the age—you may be asked to show identification when you arrive in person.
- Travel with a group to take advantage of group discounts.
- If your budget is really tight, think about day trips or short week-day vacations during off-peak times. (I stayed Sunday through Wednesday at a $250 Myrtle Beach, South Carolina, condo in early December and paid only $69 per night. The added bonus of coming in December was that there were no tourists jamming the beaches, streets, stores, and restaurants. There is nothing like watching the sunrise from a sixth-floor balcony overlooking the Atlantic Ocean.)

To sum up, retirees must be proud to tell their age if they want deals and discounts. They must also think outside the box and not be timid in initiating a conversation about why a senior discount is *not* available. Some goods and services that may not automatically come to mind when thinking "senior deals" are dry cleaners, gym memberships, car dealerships, car washing and detailing, lawn service, and pet grooming—to name a few. Moreover, do not forget to inquire at banks and credit unions. (I am over 55, so I do not pay an annual credit union fee, nor do I pay for checking.) If retirees want to be culturally engaged, intellectually stimulated, healthy and physically active, well groomed, and well fed without breaking the bank, they need to ask for a senior discount everywhere they go. And if no discount is available, ask why not. The Administration on Aging estimated that between 76 and 79 million baby boomers have or will retire soon. That's a lot of power! I wish you a happy retirement.

Please note that inclusion of a website in this article is not an endorsement of that company. I have used most of the websites included in the last few years, but a few others were discovered in my research.

REFERENCES

Brandon, Emily. Senior discounts aren't always the best deals for retirees: Here's how to get the best prices in 4 key areas. *U.S. News & World Report,* 18 July 2008.

Deals: Passenger discounts, seniors. *Amtrak.com.*

Good shop: Coupons and deals. *GoodSearch.com.*

Hotel deals. *Hotels.com.*

Lagier, Sydney. 7 secrets to a happy retirement. *U.S. News Money & World Report Money,* 22 July 2010.

Rogers, Alison. How to get great freebies and discounts. *Money* 25.2 (1996): B6.

8

MAINTAINING, REPAIRING, AND PROTECTING YOUR CREDIT AFTER RETIREMENT

Jennifer Boxen

WHAT IS A CREDIT SCORE AND WHY IS IT IMPORTANT?

Now that you are retiring, keeping an eye on your finances is imperative. Many retirees are on strictly regulated monthly incomes, making budgeting more important than ever. One of the keys to keeping within that budget is keeping expenses as low as possible, in as many ways as possible. One very effective way to keep expenses manageable is to have and maintain a good credit rating, which can be represented by a score.

A credit score is the calculation that credit bureaus utilize to help lenders determine your worthiness to receive loans. Your credit score may be the deciding factor in whether you are given insurance or get a job or an apartment, or it might determine whether you have to pay deposits on certain utilities. It can also make a big impact on the amount of interest you are charged on a loan. That difference in interest can equal big bucks. A good example is a car loan. Say you decide you want to finance a new car worth $20,000 for five years. If you have excellent credit, your interest rate is 6.99 percent, and your payment is $396 a month. If instead you have fair credit, your rate would be 10.99 percent, making the payment on the same car $435 a month, costing you $2,329 more over the life of the loan.[1] Should you be unlucky enough to have a credit score under 620, you may be considered what is called a "subprime" customer. You may have to pay as much as 17.99 percent interest, making your payment a whopping $508 a month. That is $10,466 you would pay in interest over the life of the loan; $6,710 more than you would have paid in interest with perfect credit. Multiply that by the two or three cars you may buy after you retire and you can see how a credit score can greatly influence your budget.

You may not remember what your credit score was when you bought your first house or car, and there is a reason for that. Credit scores are a comparatively recent invention. Bill Fair and Earl Isaac created the formula used to determine scores in the mid-1950s. Scores were not used widely by lenders until the formula Fair and Isaac created was applied to the three major credit bureaus (companies that track your credit usage) in the early 1980s. By the 1990s, credit scores were used widely by lenders.[2] The Fair-Isaac formula, now called FICO, is not the only one used to calculate a credit score, but it is currently the most popular with loan companies in the United States.

HOW IS A CREDIT SCORE DETERMINED?

There are currently three main credit reporting agencies: Experian, TransUnion, and Equifax (see contact information at the end of this chapter). Your score may be different depending on what formula is applied and which credit bureau is providing the information used to calculate it. The credit card that you had back in 1999 may still show up in one bureau, but because it is missing from the other two this will make a difference in the calculations. With the current FICO formulary there are twenty-two factors that are used to calculate most credit, and some have greater weight than others. They are subdivided into the following five categories[3]:

1. PAYMENT HISTORY (35%). Payment history will include any late pay-ments you made on accounts like installment loans (such as a car loan or mortgage), credit cards, and lines of credit. Any judgments you may have, bankruptcies, foreclosures, and delinquent taxes or child support will be reflected in this area. Scoring will depend on the severity of the delinquencies, how long it has been since you were last behind on a payment, how many payments you were behind on, and the amount the delinquencies were. It will also factor in the amount of accounts you have paid as agreed.

2. AMOUNTS OWED (30%). This area looks at the amount you currently owe versus the maximum credit that was extended. For example,

an individual with seven credit cards that are all near their spending limit will be negatively affected versus someone with a car loan that is two payments away from a zero balance. Amounts owed also reflect how many accounts still have balances compared to the total number of accounts on record, as well as accounts that do not report a balance.

3. LENGTH OF CREDIT HISTORY (15%). Simply put, the length of your credit history shows how long all of your accounts have been open; for scoring purposes longer is generally better. That is why it is very hard for younger people to have near perfect credit.

4. NEW CREDIT (10%). This takes into consideration both how many and what type of accounts you recently opened. This is also where credit inquiries are calculated. There are generally three kinds of inquiries. The first are those you make yourself, the second are "promotional inquiries" from companies that are considering offering you credit but that you did not solicit, and the third are inquiries you initiate because you are trying to apply for credit, such as a mortgage. The first two types do not affect your score, but the third type does.

5. TYPES OF CREDIT YOU USE (10%). This section looks at the types of credit you utilize, such as mortgages and auto loans, versus the less desirable credit card or unsecured personal loans.

The following are not used to calculate your score, although they may show up on the report:

- Location or length of time at home addresses and type of residence you have
- Place or length of employment
- The names of the companies you have or had accounts with
- The interest rate that you are paying on accounts

The following will not or should not be on your report at all:

- The number of children you have
- Your marital status
- Your income
- Any criminal history that does not involve your finances

- Your religion, ethnicity, or sex
- Your medical history (not counting medical bills in collection)

Certain people have little or no reported account history and will not generate a score. This is often the case with individuals who are financially just starting out. In the case of older individuals it can be because they never used loans and paid for things predominantly in cash. Little or no credit can also be due to how credit has historically been obtained. Some people receive loans through "buy here, pay here" auto lenders, pawn brokers, or some smaller credit unions, none of which may report to the credit bureaus. Apartment rental agencies and landlords seldom report accounts either, unless the account is delinquent. Debit cards that have the Visa or MasterCard logo may work as credit cards in most respects, but since they are still tied into a bank account they will not show up on a credit report, nor will some prepaid credit cards.

YOUR REPORT, YOUR SCORE, AND YOU

Now that you understand the basics of how scores are calculated, it is also important to know how to keep your scores as high as possible. It is vital that you start by reviewing what is on your credit reports so that you are aware of what lenders see and so you can spot any potential inaccuracies or identity theft. There are websites that offer you a free credit report or score, but usually the company wants you to sign up for a credit monitoring service, and if you do not cancel in time you will be billed a monthly fee automatically. Each of the credit bureaus and myFICO offers this type of "free" report. The Fair Credit Reporting Act entitles you to receive a genuine free copy of each of the three credit reports every year. This can be done online at www.annualcreditreport.com, but reports can also be requested by phone or mail. If requested online the report can be downloaded immediately; mail or phone requests can take up to fifteen days. These are the reports only and will not feature your scores. A good tactic is to spread out your free requests over the course of the year, one every four months. If you see anything unusual on the single report, then order the other two. It is also good to remember that if you are turned down for credit you are legally entitled to an explanation for your denial within thirty days, as well as free copies of the credit reports used to make the loan decision.

There are things that you can do to help keep your score healthy. Obviously, paying all of your bills in full and on time is the best suggestion. Make sure that you maintain low balances on your credit cards (if any at all), and refrain from applying for store cards just so you can get a discount. A common mistake that people make is to simultaneously cancel all of their credit cards, which can cause their score to plummet. If you feel you have too many open accounts, just close them gradually instead. If you decide to apply for a loan it is acceptable to shop around, but try to do it within a defined period to limit any possible inquiry penalties. It is generally not a good idea to cosign for anyone, not even your children or grandchildren. If they miss payments or default on the loan not only will your score drop if payments are missed or late, but the amount of the monthly payments and loan balance will also factor into the calculations of your score. You could also be held responsible for the loan balance if they default.

WHAT TO DO IF YOU ARE THE VICTIM OF IDENTITY THEFT

Identity theft happens more often than you think. According to the Federal Trade Commission, consumers reported identity theft as the number one complaint in 2009, with 278,078 cases.[4] In October 2010, a bank employee in Lake County, Florida, specifically targeted the elderly when stolen credit card information from clients was used to open loan accounts in order to funnel money.[5] In November 2010, AARP Insurance accidentally sent a customer another customer's personal data in the mail. Thieves love to go after older individuals because they assume these individuals are not paying attention. Hospitals and doctors' offices are the most frequent locations for records to be stolen, although no business is immune. Part of the reason identity thieves like to steal medical records is because the federal government still uses Social Security numbers as a patient's official identification for Medicare and Medicaid claims. There are some very helpful tips later in the chapter to help you protect your credit from thieves in the future, but what should you do if the theft has already happened? The steps you take if your identity is stolen are a little different from those you take when you merely find an error. If your identity is stolen, your very first step is to put a fraud alert on your credit.

This can be done by contacting one of the three credit bureaus (see contact information below), which is then legally responsible to contact the other two. There are two types of fraud alerts, initial and extended. Either alert will appear on your credit report and will instruct companies to take extra measures in verification before credit is approved. Remember, placing an alert may prevent you from temporarily being able to acquire credit in certain situations. An initial alert will

WORKING WITH CREDIT AGENCIES

Trying to correct your credit will be a frustrating and time-consuming process. It is very important that you to keep careful track of all the paperwork that you are sending and receiving. Get everything in writing if you can, and if that is not possible, keep written notes of all of the phone conversations you have with representatives. In your notes include the names of everyone you speak to (including their employee ID if possible) and the date and time of the conversation. Follow up the phone call with a letter to the company summarizing your notes. All mail should be sent certified with a return receipt requested. Include copies of all of your documentation, but do not send original signed documents. Always try to communicate with the fraud department of a company if it has one. Be friendly, but be persistent.

stay on file for ninety days and will allow you to get a free copy of your credit report from each bureau. An extended alert will get you two free copies of each bureau's report for the first year after you file. Extended alerts will stay on your credit report for seven years but will require you to file an identity theft report, which I will get to a little later in the chapter.

You should carefully review all three copies of your credit reports, noting any accounts that you did not open and any inquiries by companies you did not initiate contact with. Your next step is to then contact any of the companies with which these fraudulent accounts have been established (the contact information should be on the report). Let the fraudulent account holders know what accounts you did not open and inquire as to what specific procedures these companies may have when filing a fraud claim with them. You next move will be to file a complaint with the Federal Trade Commission; a complaint form can be found at www.ftccomplaint assistant.gov/. You should send a completed copy of the complaint form to all of the involved parties. Finally, you should file a report with all of the relevant criminal authorities, whether police, sheriff's office, or FBI. Make sure that you get an actual report with a case number, and ask for the department's fraud or ID theft division. This may be difficult, since some authorities are hesitant to report ID theft as an actual theft and not all police are required to report ID theft crimes.

This is now the point where you get an identity theft report. An identity theft report is a police report that contains detailed information about the crime, such as the account numbers of fraudulent claims, addresses, phone numbers, and descriptions of items acquired using your stolen information. It is best if you can give the greatest detail possible on these reports. The process now starts over as you send the copy of your identity theft report with any other relevant paperwork to the credit bureaus and fraudulent account holding companies in order to facilitate getting the fraudulent claims removed.

WHAT TO DO IF THERE ARE INACCURACIES IN YOUR REPORT

If the information that is listed on your report is inaccurate, such as a balance being listed on an account you know is paid, there are actions you can take to correct your report. Remember, it is considered fraud to try and remove legitimate delinquencies and other defaults from your credit report. The only exceptions to this rule are items that are over seven years old (ten years if it was a bankruptcy). If the information listed on the report is indeed incorrect, following are steps you can take to correct them.

Take copies of all of the information that you have regarding the account, including any statements and cancelled checks, and send them to both the account holding company and the credit bureau(s) in order to file a dispute. Let them know that you see an inaccuracy in the credit report and that you would like it corrected. Another solution may be to get both a representative of the credit bureau and a representative from the company on the phone at the same time and have a conference call. E-mail can be useful in speeding up communication, particularly if you have a scanner and can send documents instantaneously to the parties in question. Just be sure to follow up by also sending the documents by certified mail with return receipt requested.

As previously stated, if you have bad credit or inaccuracies in your report, in the majority of instances these are items you can dispute yourself. Unfortunately, some people fall prey to companies that claim that they can repair or fix a person's credit. These companies sometimes call themselves "credit doctors" or "credit repair centers." For a fee, these companies will offer to clean up your credit and bring up your credit score. The Credit Repair Organizations Act, a federal law, protects your rights in this situation. It makes it illegal for anyone to ask you for compensation before credit repair is completed. Potential credit repair companies must also have you sign a written contract.[6]

If you do sign up with one of these companies, keep in mind that many of them do not really remove your bad credit, they simply dispute various items (or all of them) on your report. As long as a dispute is being investigated, a reporting agency will temporarily remove the bad mark, which will bring up your score. If it is discovered that a disputed item is legitimate, the black mark returns and the score drops back down again. Another trick, which is a federal offense, occurs when credit repair companies try to get you to "create" a new credit record, which is really applying for an EIN (employee identification number) through the IRS.

PROTECTING YOUR CREDIT SCORE IN THE FUTURE

Here are some useful tips for keeping your identity (and credit score) safe from theft:

- Order your credit report at least twice a year to check for suspicious inquiries and to verify that the information on the report is accurate.
- Libraries and college computers are often targets for hackers. If you use a public computer or wireless Internet, do not use it to make purchases or log into accounts.
- Invest in a good-quality crosscut paper shredder that is capable of shredding not only multiple sheets of paper but also credit cards. Mix the shredded items with the household garbage.
- Shred cancelled checks, deposit slips, and any applications that you receive in the mail that contain personal information.
- Break yourself of the habit of keeping your Social Security card in your wallet. Keep it at home in a fire safe or other secure place instead.
- Never put your Social Security number on checks.
- If you are filling out an application or form that asks for your Social Security number, write "upon request" on the line, or at the minimum, give the last four digits.
- Do not be afraid to ask how personal information is stored and disposed of at places you do business with, and do not be afraid to refuse to give out your Social Security number.
- Never leave outgoing mail containing personal information, such as Social Security numbers or checks, in your household mailbox for pickup. Take it to a mailbox or directly to an official post office location. If you live in a high crime area, opt for a post office box for delivered mail as well.
- Make sure that you get someone to pick up your mail if you are going to be away for more than a day.

- Never give out your personal information over the phone. It is not the policy of most companies, nor is it the policy if the IRS, FBI, or police to ask you for it.
- Do not reply to e-mail requests (phishing) or texts (smishing) to update accounts or for personal information. Log into the web address of the company through its official web page.
- Do not post your birthday, place of birth, or middle name on social networking websites like Facebook.
- A large percentage of identity theft is perpetrated by someone that the victim knows. Keep your mail and other personal documents out of plain sight in your home.
- Before you recycle or donate computers or cell phones, make sure that all hard drives and other memory have been "wiped" clean.

You credit is one of your most precious assets. Because thieves are constantly finding new ways to try to take your money, you should always be aware of new ways to protect yourself. Remember that the Federal Trade Commission, Department of Justice, Federal Deposit Insurance Corporation, and Social Security Administration all have great resources you can utilize for information. Now that you understand what your credit score is, how it is calculated, how to protect it, and actions you can take if your identity is stolen, you are empowered to begin your retirement feeling more secure.

Following is contact information for the three main credit agencies:

- Equifax: 800-525-6285, www.equifax.com, P.O. Box 740241, Atlanta, GA 30374-0241
- Experian: 888-397-3742, www.experian.com, P.O. Box 9554, Allen, TX 75013
- TransUnion: 800-680-7289, www.transunion.com, Fraud Victim Assistance Division, P.O. Box 6790, Fullerton, CA 92834-6790

NOTES

1. Several good loan calculators can be found at http://www.bankrate.com/calculators.aspx.
2. Liz Pulliam Weston, *Your Credit Score: How to Fix, Improve, and Protect the 3-Digit Number That Shapes Your Financial Future* (Upper Saddle River, NJ: Pearson/Prentice Hall, 2005), 6–8.

3. Fair Isaac Corporation, "What's in Your Fico Score," http://www.myfico.com/CreditEducation/WhatsInYourScore.aspx.

4. Federal Trade Commission, *Consumer Sentinel Network Data Book for January–December 2009* (Washington, DC: Federal Trade Commission, 2010), 5.

5. Privacy Rights Clearinghouse, "Chronology of Data Breaches Security Breaches 2005–Present," http://www.privacyrights.org/data-breach.

6. *Consumer Credit Protection Act,* Public Law 90–321, *U.S. Statutes at Large* 82: 164, http://www.ftc.gov/os/statutes/croa/croa.shtm.

EXPLORING NEW ROADS

9

FOLLOWING YOUR PASSION
A DREAM DEFERRED

Dahlma Llanos-Figueroa

As CHILDREN OUR imaginations know no bounds. Our minds are awhirl with fantasies, dreams, and possibilities. We spend hours creating our own worlds, peopled with fantastic characters living fantastic lives.

By the time we are young adults and about to enter the adult world, we have been influenced by societal norms, parental expectations, responsibilities, duties, practicalities, and the need to provide for basic necessities. Many of us, in our effort to "do the right thing," put aside the dreams that filled our early years and build a life of expediency and responsible behavior. If we are lucky, in later years, some of us rediscover old dreams and almost-forgotten passions.

REDISCOVERING MY LOST PASSION

For me, writing was a passion that began in my high school library and was a part of my private life for many years. Nothing in my world indicated that anyone would be interested in the writings of a young, Afro-Puerto Rican girl from the South Bronx. My parents stressed education and encouraged me to become a teacher. That was a profession that would give me security and the time and economic wherewithal to start a family, contribute to a solidly middle-class life, and help build a comfortable home for my husband and children. Writing was a nice hobby, but I had to live in the real world, they said, and the real world treated writers very poorly.

I was a good teacher and later an even better librarian. I worked for the New York City Board of Education for decades. But after twenty years, I found myself not recognizing the public school system I had committed to as an idealistic young woman.

My years as a librarian served me well. Planning and organization had been my lifeblood. So I used those skills to find a new direction. I started by asking myself a lot of questions: What would be my first step? How would I craft my life after decades of it being ruled by external schedules, unexplained decisions, and the political whims of an often unheeding leadership? If not an educator, a lover of books, a trusted librarian, who was I?

When I went to the local bookstore and asked for books on retirement, I was referred to the Finances section and found many books, written by mostly by men, about creating a plan for personal short- and long-term economic independence. Not quite what I was looking for.

Then I was referred to the Pop Psych section, where I found books written primarily by women about self-actualization. Closer. Useful. Interesting. But still not quite what I thought I needed. Rudderless and lost in my thoughts and self-questioning, I explored the aisles until I found Christiane Northrup's *The Wisdom of Menopause: Creating Physical and Emotional Healing during the Change*. This book didn't seem to address my most critical needs either. But after a quick glance through the table of contents, I bought the book anyway. After all, my body was beginning to undergo physical changes that needed addressing as well. And there was something in the introduction about redefining creativity. What did I have to lose?

As I read the book on the way home, I was amazed at the very familiar portrait of myself that I found in those pages. The physical changes in this time of my life were important, but even more critical were the emotional and psychological issues that Dr. Northrup targeted so honestly and expertly. Her words crystallized so much of what I had been feeling:

> In the second half of our cycles, we prepare to give birth to nothing less than ourselves. It is at this time that the more intuitive parts of our brain become activated, giving us feedback and guidance about the state of our inner lives. (Northrup 2001, 44)

I read on. By connecting with the coming physical and emotional changes, I opened myself up for new ideas and a different way of looking at the world. The sections on the rewiring of the brain during this time of a woman's life were especially informative. I began to recognize much of my own behavior and many of the feelings that were becoming a part of my daily life.

About this time, I found another life-changing book that helped me navigate through this period. Julia Cameron's *The Artist's Way: A Spiritual Path to Higher Creativity* was pivotal in my life. I had never been particularly religious, at least not in the traditional sense. So it was with some hesitation that I read the first few pages. But Ms. Cameron spoke to my creative center and helped me find a path to that critical part of myself that I had shelved so many years before. The book is about rediscovering the artistic or creative nature that lives within each of us.

For Julia Cameron, the key to rediscovering your creative self lies in following a simple process—(1) recording your thoughts on a daily basis in what she calls morning pages and (2) creating artist's dates where you explore your interests in quiet and solitude. Her book takes you step by step through this process and provides exercises for sparking thoughts and feelings that may have been held at bay or buried for years or (as in my case) decades.

> Growth is an erratic forward movement: two steps forward, one step back. Remember that and be very gentle with yourself. A creative recovery is a healing process. You are capable of great things on Tuesday, but on Wednesday you may slide backwards. This is normal. Growth occurs in spurts. You may lie dormant sometimes. Do not be discouraged. Think of it as resting. (Cameron and Bryan 1992, 74)

She gives the reader permission to explore, play, investigate, and reconsider and revisit. That is how I rediscovered my writing self. I had pushed it aside when I left school and became a teacher and later a librarian. I had followed all the rules, found a good job with rock solid security. I had devoted myself to my profession. I had given back to my community and beyond. I had become a responsible adult, a respected educator. I had traveled, created a family of my own. And at the end of it all, I still felt unfulfilled and yearning for something else. Now I had finally found it again.

Once I made writing the center of my life, I invested time and money to become the best writer I could. I took workshops, listened, and learned. It wasn't easy to go from being a teacher to being a student again. And there was much that I had to learn or relearn.

Right from the start I decided that if I was going to write, then the work had to be substantive, something that touched my inner world. So when it was my turn to read in a workshop to a group of absolute strangers, I was a bundle of nerves. It was tough. But I didn't give up. I began reading like a writer. I kept writing. I stumbled and I learned. And I kept writing.

In truth, I had been quietly writing all along during vacations, holidays, and whenever my schedule allowed. But now it was different. I felt an urgency as I filled journal after journal with my morning pages. These entries became second nature to me. I wrote whether I felt well or was ailing. I wrote through tragedy, celebrations, disappointment, wonder, love, insecurities, anger, triumphs, and failures. I wrote about the joys and frustrations of my childhood and my accomplishments and disillusionments as an adult. I wrote about the life I experienced in Puerto Rico and of my youth in the Bronx. I wrote in the morning and at every opportunity. I started travel journals and took them all over the world with me. These journals started piling up. I spent money on beautiful blank books and began a pen collection. These were more than just collections. They were the tools I would need in my journey. I created a quiet corner where I went at five o'clock every morning before going to work. There I meditated and recorded every image that came to me. I was creating a writing process that serves me well to this day.

I taught creative writing to teenagers on the weekends. I started reaching out to community and arts agencies. I conducted writing workshops in local libraries for senior citizens. Working adults came to me after putting in a hard day's work to write their stories of urban struggles and immigrant experiences.

I hadn't been published yet, but that became my goal. I bought the Tony Robbins (2000) motivational materials, *Get the Edge: 7 Days to Transform Your Life,* and used those techniques to start making concrete, short- and long-term plans. In the process something in me shifted. It wasn't a matter of if I would get published anymore, but when. I went from thinking someday I'd write, to knowing I am a writer. It took a long time to say it out loud. Once spoken, it took on a life of its own, and there was no turning back.

When I did retire in 2004, I became a full-time student all over again. I used my library research and computer skills to identify and contact community arts agencies—the Bronx Council for the Arts, Association of Hispanic Artists, Center for Puerto Rican Studies Library, and International Women's Writing Guild were valuable contacts that helped me move forward. Through these organizations I participated in events that led to my meeting my agent as well as my editor. I used the Internet to find out about and apply to writing workshops all over the country. I gained more confidence in my work and reached out to international writing workshops. By sharing with and learning from writers from all over the world, I acquired a more global outlook and could place myself within the realm of other writers who were themselves navigating their creative journeys. Similarly, I found outlets for my short pieces and began building a writing resume. Along the way I also made important connections that placed me within a community of writing professionals, many of whom became mentors and colleagues in the years that followed.

In 2005 I had several pieces published in short story anthologies and on a prestigious online literary journal. In 2009, St. Martin's Press published my first novel, *Daughters of the Stone.* As I write these words, PEN America named me as one of two runners-up in the 2009 PEN America Bingham Fellowship for Writers.

I have come a very long way. My journey hasn't always been a smooth one. And it certainly isn't over. Since I reached my first goal—getting my novel published—I had to learn a whole new career, self-promotion. I have never wanted to be a businesswoman, but that was exactly what I have become. I've learned that if I don't sell this book, there probably won't be any new ones to follow it. I learned, and I learned quickly. I set up a website, opened a Facebook page, and started a newsletter. I hired and fired publicists, and learned how to reach out to the public on my own and how to follow up on new possibilities. The planning, researching, and organizational skills that were the backbone of my years in the library have been invaluable in this process. Some people bemoan having wasted years before rediscovering their dream. I have learned that my long years of experience, and the maturity that came with those years, serve me well. The truth is, I have needed those years in order to do what I am doing today.

MY CONTINUING JOURNEY

One of the many lessons I've learned on my journey is that once I opened the door to long-deferred dreams, I found a wealth of old, unexplored passions and quite a number of newly discovered ones. Here are some that came flooding out:

- Taking care of my body—my dreams will go nowhere if I don't have a healthy body to energize them.
- Making financial adjustments and readjustments—getting a temporary day job may be necessary to support my journey.

- Sharing my story—my agent suggests that I write about my journey in the world of publishing and self-promotion, so that others can benefit from my experience.
- Feeding my creative force—international conferences and workshops are opportunities for traveling and exploring new ideas.
- Teaching—going back to the enthusiasm of my early years with the wisdom of maturity is incredibly satisfying.
- Dancing—movement and play just for the pure joy of it makes me smile just thinking about it.
- Networking—setting up a support team that will sustain me into the future is a must.
- Writing—in the bottom drawer a nascent dramatic monologue, a collection of short stories, memoir travel pieces, and a new novel are all lying in wait for me.

CRAFTING THE FUTURE

In terms of my novel, I have a feeling it's not finished with me yet. The Kindle e-book version is available and makes the novel more affordable to students and community readers who might not be able to afford the hardcover copy.

I will continue reaching out to the academic community and doing college presentations of my work. My book is closely tied with any number of seasonal and thematic calendar events. So I'm already committed to a number of events highlighting Latino Heritage month. I anticipate the same will be true for Black History and Women's History months. My publicist is working on some events tied to Mother's Day celebrations, as the mother-daughter relationship is an important theme in the novel. We are also exploring collaboration with performing artists who can bring my words to a theater audience.

On a broader scale, I'm looking forward to the fall and winter, my most creative times of the year. I will hibernate and feed on what has come before. I look forward to getting up at four or five in the morning while it's still dark out and the day's activities have not overtaken me. I'll light my candles and my incense and meditate for a half-hour or so . . . and wait. Then I'll turn to my journal and record whatever emerges. Whatever emerges will be the foundation for the next step. My new project is already percolating in there, I know it. I'm excited to see what it will be.

CRAFTING YOUR OWN JOURNEY

STEP ONE

- Go within.
- Create a passion journal—buy a blank book you are attracted to and keep it by your bed.
- Dream—day or night, journaling opens the door, so write before you go to sleep and when you wake up.
- Record your dreams—nothing is too trivial or silly, so give yourself permission to fly!

STEP TWO

- Be open to surprises.
- Recall images; they are the wonderful keys to more doors—write about what you were doing or what was going on when you experienced your favorite...

  » Scent—food? Perfume? Paint? Let whatever scents appeal to you lead the way. Maybe take a cooking course? Volunteer at botanic gardens or join a local gardening club?

  » Vision—take an art course, volunteer at a museum, work at a gallery, or cut out pictures you love and begin making minicollages in your journal. It'll feed your creative side and provide a way to track your emotional journey. Also, framing your vision in this way will give you a visual record of your passions even if you think you don't have any.

  » Sounds—music? Go to library listening booths and check out new artists. Many music retailers have earphones for sampling recordings before you buy. Sampling Internet sources for music is only a click away.

  » Touch—love textures? Join a knitting or quilting association or attend conferences. Men are welcome, too!

- Brainstorm—the wilder the better. Nothing is out of bounds, and be sure to record everything in your journal.
- Ask for help—talk to older retirees. Most will be more than happy to share their journey with you. This is a great way of finding the dos and don'ts without pain.

- Network—find a support group among like-minded people. Join organizations or take college courses (many universities give seniors special discounts if you ask). Most continuing education courses are stress-free and can be a lot of fun.
- Share—pass on what you've learned to younger retirees. In giving, you will receive.
- Celebrate everything at every step—life is too short not to do so.

SUGGESTED READING

Beilenson, John. *The Future Me: Authoring the Second Half of Your Life: A Guided Journal*. White Plains, NY: Peter Pauper Press, 2003.

Braun Levine, Suzanne. *Inventing the Rest of Our Lives: Women in Second Adulthood*. New York: Plume, 2005.

Cameron, Julia. *The Vein of Gold: A Journey to Your Creative Heart*. New York: Penguin, 1996.

———. *Finding Water: The Art of Perseverance*. New York: Penguin, 2006.

———. *The Complete Artists' Way: Creativity as Spiritual Practice*. New York: Tarcher/Penguin, 2007.

Cameron, Julia, and Mark Bryan. *The Artist's Way: A Spiritual Path to Higher Creativity*. New York: Putnam, 1992.

Lawrence-Lightfoot, Sara. *The Third Chapter: Passion, Risk and Adventure in the 25 Years after 50*. New York: Farrar, Straus and Giroux, 2009.

Northrup, Christiane. *The Wisdom of Menopause: Creating Physical and Emotional Health and Healing During Menopause*. New York: Bantam, 2006.

REFERENCES

Cameron, Julia, and Mark Bryan. 1992. *The artist's way: A spiritual path to higher creativity*. New York: Putnam, 74.

Northrup, Christiane. 2001. *The wisdom of menopause: Creating physical and emotional health and healing during menopause*. New York: Bantam, 44.

Robbins, Anthony. 2000. *Get the edge: 7 days to transform your life*. Audio CD. Guthy-Renker.

10

GOING BACK TO SCHOOL

Louise F. Benke

DURING THE LIBRARY's farewell party for me, I smiled often. It had been two decades of satisfying, productive, and exhausting work with a terrific, innovative staff I knew I would miss. Most of those years were as a very involved middle manager and head of children's services. Now at age 61, I was willingly leaving a job I loved. And no, there were no grandchildren or cruises awaiting me, helping to ease such a major life change.

Two years prior, I had contemplated the path new library leaders were likely to take as we grew into a much larger regional system, such as reorganizing management and moving children's services into a less prominent role. If I were correct, could I be comfortable taking a less involved management role? Or could I see myself leaving children's services behind to become strictly management?

With the economy in recession, finding a good fit in another library in the region was unrealistic. What besides children's services in public libraries could maximize my talents and ignite my passions as completely and effectively? I headed off to the counseling center at a nearby university to take the Strong Interest Inventory and the Myers-Briggs personality profile, hoping results would reveal options for me.

At age 60, with good health and lots of energy, even contemplating retirement felt a bit premature, but I examined that feeling as well. Fortunately, our finances could support both my husband and my retiring if we wished. I followed my usual librarian pattern of checking out all of the most recent books on retirement, asking my husband to discreetly check out the books for me lest fellow staff members notice the change in my reading interests.

OLD DOGS, NEW TRICKS; OLD DREAMS, NEW NEURONAL PATHWAYS

I loved being a librarian, the feeling of never being far from life-changing ideas. As I wracked my brain for the title to the next chapter of my life, friends recommended two books that had nothing to do with retirement or a specific career. One was Norman Doidge's (2007) *The Brain That Changes Itself: Stories of Personal Triumph from the Frontiers of Brain Science.* This book introduced me to the recent neuroplasticity research on how even the "aging" brain can continue to create new neuronal pathways and learn new skills. The other book, *Proust and the Squid: The Story and Science of the Reading Brain* by Maryanne Wolf (2008), examined the intriguing ways our brains learn language and reading. Lightbulb! The combination of these two books allowed me to resurrect a dream I had experimented with decades earlier, of learning more about the reading process to better serve young readers—a dream I thought I was too busy, too old, and too set in my ways to pursue successfully.

For the first time in months, I felt some excitement about my future endeavors. Possibilities of how I could apply an advanced degree in reading cropped up nightly. I met with the head of the master's in reading department at a respected university in our area with a list of questions about possible obstacles at the ready. That hour spent tentatively exploring my options was pivotal. Not only did I come away with concrete steps, but I also drove home feeling as if someone had just invited me into a new universe where I could feel valued for my knowledge and experience, intellectually stimulated, and challenged to go even further in making a difference in the lives of young readers. Key to that response was the department head already knowing and respecting the importance of public libraries in children's lives and sharing about other women who had successfully returned to school at older ages.

"WHAT? YOU DON'T KNOW HOW TO READ YET?!"

Still, leaving a job that defined my identity was not going to be easy. Each step I took toward returning to school to get a master's in reading helped me over rough spots. When the results of the Strong Interest Inventory and Myers-Briggs Type

Indicator finally arrived, they underscored each part of my plan, telling me that I indeed would do well with both going back to school and with the career options that could follow. Tentatively, I tried the idea out on family members and close friends and, aside from surprise that I could leave a job that had been my passion, all were supportive. My 27-year-old son was bemused and asked, "What?! You don't know how to read yet?!"

The application process for graduate school was online and surprisingly painless. Forty-year-old transcripts from around the country were easily ordered online. The three required recommendations could be conveniently completed with an online form. Even the painful and complicated updating of my twenty-year-old resume served to remind me of the skills and knowledge I had gained over three decades in library work and reinforced why this career shift was a good idea.

Quietly moving forward on graduate school before making the final decision to leave my job helped. I gave myself the option of backing out at any time that it didn't feel right. Gradually, the cons and pros were all explored and I was ready when the new director shared less-than-exciting options for my new role within the reorganization. "Thank you. But I feel my talents and passions will be better applied by my going back to school."

OBSTACLES TO RETURNING TO THE CLASSROOM

Remember when you finished that last exam in graduate school and you swore you would never go back to school? While the comments I received when I shared my news were overwhelmingly positive, among my contemporaries remarks were usually followed with "I could never do that!" My response was always, "Why not?" Following are some the roadblocks my colleagues put up:

- Having to repeat courses they've already taken
- Dislike of the stereotypical classroom experiences, such as writing research papers and reading uninspiring textbooks
- Distaste for the games inherent in a grading system
- Concerns that cognitive memory losses of being older would put them at a disadvantage
- The logistics of finding a university with their program within easy driving distance
- Investigating the online education route

- Learning other new technologies of higher education—Blackboard, online grades, tests, group discussions, and more
- A new identity and fitting in with traditional students
- The expense

For me, none of these challenges is turning out to be significant. While I did have to repeat two courses, generally speaking, education requirements seem to be a lot more flexible now than they used to be. The reality is that educational institutions want your money, so they are somewhat willing to let you do it your way. Ultimately, I began by taking the two courses I had taken before. It helped me ease into going back to school confident I could handle the courses to come.

The classroom experience of today is much more multimodal and interactive than the classrooms of my youth. Each course has been replete with online sites and small group discussions. Checking the clock during even a four-hour class is unusual for me. Writing research papers once again was a stressor because of old demons of procrastination. But that too is no different from the deadlines for grant applications and director's reports of my career. With instructor approval, students are encouraged to flex and shape assignments to work for their particular situations. It is still a wheelbarrow load of work, but so was my job.

The arbitrary nature of grades is likewise no different than merit pay raises. If you did well in college classes before, chances are you will do as well or better this time around. After all, you won't be as likely to suffer the effects of all-night partying! I will, however, admit to being quite elated with that "A" in my first course. It put to rest that all-too-common concern that the normal short-term memory losses of later life indicate a significant decline in cognitive abilities.

While the master's program in reading I chose is an hour's drive away with an extended campus location even closer, I had other choices within a two-hour drive. Then there are the myriad options online that would let me stay home and fit my studies to my individual routines. A helpful website is eLearners.com, a clearinghouse for accredited online degrees and certificate and training courses.

As a practicing librarian, I could have crossed off the concern about new technologies immediately. If you have learned automated payroll and evaluation systems, flexed with each new ILS and database interface, and served your time on the reference desk, you will do fine with the likes of Blackboard, a common online interface for communication among class members and instructors. I found that I am probably in better shape doing research for papers and preparing for class presentations than my fellow students and even some instructors. EBSCO Academic

Search Premier and I have become even greater friends than when I was on the reference desk. It allows me to format citations according to the needed style; make notes on articles; limit my choices to the most recent, full-text, and peer-reviewed sources; and even listen to articles being read aloud. Creating bibliographies using Easybib.com was also a godsend. Late at night, being able to "search inside the book" on Amazon in a textbook that I didn't have with me was equally useful. Online texts such as classics in Project Gutenberg were conveniently accessed. As for the audiovisual technology involved in class presentations, I was amazed to find a wide variation in what students and instructors could handle, and comforting to know that there was tech help readily available when some technology eluded me. Add that to the knowledge I have of how to work the local library systems to my benefit, and I am easily as well off as my classmates.

Fitting in with my classmates worried me at the start. In my career, I had always made a conscious choice to work in public libraries rather than in school settings, and I did not have—nor did I want to get—a teaching certificate. Now, every one of my classmates has a teaching certificate and is teaching in some capacity. In addition to standing out like a sore thumb because of my senior status, I would be an outsider to the world of teachers. I was concerned that when class discussions turned to educational theory or practice, I would be totally clueless. And when groups formed to work collaboratively on a project, would I be last on the bench?

None of it was a problem, of course. Instructors and classmates alike openly request my input in discussions from the unique vantage point I have. As for age making a difference in fitting in, I've actually had the opposite experience: the two or three other older students seek me out perhaps because they feel a kinship. Younger students are appreciative of my wanting to learn more in their field and say so. They frequently share their frustrations and successes in using their local public library and ask my opinion. My contributions to class discussions, particularly on topics such as intellectual freedom, are encouraged. Even the informal chatter during breaks has been fun and inclusive of my situation. In one conversation, I happened to mention the age of my son and one of the students volunteered with enthusiasm she was that age as well.

The only negative possibly connected to age difference has come from my desire for the learning perspective to be more content-oriented than grade-oriented, which is just the opposite for many of my classmates. Occasionally, I have felt an inordinate amount of time in class was spent answering questions about how many pages the assignment should be or what information will be on the test, when I preferred learning more about the topic or discussing new ideas.

Finally, let's examine the obstacle many would consider the first to overcome—the expense.

FLEX YOUR BOOMER FINANCIAL AND POLITICAL MUSCLE

Despite a relatively secure financial prognosis, there were some preparations I felt I needed to make before leaving the economic stability of my job.

- Clarify and confirm your health insurance and retirement plans. One of the first resources I used was the confidential services of our Human Resources retirement specialist. Her emphatic warning was to not even consider leaving my job until I had a clear plan for health insurance for the rest of my life.
- Check in with your financial advisors. Our Certified Financial Planner™ and accountant were invaluable in running the numbers for the possible scenarios of retirement and partial retirement, and even the disadvantages to earning an income later when retirement accounts must start paying out.
- Use even the simple ways to cut costs. A little digging revealed a variety of sources for cost-cutting. My husband's alumnus status at a nearby university gave us free access to its career counseling center services. If I had chosen to attend the university where my husband is a faculty member, there would have been a tuition break. My familiarity with interlibrary loan allowed me to easily borrow the less essential textbooks for the summer courses that lasted only a few weeks. Finally, I am currently investigating graduate assistantships that could cover part of the tuition and award a stipend.

Many more options exist to help financially:

- Some institutions have better deals. Sometimes even private universities offer special programs for older adults. Others may allow free or reduced-cost auditing for older adults, allowing you to test out your interest before committing to a full course of study.
- Some employers offer assistance to older workers returning to school. Larger corporations are beginning to recognize the value of offering

everything from tuition to book reimbursement to flexible scheduling, especially if you plan to go into areas of public service. Of course, this may mean you have to stay in the job for several years following your degree.

- Federal tax breaks, grants, and loans are available and more are coming. Tax credits reduce your tax bill dollar-for-dollar. The Lifetime Learning Credit offers up to $2,000 if you qualify. A tax deduction might allow you to deduct up to $4,000 for tuition and fees. Moreover, the Obama administration has a website with support for unemployed workers who want to go back to school at www.opportunity.gov. It also covers how to apply for federal grants and student loans.

- Some scholarships target adults returning to school. An excellent resource for more information on the ever-changing landscape of financing education is the book *501 Ways for Adult Students to Pay for College: Going Back to School without Going Broke* by Gen and Kelly Tanabe (2004).

- It's good to be a baby boomer. Because many companies are examining baby boomer consumer and political choices, the near future promises programs and legislation tailored to our burgeoning interest in being productive during the last third of our lives, such as the following:

  » Making second career, short-term training, and hands-on learning opportunities desirable, affordable, and convenient
  » Offering accelerated degree programs, short-term credentialed-learning opportunities, expanded prior learning assessment practices, financial aid, and satellite programs for mature workers and students
  » Developing workshops that help alleviate fears of lifelong learning, dispel misconceptions about the economy, explore skill-building and second-career options, and facilitate referrals to institutions of higher learning

If you had affirmative responses to seven or more of the inquiries above, you are ready to go back to school. Granted, I am only three courses into this new chapter of my life, but I continue to feel clear that this is the correct choice. Despite the usual academic pressures of heavy reading loads and late night writing of papers, the overall stress is much less than in my former library job, and I am confident I will head back to the workforce in another satisfying job. How did I ultimately know that this was going to be the correct choice for me?

- Dissatisfaction with the direction my career was taking. I am grateful that what could have been a career disaster has instead been a portal to a promising next stage. It has made it much easier to let go of my former job responsibilities.
- My passion and desire to continue to serve children. I am energized by the research frontiers on the neuroplasticity of the brain and the reading process, and passionate about how libraries and schools can help children benefit from this research.
- A degree program that meets my needs. I am enjoying taking my time to read and write about what interests me. Connecting with others who share my interests is an added plus.
- The satisfying, realistic career options upon completion of the degree. When I am finished with my master's, I might go on for a doctorate, reenter full-time work, do hourly or part-time work, tutor, consult, volunteer, or even go into politics armed with new information and experiences. Pragmatically, I recognize that going back to school gives me time to figure out what is next and gives the economy a chance to settle down—or crank up, depending on how you look at it.
- The success of those going before me. And many more of us are coming down the pike. The baby boomer generation is reinventing notions of retirement. According to *Retirement Rx: The Retirement Docs' Proven Prescription for Living a Happy, Fulfilling Rest of Your Life* by Frederick T. Fraunfelder and James H. Gilbaugh, Jr. (2008), "Seniors healthy at age 60 can easily make it to their eighties or nineties. We may end up spending as much time in our second careers as our first."

One report in particular, A MetLife Foundation/Civic Ventures Encore Career Survey (2008), resonated with my situation. It provides a wealth of information on how almost 3,600 seniors who have already created a second or "encore" career for themselves reaped many rewards:

- Eighty-four percent of those in encore careers say they get either a "tremendous amount of satisfaction" (38%) or "quite a bit of satisfaction" (46%) from their encore careers.
- Nine in ten of those in encore careers say it is "definitely true" (54%) or "somewhat true" (40%) that they have seen the positive results of their work and know they are making a difference.

- People in encore careers have much in common. Most of those in encore careers come from professional and white-collar jobs (88%), have at least a college education (67%), and tend to live in cities and their surrounding suburbs (72%). Most (60%) are leading-edge boomers between the ages of 51 and 62. Most (56%) are women.
- Beyond demographic characteristics, people currently in encore careers also are somewhat more likely to say they have placed "a great deal" or "quite a bit" of emphasis on their work lives (81%) compared to the population of 44- to 70-year-olds in general (75%).
- Three-quarters (76%) of those in encore careers say they are earning the income or benefits they need.
- Not only do I need and appreciate the support of my family, I need to remember my responsibility to them. Modeling for our children and the next generation does not stop when they reach adulthood. As the baby boomer wave enters retirement age, we have the opportunity to work toward a better society in much the same way that we did as adolescents in the 60s and 70s.

As any good librarian knows, there are more resources if you need them. Some of them do provide checklists to help you decide if you are ready to go back to school, retire, or start a new career. Undoubtedly, there are pros and cons either way you choose to go, and ultimately, you must shape your own path.

REFERENCES

A MetLife Foundation/Civic Ventures Encore Career Survey. 2008. http://www.encore.org/learn/research/publications#surveys.

Doidge, Norman. 2007. *The brain that changes itself: Stories of personal triumph from the frontiers of brain science.* New York: Viking Penguin.

Fraunfelder, Frederick T., and James H. Gilbaugh, Jr. 2008. *Retirement Rx: The retirement docs' proven prescription for living a happy, fulfilling rest of your life.* New York: Avery Penguin.

Tanabe, Gen and Kelly. 2004. *501 ways for adult students to pay for college: Going back to school without going broke.* Los Altos, CA: SuperCollege.

Wolf, Maryanne. 2008. *Proust and the squid: The story and science of the reading brain.* New York: HarperCollins.

11

PARTICIPATING IN ORAL HISTORIES OR DONATING PAPERS TO ARCHIVES

Dorothea J. Coiffe

LET YOUR LIBRARY memories and experiences live on, and let future researchers learn either by participating in an oral history project or by donating your papers to an archive. Know how each process works before you make your decision. Find out about the "before, during, and after" of the interview for the oral history process and the "about" of the archival process. Understand the ethical and legal obligations beforehand both on your part and that of the agency collecting your memories. There are many things to do and think about when you are about to retire. You wonder whether you are financially able to retire, about where you want to live, where you want to travel, what you want to research, what you want to write, and whether to continue working in some capacity. One thing many people do not typically think of as part of their retirement preparation is recording their career (and life) experiences by donating their papers to an archive or participating in an oral history project.

ORAL HISTORY —

In the spirit of "everyone has a story," your years as a woman/man, as a mother/father, as a sister/brother, as a parent, as an immigrant, as a minority, as an educator, as a librarian, as an artist, as a writer, or any other facet of your life may prove rewarding to others in the future.

> Everyone has a story, and you are no exception. Your life story may prove inspiring and useful to others in the future.

The life stories of those in our profession echo and parallel the Civil Rights movement, the Women's Liberation and Gay Rights movements, and the dawning of the Information Age. It is at retirement that you feel freer to reveal your joys, regrets, and accomplishments. Who knows what your knowledge, memories, experiences, background, traditions, customs, or skills may spark in someone? The Oral History Society's website best describes the reasons why to contribute your voice:

> . . . historical documents and books can't tell us everything about our past. Often they concentrate on famous people and big events, and tend to miss out on ordinary people talking about everyday events. They also neglect people on the margins of society—ethnic communities, disabled and unemployed people for example—voices . . . hidden from history. Oral history fills in the gaps and gives us history, which includes everyone. Unfortunately, memories die when people do; if we don't record peoples' life histories they are lost forever. (Perks 2008)

Now that you decided to participate, you will be "a primary source" and a "bearer of tradition" (Hunt 2003). Does the project choose you or do you choose it? There are methods for choosing candidates for interviews, including random and systematic sampling techniques. The methods used should be clearly stated, followed precisely, and appropriate for the project's goals according to the South Dakota State Historical Society (2004). Here are a few places to check to find a suitable oral history project for you:

- Your alma mater(s)/fraternity/sorority
- Your unions
- Your clubs/societies/charities
- Your place(s) of work/where you volunteer
- Government veteran associations
- Public library/community center(s)
- Museums/Local historical societies
- Television/radio stations

BEFORE THE INTERVIEW

You know the most about your own life story and your community, not the interviewer/researcher. As the interviewee or narrator, you should understand the purpose of the interview and be comfortable with the person interviewing you. You should know approximately how long the interview(s) might take. You may want a friend or relative along with you when you interview, especially if your native language is different from that of the interviewer's. Many oral history project interviewers go over some questions well before the interview to get their memory juices flowing. This also lets both parties know if there are any sensitive or traumatic questions or issues, so no one will be surprised.

Prior to your interview, your interviewer underwent training for this particular oral history project and signed an interviewer agreement. He or she will be familiar with its goals and purposes, as well as the legal, ethical, and confidentiality aspects in conducting an interview. The interviewer agreement obligates the interviewer to commit to the project and the interviewing process. The interviewer should have prepared for the interview by doing background research on you and/or the project as well as know how to work and troubleshoot the recording equipment (Nebraska State Historical Society 2009).

THE INTERVIEW

It is best that your interview take place in a comfortable, familiar, and quiet setting. Both interviewer and narrator should have blocked off an appropriate amount of time so neither feels rushed.

Interviewers usually have a set of planned questions, though they will be listening for leads or cues to tangentially interesting topics or for other potential people to interview. Oral history interviews are spontaneous and conversational. If you may

---

FOR YOUR INTERVIEW

- Choose a comfortable, familiar, and quiet setting.
- Neither you nor the interviewer should feel pressed for time.
- Bring documents or photos to jog your memory.
- Know that sensitive portions can be released later, according to your stipulation(s).

go beyond the specific focus of the project, the interviewer will steer the interview back in due course (South Dakota State Historical Society 2004). Since the interviewer did background research, he or she might even ask you to expand on a topic.

The best of us mix up names, places, dates, and so on, so in order jog your memory, bring documents or photos with you. The interviewer may ask you to spell unfamiliar names or words; this will help future researchers. Know that you may *always* refuse to talk about a particular topic with which you feel uncomfortable. You may ask to speak off-the-record on these matters, but the interviewer most likely will encourage you not to do so. Remember, you may stipulate *not* to release that portion until an agreed-on date years in the future. Oral histories are not anonymous, but if your story is about, say, classified information from a recent war or someone who is currently involved in organized crime, it can be.

AFTER THE INTERVIEW

Once the interview is finished, you will need to fill out, read, and sign a written release form. This is a matter of copyright and permission between you, the narrator, the interviewer, and the respective project's agency. This release is a document that transfers the copyright of an interview to a designated owner and also gives permission to use the interview information for publication, public programming, or other public dissemination (Nebraska State Historical Society 2009). The release form should clearly define ownership of the materials, transfer of copyright, and expected uses of the materials. For instance, you should know whether the interview would be on the Internet or part of a future commercial product. You may include any restrictions on use of the materials. The release form need not be complicated, full of legalese, or particularly long. A simple release form includes wording like that used by the Smithsonian Center for Folklife and Cultural Heritage:

> By signing the form below, you give your permission for any tapes and/
> or photographs made during this project to be used by researchers and
> the public for educational purposes including publications, exhibitions,
> World Wide Web, and presentations. By giving your permission, you
> do not give up any copyright or performance rights that you may hold.
> (Hunt 2003)

After going over the interview later, the interviewer may contact you with follow-up questions. Know that oral histories are transcribed literally, meaning they will include all hesitations, slang, and grammatical errors. Both you and the interviewer should review the transcripts and make corrections, if possible. Editing of oral history tapes and transcripts are minimal. You have a say in editing and deciding on the final content of recordings or transcripts. Reasons to edit these before use or distribution are usually for length, repetition, and appropriateness for a target audience.

> Your story *will* enrich history!

Both the actual tapes and the transcription of your interviews will be stored in a repository such as an archive or library. There it will be available for use and valued by the public and researchers.

In keeping with copyright, you should receive proper recognition for your contribution. The Smithsonian's Center for Folklife and Cultural Heritage (Hunt 2003, 12) tells us why participating in an oral history project is a good thing: "The stories collected are valuable not necessarily because they represent historical facts, but because they embody human truths—a particular way of looking at the world." Your story *will* enrich history.

DONATING YOUR PAPERS TO AN ARCHIVE OR SPECIAL COLLECTIONS REPOSITORY

The Society of American Archivists (SAA) writes eloquently on why you might look into donating your papers to an archive:

> For millennia, written records have provided essential clues to the past. Through letters, diaries, and unpublished writings of many types, and also through the audible and visual records of recent times, researchers have been able to study and understand much about the history of particular families, communities, businesses, and organizations, the history of specific events and broader societal trends, and history in general.

To perpetuate the memory and continuing the value of a person's experiences, archivists think long term. They think of potential researchers of the future, twenty-five, fifty, one hundred years, or more. It is the archivists' charge to select, organize, and preserve artifacts of individuals, events, or an organization. According to the archives of the Wisconsin Department of Veterans Affairs, "Donating materials to an archives is an act of civic-mindedness and one that the prospective donor should take pride in." Nowadays most oral histories are digital, whereas archives always deal with physical items. These are collectively known as "papers" of a person's life or of an institution's history (or one of its departments or divisions).

Archives are interested in materials stating the purpose, policies, and activities of churches, political organizations, businesses, economic interest groups, community groups, voluntary associations, professional associations, or other collective enterprises (e.g., a rock band). Individuals or families may have stored records of these organizations, which may also be significant. Here are a few tips on which archive to approach (or that may approach you), what archivists accept, and what legalities may be involved.

WHAT ITEMS DO ARCHIVISTS COLLECT?

Items typically donated are letters, e-mail printouts, diaries, journals, logs, date books, clothing, personal objects, photographs, film, slides, videos, scrapbooks, ephemera, as well as artifacts, artwork, books, maps, and music scores. Teaching materials include lecture notes, syllabi, course assignments, lab manuals, and correspondence with colleagues and students. Research materials include notes and final drafts of unpublished articles and reports as well as drafts of published works. Biographical info such as old curriculum vitae, correspondence, and other documents relating to professional or research organizations with which one has been involved. Archivists love doodles, the scribbled marginal notes, and the miscellaneous reminders on scraps of paper.

SELECTING AN ARCHIVE

A professional, such as an archivist, curator, or librarian, should head the archives of his or her institution. It is that person's duty to preserve items of historical importance. However, many people have made mistakes donating their papers to the wrong place.

The archivist can discuss with you the historical value of your papers and advise you on which archive would be best for your papers. Before signing a donor form, you may want to ask the following questions from the Wisconsin Veterans Museum:

- Does the institution actually have an archives program/facility?
- Does it employ at least one full-time professional archivist? Does this archivist have a master's degree in either library science or history?

If you are unsure how to contact a repository in your area, you may wish to begin by speaking with someone at your state historical society or state archives. The Society of American Archivists (e-mail servicecenter@archivists.org) can also provide you with suggestions.

- Does the archive keep regular hours?
- Does the archive have adequate funding? Are these funding sources secure?
- Where is the facility located? Generally, your items will get the most use if you donate them to an archives program with an appropriate subject focus in a suitable geographic location.
- Does the archive advertise its holdings and/or have a website?
- Does the archive make descriptive information available about its collections in national library databases, like OCLC and/or RLIN, so that researchers from all over can find them?

WHAT TO DONATE AND WHAT ARCHIVES ACCEPT

Though most archivists have limitations on what they accept according to their institution's mission, budget, and space, they usually accept donations of as small as a single item or as large as dozens of boxes. Archives generally are more interested in a "coherent body of material rather than individual items" (SAA). If items are not appropriate for an institution's archives, the archivist may be able to refer you to another more suitable archive. The material need not be organized, nor does it need to be "old" or by or about a famous individual, event, or organization to be historically significant (SAA). Most archivists are happy to review all items beforehand. So, contact your institution's archives before discarding or reorganizing your papers, photos, or ephemera. Ephemera are items that when produced or used (usually for a specific, limited use) were never meant to be kept. These could be anything from "a bus ticket to a poster" (PBS).

To increase your item's usefulness to researchers of generations to come, it is best to identify it with as much detail as possible—photographic, videographic, and audio. Items removed or rearranged prior to donation could diminish the potential research value. Archivists love the doodles, the scribbled marginal notes, and the miscellaneous paper reminders on napkins. Again, before weeding, discarding, or reorganizing papers and records, donors are encouraged to contact the archivist beforehand.

Getting your donation to the archive is another matter. Some items and collections require more care than others. The archivist can recommend to you how best to pack and ship your papers. Some archives will arrange transportation for a donation. It is bad etiquette to send items to the repository before consulting its archivist first. After you donate your papers, archivists usually stay in touch to locate and/or identify other potential archival materials.

ETHICS AND LEGALITIES OF DONATING

Donating to an archive has several legal issues associated with it, such as the rights of ownership, privacy issues, conditional stipulations, and copyright. The donation agreement for an archive is called a "deed of gift." It is a signed formal document that allows the papers you donate to become the property of that institution. Once officially donated, you may not take anything out, and if you want to add material later, it usually is treated as a separate donation. Therefore, prospective donors should familiarize themselves with these policies by talking with the archivist. You should be clear about any special needs or concerns before signing the deed of gift. U.S. laws prohibit the archivists from assessing the value of donations or providing advice about tax deductions. Donors should speak with their own accountants or lawyers about such information (Amherst College Library). Those items not selected to be part of the archival collection are another negotiated specification of the deed of gift. These items are usually returned to the donor or their family, or they can be destroyed.

Copyright issues are always complex. You should work with the institution's archivist to clarify issues of copyright ownership. Generally, copyright belongs to the creator of writings and other original material (such as photos and music), but it can be legally transferred to heirs or others. An example would be Michael Jackson owning the rights to the Beatles music. Copyright ownership is a separate issue from ownership of the physical item (the letter or photo). As part of the deed of gift, you may want to include granting the copyright ownership with selected or all items of your donated materials (American Alpine Club). By donating the copyright along with an item, future researchers who wish to quote from an archival collection in their published works need only ask one owner for permission.

Unlike most museums, archives generally do not accept items on loan. Each donation in an archive is backed by a legally binding deed of gift that is tailored to the donor's stipulations. Instead of removing any sensitive material from your donation, you and the archivist should discuss how to restrict parts of the collection to protect your privacy or the privacy of others. These negotiated time restrictions should be of a fixed and specified duration (measured in months, years, or decades) as part of the deed of gift contract.

Every archive should have established policies governing access to its collections regarding availability, copying, and publication. Once donated to a special collections repository materials never circulate. This is to ensure its preservation for as long as humanly possible. It is reasonable to expect your donation may be investigated by researchers and scholars, featured digitally online, or included as part of a museum or institution exhibit. Conversely, archivists cannot accept as a condition of donation that some or all of your donation will definitely be used in a specific exhibition or manner.

Caring for collections and preparing them for use by researchers is the most expensive operation in an archive. Therefore, most archives are amenable of the inclusion of grants toward the arrangement, cataloging, and conservation of donated papers in the deed of gift. However, Society of American Archivists says that this is "rarely a prerequisite for the acceptance of a collection." Donors may also make a one-time monetary donation toward the cataloging and conservation of their papers if they feel moved to do so.

> Donating papers to an archive, your history becomes a part of a bigger collective memory.

Your letters, diaries, photos, and other material collected over the years may give vital and unique information regarding you, the history of your family, and/or your organization.

While these papers are dear and hold sentimental value to you, they also shed light about your community, state, or nation. Even if you or those in your family were not famous, you did contribute to the culture, heritage, and history of a certain place and/or time. When you donate your papers to an archive, your history becomes part of a bigger collective memory.

REFERENCES

American Alpine Club. *Archives donation guide.* http://www.americanalpineclub
.org/p/archives-donation-guide.

Amherst College Library. *Giving to the Amherst College Library.* https://www
.amherst.edu/library/about/support.

Hunt, Marjorie. 2003. *The Smithsonian folklife and oral history interviewing
guide.* Washington, DC: Smithsonian Institute. http://www.scribd.com/
doc/27072477/Folklife-and-Oral-History-Interviewing-Guide.

Nebraska State Historical Society. 2009. Legal and ethical issues: First things first. *Capturing the living past: An oral history primer*. http://www.nebraskahistory .org/lib-arch/research/audiovis/oral_history/legal.htm.

Morton, Sunny McClellan. 2010. Tools for taking care of your family's legacy: Donating your research, storing textiles, and making heirloom IDs. *Family Tree Magazine*, January. http://www.familytreemagazine.com/article/January -2010-Family-Archivist.

PBS. *Detective technique glossary*. *History Detectives*. http://www.pbs.org/opb/ historydetectives/techniques/glossary.html.

Perks, Rob. 2008. Practical advice: Getting started. Oral History Society. Updated June 2009. http://www.ohs.org.uk/advice/.

The Society of American Archivists (SAA). *A guide to donating your personal or family papers to a repository*. http://www.archivists.org/publications/donating -familyrecs.asp.

South Dakota State Historical Society. 2004. *A beginner's guide to oral history*. http:// history.sd.gov/archives/forms/SHRAB/oralbook1.pdf.

University of Western Ontario Libraries. 2011. Frequently asked questions— Personal papers of individual faculty members. http://www.lib.uwo.ca/ archives/faq_faculty_papers.shtml.

Wisconsin Department of Veterans Affairs—Wisconsin Veterans Museum. Choosing an archives. http://museum.dva.state.wi.us/RC_Archives.asp.

WORKING AFTER RETIRING

12

CHOOSING TO GO BACK TO WORK

Sharon Nottingham

USA TODAY REPORTS that in an AARP survey 79 percent of baby boomers indicated they plan to pursue some kind of work after the age of 65 (Kornblum 2007). One reason is financial, as indicated in a 2009 survey by Gallup, which found that 52 percent of Americans say they won't have enough money in retirement (Newport 2009). But it isn't only the need for money that sends people back to work. Work provides daily structure and activity, recognition, mental challenges, shared accomplishments, and a sense of belonging. It is, in fact, that sense of belonging that many retirees experience as the greatest loss when they retire from a career. Social isolation leads many retirees to work as greeters at Wal-Mart or baristas at Starbucks.

Financial guru Warren Buffett believes that a key to a long and happy life is to have work that connects you to others, challenges you on many levels, and makes a difference (Clyatt 2005, 224). At the age of 80 Buffett is still actively involved in both work and philanthropy. Marc Freedman explains an effect of the busyness of so many retirement communities: "The problem was that the new focus on activity was not able to close the gulf in meaning and roles between the end of work and the end of life, to fill the void produced by the absence of work" (Freedman 2007, 54).

What does it take for happiness and contentment in retirement? The aspects of life most often mentioned as requirements for happiness in the later years of life are not so different from the qualities that lead to happiness at any stage of life:

- Enough money
- Good health
- Network of family and friends
- Enjoyable and engaging activities
- Intellectual stimulation
- Balance between freedom and engagement

Chances are excellent that the next stage of life will include working in retirement, whether because of economic necessity, reprise of the camaraderie of the workplace, or satisfying an inner need to be useful. Retirement used to be a going away from the workplace to a life of leisure for a few years, but now so much has changed that we no longer hear a contradiction in the phrase "working in retirement."

The Social Security program was designed at a time when a mandatory retirement age led to increasing numbers of people who were too old to work and too young to die, the time between disability and death. We now find that too old to work is not a function of arithmetic, but one of physical and mental health and well-being. A person today at the age of 60 has a strong potential to reach the age of 90.

The concept of traditional retirement as we think of it has existed only since the 1960s, when increases in longevity and economic security combined to bring about a new era (Freedman 2007, 44). It is a nameless era that now can stretch through three or even four decades between a long career and cessation of work for a final time. When future generations look back, I predict they will say, "What were they thinking? How could an entire generation have thought that they could work for three or four decades and then keep themselves fulfilled and financially solvent through four decades of nothing but leisure, being self-indulgent and satisfying only selfish needs?"

In 2006, the first of the baby boomers turned 60, and every day 8,000 more join them (Freedman 2007, 70). Now called by some "the great gray wave," they are changing things again. Boomers are the people who created a youth culture, changed the role of women at work, and are now setting about redefining this new stage of life. It used to be that people passed from childhood to adulthood and then to something called old age, a period of time that typically would last only a few years. With increased life expectancy that period of time has stretched to become decades. The reality is that very few people have the resources to sustain thirty or forty years of full-time absence from the workplace.

Going beyond seeking continued or additional income, baby boomers retiring want to take advantage of their new freedom to make a difference in the world, to leave the world better for their having been here.

MAKING DECISIONS

As you approach retirement age, you may find yourself faced with a number of possible futures and feel like an adolescent in many ways. You may experience personal upheaval, feel unsure of yourself, and cast about for who you are or should be during the transition. The more work has been the defining element of a person's life, the more intense these feelings will be. The process of moving to another stage of life can itself take a long time and has been made more complicated by extended life spans, the demise of traditional pensions for many, women in the labor force, and the rising cost of medical care and the possibility of a need for long-term care.

Following are few suggestions to help with making so many decisions about finances and lifestyle:

- Find someone whose opinion and objective advice you can rely upon.
- Create a list of the websites, books, and other resources and study them to inform your decision making.
- Interview people in various situations as you try out what appeals most to you and question your own goals and values.
- Join professional associations and online communities.
- Participate in social media websites.
- Create a team of advisors to serve as gurus in your niche and as experts in areas such as personal finances and investments and small business operations.

Many resources provide insights, exercises, and advice to those contemplating retirement. *The Wall Street Journal Complete Retirement Guidebook: How to Plan It, Live It and Enjoy It* offers advice about making your way through what "has become for many a puzzle—with dozens of decisions and far too much guesswork" (Ruffenach and Greene 2007, 3). Four of the twelve chapters, including "To Work or Not to Work," are directly relevant to making choices about working in retirement.

BEGIN NOW

There is agreement about the wisdom of beginning your search about life in the next stage while still employed. You may need to invest time, money, and energy in developing skills and contacts before you retire while you can utilize the resources available to you in your current situation. For instance, you can use your employment to leverage your ability to prepare for an entrepreneurial enterprise. This does not suggest that you would be working on your business on your employer's time, but that you would take advantage of the opportunities offered through your current employment—opportunities such as using current income to pay for start-up needs or using your income as the basis for obtaining loans more easily. Use your own time to write a business plan and to see if current work contacts can lead you to prospective clients in a different field. Use your network to obtain complimentary letters and recommendations on paper or on social network sites like LinkedIn. Compile samples of writing, published work, or whatever demonstrates what your strengths are while you have access to workplace files. If you will be relocating, ask for introductions from your current network. It is astonishing how quickly people in your current network will make changes and move on to other positions. Bear in mind that when you leave your profession, you will most likely earn less money, so be sure that you have calculated your financial needs and can afford to pursue your passion in another field if that is what appeals to you.

Finding work may be harder than you anticipate, regardless of the economic climate, and a job search will be easier with your current network still in place. If you choose an entrepreneurial path, you may have to learn the skills required to run a small business. If you decide to change fields, you may have to get additional training or even training and experience to be able to do what you really envision for yourself. You may need an extended period of time to explore your options to discover what will provide you with the greatest satisfaction. Will you work for someone, buy a business, start a business, or volunteer? If you choose to be self-employed, be prepared for working three to five years before your business becomes established.

In the book *Retire Happy: What You Can Do Now to Guarantee a Great Retirement,* authors Richard Stim and Ralph Warner (2008) cover all the aspects of retirement planning that you ought to consider, including the chapter "Working after Retirement." Particularly valuable is the list of online resources available for searching the senior job market.

DO THE RESEARCH

You will find an abundance of books, websites, coaches, classes, and training opportunities when you search for information to guide your decision making. One of the best resources to assist you in making a wise decision about your future is "Your Encore: An Introductory Guide to Finding Your Encore Career," an appendix in *Encore: Finding Work That Matters in the Second Half of Life* (Freedman 2007). Freedman offers questions and resources to guide you from getting started to narrowing your choices to the one that is the best fit for you. (The guide is also available at www.encore.org/work.)

What will you research to help you to find your path for the next stage of your life? There is a wide range of information you will want to gather, depending on what information and skills you already have. How well do you know yourself? Do you want to explore your interests to discover what motivates you? Have you already determined how you will approach your own retirement, and how you will balance work and freedom, family and friends?

How long do you expect to live? Having some estimation of your longevity will be helpful to you in deciding a path for your next working experience. At the age of 65 you may have twenty to thirty or more healthy years ahead. Since the duration of this stage of life will have a significant impact on your decisions, it is the time for some honest assessment. If your health is not good, for instance, and if it is an option, you may choose to either work less or find less stressful work in a full-time position. Of course, no one knows how long any individual will live, but there are longevity calculators to provide an estimate for you. Two starting places are www.livingt0100.com/ and https://personal.vanguard.com/us/insights/retirement/plan-for-a-long-retirement.

MANY CHOICES

Continue to work at your career, work less, take a year or two off and then work again, begin an entirely new career, volunteer—these are just some of the possibilities to consider. You may opt to work part-time. Some advise that work in this new stage of life should avoid stress and allow greater time flexibility, qualities that seem for most people to average working two days, or about sixteen hours a week. Not all of the resources you will find helpful are directed specifically to retirees. Books like *I Don't Know What I Want, But I Know It's Not This: A Step-by-Step Guide to*

Finding Gratifying Work by Julie Jansen (2010, 182) offer career changing advice to job seekers of any age. Jansen does, however, include a chapter, "One Toe in the Retirement Pool," that provides a three-step assessment tool to guide your thinking about working in retirement. Jansen notes: "You must prepare yourself emotionally, psychologically, and financially for this new phase whether it means you're working or not. To do so you must talk to people, research, and be very thoughtful about who you are. You must know what your goals are in life and what makes you happy as well as fulfilled." (Jansen 2010, 188)

PERSONAL STORIES

William Safire, longtime columnist for the *New York Times,* added his own advice to the wisdom of James Watson, famous as a discoverer of DNA, who had told him: "Never retire. Your brain needs exercise or it will atrophy." In his final op-ed column, Safire said, "We can quit a job, but we quit fresh involvement at our mental peril" (Safire 2005).

People I am personally familiar with offer suggestions of the range of choices in their examples of some later-life career changes:

- An entomologist who emigrated from the United States to New Zealand and creates award-winning turned-wood bowls
- An award-winning public relations professional who works pro bono for causes she supports
- A library administrator who became a financial planner
- A high school teacher now a yoga instructor
- A school administrator who works part-time to mentor new high school teachers
- A corporate librarian now an independent information professional

My own story brings to mind the saying "Do as I say, not as I do," or in my case did. I reluctantly retired to relocate for personal reasons without giving much thought to my future. The truth is that I had put more effort into planning a two-week vacation than into what might be a third or more of my life. In the beginning, I kept busy volunteering to lead a nonprofit fundraising group, creating ceramics, making quilts, taking water aerobics and yoga classes, writing a cookbook and maintaining a cooking blog, and traveling. I was busy, very busy, yet something was missing. I missed the people, the group I worked with for decades, and the emotional benefits of being part of a team engaged in a shared mission. Gone were collegial camaraderie, lunches, a sense of accomplishment, positive feedback, and a larger paycheck. I realized that keeping busy was not enough for me.

Returning to full-time employee status was not appealing to me after a few months of freedom. What did appeal to me was being an entrepreneur with an independent information research business. In contrast to my lack of preparation for retirement, I applied the skills I had built over decades as a librarian to going back to work. I began my search by attending an ALA conference to reconnect with the industry and former colleagues and to begin building a new network.

Not only did I do the research, I let my network know of my plans. One of my former colleagues did research that led to the Association of Independent Information Professionals (AIIP) and Mary Ellen Bates's (2010) *Building and Running a Successful Research Business*. Bates's book is essential reading for anyone considering this field. After joining the AIIP, I had the member benefit of working with a mentor who helped me focus on narrowing my niche.

Following the advice of my accountant, I registered a fictitious name for my business with the Florida Department of State. I set up office space in my home, keeping my overhead low by being satisfied with what I already had for furniture and equipment. I took care of the visible aspects of having a business: a professionally designed logo, printed business cards, a website, and accounts on social networking sites.

It has been difficult to transfer my management and leadership skills in a not-for-profit position to being a sole proprietor of an independent information business. After an entire career receiving a paycheck, I needed to learn to charge for what I do. Although my searching skills were superior to entering a few words into Google, my skills needed to be updated to merit the fees I intended to charge. I needed to learn how to use different search tools and strategies and to have access to fee-based databases.

At first I practiced by researching for family members. I assure you there is abundant work available pro bono, which somehow sounds more professional than doing the work for free. My first client was a referral from a person I had met socially. I can say that 100 percent of my clients have given me repeat business. We do business not with strangers but with a brand we know or with a person we know directly or because of a recommendation from someone we trust.

I have a plan and a strategy to grow my business. There is now balance in my life between having freedom and having work that is satisfying. I have discovered that my passion remains the same: putting together people with the information they need. Creating your own plan can lead to balancing freedom and commitment and to discovering your own path to making a contribution at any age.

Marc Freedman says with an encore career, as he calls working in retirement, we can "break through to a new era of individual and social renewal, to ride the wave of longevity and health toward a future that works better for all generations" (Freedman 2007, 12).

REFERENCES

Bates, Mary Ellen. 2010. *Building and running a successful research business.* Medford, NJ: Information Today.

Clyatt, Bob. 2005. *Work less, live more: The new way to retire early.* Berkeley, CA: Nolo.

Freedman, Marc. 2007. *Encore: Finding work that matters in the second half of life.* New York: Public Affairs.

Jansen, Julie. 2010. *I don't know what I want, but I know it is not this: A step-by-step guide to finding gratifying work.* New York: Penguin.

Kornblum, Janet. 2007. Community colleges take the lead in retraining retirees for new jobs. *USA Today.* October 3.

Newport, Frank. 2009. Americans increasingly concerned about retirement income. *Gallup Hot Topics,* April 20. http://www.gallup.com/poll/117703/Americans-Increasingly-Concerned-Retirement-Income.aspx?utm_source=email%2Ba%2Bfriend&utm_medium=email&utm_campaign=sharing&utm_term=Americans-Increasingly-Concerned-Retirement-Income&utm_content=morelink.

Ruffenach, Glenn, and Kelly Greene. 2007. *The Wall Street Journal complete retirement guidebook: How to plan it, live it and enjoy it.* New York: Three Rivers Press.

Safire, William. 2005. Never retire. *The New York Times,* January 24, 2005, Opinion. http://www.nytimes.com/2005/01/24/opinion/24safire2.html?emc=eta1.

Stim, Richard, and Ralph Warner. 2008. *Retire happy: What you can do now to guarantee a great retirement.* Berkeley, CA: Nolo.

13

COLLECTING AND SELLING ON EBAY
A GREAT CAREER FOR RETIRED LIBRARIANS

Jennifer Tang

PEOPLE HAVE DESCRIBED eBay as the world's largest marketplace. On any given day, millions of people, from collectors to bargain hunters, buy and sell items from this worldwide flea market. In addition, Europe, Asia, and Mexico have their own sites as well.

Unlike online vendors such as Amazon, eBay depends on its sellers to supply its inventory. Ebay makes its profits not by creating goods itself, but by offering an online forum in which people can post items for sale. Organized like a giant database, eBay allows sellers to categorize their items, making it fairly easy for buyers to find them. The company makes money by charging people three times—once through "listing fees" (similar to someone putting an ad in a newspaper); another via its payment service, PayPal (by charging sellers for a service that allows them to accept credit card payments); and thirdly, by taking a percentage of the final item price (known as a final value fee, or FVF).

Despite the drawback of having to pay eBay three times, many people have managed to make extra income on the site by knowing what to sell and how to pitch the item to buyers. Since eBay doesn't require a license for anyone to open up a storefront, eBay businesses can be run entirely from home. Since its inception, everyone from stay-at-home moms to retirees have created second careers by just sitting at a desk and clicking a mouse. To become a successful seller, following is everything you need:

- Home office equipped with a computer with decent Internet access
- Nearby post office
- Credit card account
- Good digital camera
- Familiarity with the Internet
- The ability to do research online and search databases

I started buying and selling on eBay in May 2000, a few years after I graduated from library school. Though I had heard of the site years before, I had no interest in it until I learned that eBay sold vintage Barbies. As a collector, I was intrigued that my old childhood dolls, once dumped in the trash by my mother, could be bought again for a low price on eBay. After registering for an account, I learned that eBay listed sale items in one of two ways: either a seller offered the item at a fixed price (BIN, which means "buy it now") or the item was offered in an open auction where you had to bid and compete with other buyers (like an auction house).

In my case, I wanted a 1977 Superstar Barbie that had been put up for auction. Since the doll was used, was missing two earrings, and had no original packaging, I assumed it would cost less. The auction was composed of the following elements:

- A description of the item
- A photo
- An opening bid
- The date and time the auction was supposed to end (Because eBay headquarters are located on the West Coast, auction times are stated in Pacific Standard Time.)

I noted that the highest bid was $10, the same price I had paid thirty years ago. I entered my bid of $15 and immediately got a dialog box—"You are the high bidder!" Because another person could outbid me at the auction's close, however, I noted down the time the auction ended. I had to be ready to shoot down any last-minute bids with one of my own (a technique eBay veterans call "sniping").

When I checked back a few days later, the bidding had gone up to $18. I waited until the last seconds of the bid and won the doll for $25. The seller e-mailed me with a congratulatory message that I had "won" the Barbie. Ecstatic, I signed up for PayPal and registered my credit card information so that I could send the seller my payment. A week later, I got the doll and it now sits happily on my shelf.

But this was not the last step of the process. Ebay e-mailed me with a reminder that I had to give the seller feedback. Because eBay is a community made of inexperienced and experienced sellers, the feedback system was created to help buyers decide which sellers they would feel most comfortable dealing with. Though PayPal and eBay offer buyer protection programs in case a transaction doesn't work out, feedback ratings remain the single most important guide for buyers to use in gauging a seller's trustworthiness. Some sellers get high marks for fast shipping, others for the quality of item and the packaging. Writing a one-line statement is usually sufficient. For example, my feedback statement read: "Fast shipping, great item, very happy." In return, the seller gave me a positive feedback: "Fast payment, great buyer!"

After I had accumulated twenty-five feedbacks, I decided it was time to try my hand at selling. To prepare, I studied other auctions on the site, noting word choices and use of photos. Many sellers used annotations such as NWT (new with tags), NWOT (new without tags), HTF (hard to find), OOP (out of print), and other shorthand notations.

After rummaging through my closet, I decided a Smurf video game I had bought from Odd-Lot would be my eBay guinea pig. I had bought it eight years ago and had been too lazy to take it to Goodwill. To make sure that this item was popular enough to garner a sale, I searched eBay's "Completed Auctions" site and scrutinized all the auctions that had ended with a sale. By doing this, I was able to ascertain that, while many people had Smurf games for sale, nobody had mine. I wrote a simple description:

> You are bidding on a rare, HTF Smurf video game. Box is in good condition with a few tears and the game was played very little. See photos. Great for collectors! I haven't seen another one on eBay like it. Shipping is $5 to U.S., add $2 for insurance. PayPal accepted; payment due within 7 days.

Like any online store, I expected the buyer to pay shipping and insurance. As part of my research, I had taken my box to the post office, weighed it, and figured out what the shipping costs would be. In addition, I copied other sellers in their habit of specifying how long they would wait for payment. By putting in the condition "payment due within 7 days" I wouldn't have to wait an extended period of time for someone to pay me. Every eBay transaction is considered a legal, binding contract, and by spelling out the exact terms of the contract, I was protecting myself.

I supplemented my description with a few photos, striving to show the game from all angles. Since I didn't know how valuable the item was, I decided to forgo the fixed item price option and listed it for 99 cents as an opening bid. By offering such a low price, I was expressing confidence that enough bidders would be attracted to the item to drive the price up. I was also saving money. Ebay charges higher fees in accordance to how much you want for your item, so listing an item for 99 cents costs only 10 cents while listing it for $50 would be approximately $2. I also decided to set my auction to a seven-day run. I hoped this would give potential bidders enough time to look at the item and consider purchasing it.

A week later, the auction ended with twenty-one bids, the highest being $150, from a bidder in London. I nearly fell off my chair. He e-mailed me, saying he'd be happy to pay all the costs of shipping overseas. After the auction closed, I opened my PayPal account and was happy to see the $150 sitting in my account. I soon packed the item and took it down to the post office, amazed that my old toy would live out its final days with an English accent.

After that, I was hooked. How could someone pay so much for an item that I had been on the verge of tossing in the garbage or donating to Goodwill? How many treasures lurked in my apartment? As any eBay veteran might tell you, finding hidden treasures in your own house is an ordinary occurrence. All I had to do was search eBay's huge database for successful past auctions and find out that this was true.

To date, I've sold over 1,000 items on eBay and have 1,450 positive feedbacks from buyers and sellers alike. I've made thousands of dollars selling off my unwanted items as well as helping others exchange their dusty treasures for cash.

Because so much of eBay selling requires doing research and searching a giant database for information, I believe librarians are uniquely positioned to launch successful second careers on eBay. Like any other database, it requires knowledge of Boolean operators (AND, OR, NOT) as well as understanding HTML (helpful if you want to construct auction templates that include photos). Knowing how to communicate online, moreover, is essential (whether written or oral).

Other qualities that successful eBay sellers have are good organizational skills, a love for history, and an eye for collecting. Librarians who have worked in acquisitions, in particular, may do especially well, since they are used to entering orders, tracking individual purchases, and being cognizant of shipping times. These skills, if performed well, are often rewarded with excellent feedback from grateful buyers, which in turn leads to more sales.

GETTING STARTED: THE BASICS

To start selling on eBay, the first step is to familiarize yourself with how it works.

- First, register an account. Go to the eBay home page at www.ebay.com and enter your personal information. It will ask for your credit card information because eBay charges fees the minute you start listing your regular or fixed-price auction.
- Choose a username and password. *Tip:* if you want to specialize in a particular field, you might want to consider a name that reflects your specialty. Many sellers like anonymity, so be imaginative—use an ID that reflects an item you're selling, like BARBIEWORLD or ILOVEBAGS.
- Register for a PayPal account. PayPal is owned by eBay and is the preferred method of payment. Whether you're buying or selling, you need a PayPal account. While there are no fees to buy an item using this account, PayPal takes a percentage of your final sales price whenever you use it to accept credit card payments from buyers.

RESEARCH

- Before you sell on eBay, it is advisable to become a buyer first. Most people won't buy from sellers with zero feedback. The more transactions you have on eBay, whether as a buyer or a seller, the higher your reputation. Since almost anything can be found on eBay, there's no excuse not to start perusing the site and begin buying a few items, if only to get feedback.
- Get familiar with the eBay database. Items are grouped by category. Start by entering keyword searches on the main eBay page. You can also filter your results by price range, seller location, limiting your search to BIN or regular auctions, and other variables. Use your librarian expertise with Boolean operators to narrow down your search.
- After you've "won" an item, pay using PayPal and leave positive or negative feedback, depending on how happy you are with a purchase. Is the item damaged, not as described, or missing something? Buyers can leave negative feedback to warn other buyers, but sellers can't. A few years ago, eBay decided that sellers could say only positive things about a bidder (the customer is always right apparently).

- When you've accumulated enough feedback (no less than ten), start researching the market for your item. Go to "Completed Auctions" on the main eBay page and see what your item last sold for. Then you know how much it's really worth.

CREATING AN EBAY REGULAR AUCTION OR BIN (BUY IT NOW) AUCTION

- Study how other sellers word their descriptions. Pay attention to how you can highlight the best attributes of any particular item.
- Decide if you want to sell to buyers only in the United States or if you're open to selling your item to overseas customers. Some balk at doing this because (1) you need to fill out an additional customs form and (2) it's harder to track down an item in a foreign country (an unscrupulous buyer may lie and file a claim, saying he or she never received it, and you could lose money). Personally, I've had great transactions with buyers from around the world.
- Agree on the lowest price you'll accept for your item and decide whether to offer it at a set price or start with a low bid, waiting to see if it goes to the highest bidder (eBay fees for BIN sales are higher than conventional auctions).
- Take detailed photos using a digital camera. Highlight your item's best attributes. People prefer pictures that give products clear lines and definition. Put yourself in the buyer's place—since you won't see or touch the item, you will need as complete a description as possible.
- Set up an auction time. Ebay offers one-day, three-day, seven-day, and ten-day auctions. Whether you choose a quick sale or a leisurely one is up to you. Some sellers feel confident that an item is popular enough to warrant a one- or three-day auction and want the fast cash. Personally, I prefer to use the seven-day format because more people would probably prefer at least a few days to decide whether they want the item or not.
- Answer the bidder's questions promptly. Consider it a compliment when someone sends you questions about the item. Rapid response time impresses potential buyers—if you are responsive to their needs, they have more reason to trust you, the seller.
- Check with the post office for shipping rates so that you don't unintentionally undercharge or overcharge a buyer when you state shipping prices.

- Sit back and watch your auction as it progresses. Seeing bids go up is like watching a slot machine in Las Vegas. Only this time, you get to win the jackpot.
- That's all there is to it!

FIND YOUR SELLING NICHE

While many people sell what's lying around in their garage or home, I've learned that the biggest sales on eBay come from items not available anywhere else. For example, a Jason Wu–designed doll recently sold for $1,000. The doll was a collector's edition that was sold only in New York City for an event called "Fashion's Night Out." If you lived in the area, you could have bought the doll from Bergdorf Goodman's for only $150. If you had sold it for $1,000, you would have made an instant profit of nearly $800.

Like me, many people enjoy re-collecting their childhood toys or other memorabilia. This is a huge category. Before eBay, buyers had to visit hundreds of flea markets or garage sales, hoping to come across an item through pure serendipity. Ebay changed all that.

As in any other discipline, do your research. I would have never spotted rare Barbie collectibles without investing in Barbie collector's books. The same qualities that make a good antique dealer apply to someone selling used goods on eBay. The more you know, the more you'll make.

PROHIBITED ITEMS ON EBAY

During the 1990s, news headlines focused on controversial eBay auctions, such as Nazi memorabilia, organ donations, and sexual services. Even a piece of the Berlin Wall was found on eBay. Since then, the company has implemented new rules and regulations that have clamped down on the Wild Wild West that the site was in its very beginnings. If you choose to post items that fall into these aforementioned categories, be warned—eBay has the right to pull your stuff off the site and cancel the auction.

CONCLUSION

Ebay remains the most well-known website for finding obscure, hard-to-find, or unusual items. Selling on eBay is an art that involves posting an accurate description, detailed photos, and writing a persuasive sales pitch. Whether selling off personal items or buying and reselling treasures found at yard sales, thrift stores, or consignment shops, eBay sellers are advised to do their research. Since the eBay database requires knowledge of searching using Boolean operators and keywords, a skill most casual users don't have, librarians are at a distinct advantage.

In recent years, a number of sellers have fled eBay for other sites such as Amazon and Boocoo. Many have even turned to Craigslist. The reason is that eBay has been slapping smaller sellers with higher fees, amounting to as much as 13 percent of the final auction price. Whether these sites will prove as popular as eBay for hard-to-categorize items is questionable. For all its drawbacks, eBay remains immensely popular with millions of users from around the world and has been used as a means of livelihood by many.

SUGGESTED READING

Becherer, Richard C., Diane Halstead, and Albert J. Taylor. "Auction Characteristics and Outcomes: An Empirical Examination of eBay." *Journal of Internet Commerce* 7.3 (2008): 403–424. *Academic Search Complete.* EBSCO. Web. 12 Nov. 2010.

Collier, Marsha. *eBay for Dummies.* New York: Wiley, 2009.

———. *eBay for Seniors for Dummies.* New Jersey: Wiley, 2010.

Compton, Michele. "Do you eBay?" *Women in Business* 59.3 (2007): 16–19. *Academic Search Complete.* EBSCO. Web. 12 Nov. 2010.

Cornish, Randy. *Absolute Beginner's Guide to eBay.* Toronto: Que Publishing, 2008.

Dralle, Lynn A. *Home Run: The 4th 100 Best Things I've Sold on eBay.* Palm Desert: All Aboard, 2009.

Ennico, Cliff. *The eBay Business Answer Book: The 350 Most Frequently Asked Questions about Making Big Money on eBay.* New York: AMACOM Books, 2008.

Ennico, Cliff, and Cindy L. Shebley. *The eBay Marketing Bible: Everything You Need to Know to Reach More Customers and Maximize Your Profits.* New York: AMACOM Books, 2010.

Geck, Caroline. "Selling Online 2.0: Migrating from eBay to Amazon, craigslist, and Your Own E-Commerce Website." *Library Journal* 134.11 (2009): 82. *Academic Search Complete.* EBSCO. Web. 12 Nov. 2010.

Gralla, Preston. *eBay in a Snap.* Toronto: Sams Publishing, 2004.

Holahan, Catherine. "EBay Courts 'Power Sellers'." *BusinessWeek Online* (2008): 9. *Academic Search Complete.* EBSCO. Web. 12 November 2010.

Holden, Greg. *1000 Best eBay Success Secrets: Secrets from a Powerseller.* Naperville: Sourcebooks Inc., 2006.

————. *The Collector's Guide to eBay: The Ultimate Resource for Buying, Selling, and Valuing Collectibles,* New York: McGraw-Hill, 2004.

Karp, David A. "Secrets of Selling On eBay." *PC Magazine* 25.2 (2006): 72–75. *Academic Search Complete.* EBSCO. Web. 12 Nov. 2010.

Marie, Janyne Ste. "Buying on eBay: A Basic Primer." *Key Words* 17.2 (2009): 57–60. *Academic Search Complete.* EBSCO. Web. 12 Nov. 2010.

McCann, Clare. *The Beginner's Guide to Buying and Selling on eBay.* Chichester, UK: Summersdale, 2007.

Pagac, Jerry. "How I Did It: You Sold What Online?" *Parks & Recreation* 43.8 (2008): 20–21. *Academic Search Complete.* EBSCO. Web. 12 Nov. 2010.

Prince, Dennis L. *How to Sell Anything on eBay... And Make a Fortune.* New York: McGraw-Hill, 2007.

Waring, Becky. "How to Buy and Sell on eBay Scam-Free." *PC World* 26.5 (2008): 41–42. *Academic Search Complete.* EBSCO. Web. 12 Nov. 2010.

Weltman, Barbara. *The Complete Idiot's Guide to Starting an eBay Business.* Minneapolis: Alpha, 2008.

Wuorio, Jeff, and Patricia Greco. "eBay Guide." *Good Housekeeping* 246.2 (2008): 93. *Academic Search Complete.* EBSCO. Web. 12 Nov. 2010.

14

WORKING PART-TIME AFTER RETIREMENT

Rita Marsales

ART AND BOOKS have been two big passions of my life, but I was only able to combine them professionally after I was into my seventh decade. I fully enjoyed the forty-plus years that I spent working in an academic library, where I wore many hats over the years. I worked in Gifts and Exchanges, Cataloging, Serials, and Reference. I participated in the transition from cards to an online environment. My final role was most satisfying—I created a preservation department for our library. I also enjoyed being involved in related ALA committees.

However, I never forgot my interest in the art that had been my undergraduate major. Just for fun, I began taking art history classes at my university and eventually enrolled in the graduate program. It took many years to complete as I could only take one or two classes a semester, so my children had graduated from college before I received my master's in art history in 1992.

Before I knew it, I was 68 and past due for retirement in 2004. I enjoyed relaxing and traveling for a while, then tried various volunteer jobs but found them unfulfilling. I had stayed busy all of my life so I was bored with so much free time.

An old friend called and asked if I would be interested in helping out with a special project in his library—cataloging a gift collection. I have always enjoyed cataloging, but my answer was that they needed to find someone young to do it. I was by that time 71. I agreed to have lunch to talk about it and then said I would be willing to work ten to twelve hours a week. I hadn't had a lot of experience in cataloging, but I had good training from the regular cataloger in getting started.

The library is in a very prestigious art museum, so I finally have an opportunity to be associated with the art world by providing information for the curators. I enjoy the wonderful books that I handle and my art history background is invaluable. The one thing that I didn't like was that I had to file cards in a card catalog as well as catalog books. I still remembered how to file, but it was no fun.

All went well for about nine months. Then the regular cataloger decided that she could finally retire and turn over all of the cataloging to me. I increased my hours to about fifteen a week and waded in. I learned a lot and streamlined wherever I was able. After eight more months, the head librarian decided that he should retire. Our staff was down to the assistant librarian, three volunteers, and me. After six more months, the assistant librarian left to have a baby and one volunteer quit.

Undaunted, I carried on with the help of the volunteer who worked the most. We were able to clean up the rare book room by shifting the volumes and creating an oversize book area. We also transferred the circulation records from a paper file to an online file. However, this dear volunteer had to quit because her student internship was over.

It was a lonely time for me with no other employee in the library for six months. The library is under the supervision of one of the main curators of the museum. She is a lovely person but spends most of her time traveling the world or mounting exhibitions. One bright spot was the decision e to hire a new head librarian, and two able candidates were soon interviewed. When the gentleman from New York with a PhD in art history as well as an MLS accepted, I was overjoyed, but he couldn't begin work for three more months.

By this time I was really tired of filing cards and so took up the challenge of creating an online catalog. Instead of looking at systems that cost tens of thousands of dollars as had been done previously, I inquired about one I knew well from the days when I worked part-time in a school library. It cost $1,000 per year, so the museum administration was willing to try it. Happily, I ordered a disc of our records in MARC format and loaded it into the newly acquired system. It looked beautiful, but there were no call numbers! After many hours of consultation and reloading, I was able to get the new system up and running, two days before the new head librarian arrived.

I am really happy with our new head librarian and we work well together. I love that he went to library school *after* getting his PhD in art history from Harvard because he really liked research. Sometimes it seems a little strange to realize that he is younger than my youngest son, but we are pretty much in agreement on library operations. I am delighted to have him handle the planning and special projects and let me get back to pure cataloging, a lot of which is original and challenging. I also am in charge of circulation in our new system, bar coding, and interlibrary loans.

I chose to return to work because I like to have a purpose in life and enjoy being around people. Advantages for me are that I can set my own hours within the allotted time per week and can take a day off or vacation whenever I want (with due notice of course). I don't have health care or retirement benefits, so that works to the organization's advantage. Since I have Medicare, Social Security, and a pension already, I don't need benefits. Taxes are deducted from my biweekly paychecks. The extra money helps me to pay bills and travel. Most of all, I like keeping my mind active. Since I love art, I can visit the museum galleries when I need a break, get special tours, and receive discounts at the museum bookstore.

You may say that it was easy for me to find employment after retirement because I had friends. That is called networking, and I've have been doing that for years. There are other ways to find work, however. I had to work more than one job over the years because I was a single mother of three. I can offer some suggestions for finding library-related employment. Everything I will tell is something I have done myself or know someone who has.

First, you must decide how many hours you would like to work, and then the number of hours you would be willing to work. Next, decide what pay you deserve based on a lifetime of experience. Don't sell yourself short; start higher and negotiate. Once you start working it is more difficult to ask for an increase. I didn't ask for enough salary at the museum library, but I have received two substantial bonuses—something that never occurred in my academic career. Don't forget to update your resume before you start your job search. Make it simple but as impressive as you can. If you have a second master's degree or job experience in a specific field, those qualifications may open up even more possibilities. Following are some ideas to get started, but I'm sure you can come up with some of your own:

- School libraries often need extra library help for a few hours a week. They need catalogers, someone to manage the circulation desk and answer questions, and someone to read to children. Go to a school library close to you and inquire. It helps to be a grandmother, but that is not as important as the years of experience you have to offer.
- If public library work appeals to you, inquire at your city or county library. They may have limited budgets, but it may also be easier for them to hire a non-benefit-eligible part-time employee. After-school hours are when these libraries especially welcome extra help.

- I once worked part-time for our local community college as a substitute reference librarian. Community colleges hold classes at various high schools around the city and place their own librarians in the school libraries in the evenings. If the librarian assigned to that campus couldn't make it one evening or was on vacation, they called a substitute librarian. It entailed going in to work on short notice and then being able to enter a strange library and immediately start answering reference questions, even if you didn't know your way around that particular library. It was a challenge, but fun. I also worked for a community college as a cataloger during a retrospective conversion, but I suspect this is no longer an option.

- If you are able to work an evening shift, you may find a part-time job as a reference or circulation librarian in a university library. It might be only one evening a week and not too late. Saturday or Sunday afternoon shifts may be available as well. I worked like this for three years at a small private college. Remember, being around young people keeps you young!

- Being a cataloger can land you all kinds of jobs. There is one area that is really profitable: the private collector. You can more or less set your own price and hours. There are many wealthy people who have collections of books that have grown so large that they are unable to find the book they want. There are simple software programs that you can use, so try to avoid typing cards. Sometimes, people only want what amounts to a bibliography with the books being arranged by title or by author, but it usually is helpful to have them also arranged by subject. You don't have to use LC or Dewey; there is a simple Cutter Table that has been around for ages. I once arranged books for an art patron. She didn't want any marking on her books but wanted them grouped by art movements. This task didn't take long, but when she called back a couple of years later and complained that the books had gotten out of order and needed to be arranged again, I declined. Another collector who didn't want his books marked was happy to have labels on his shelves.

- Don't forget special libraries. I once paid some legal fees by cataloging a lawyer's library. I worked as a cataloger for an office of psychiatrists several hours a month for a number of years. I worked for many months at a well-known engineering firm while its regular librarian was recuperating from an automobile accident. Special libraries also receive gift collections that can't be processed in the normal work flow. The keys are flexibility and experience.

- If your specialty is reference, you can find people who want research done or bibliographies prepared. You can work for authors by proofreading their work or cross-checking their citations. Genealogical research is yet another possibility.
- Medical libraries are a special field but have many traditional library tasks where they may welcome part-time employees.
- Church and synagogue libraries depend heavily on volunteers, but when they grow large they may welcome some part-time paid help for acquisitions and cataloging.
- Many organizations have archives rather than libraries per se, but librarian skills apply in organizing these as well. Some examples are local art venues such as theaters, symphonies, operas, historical organizations, and specialty museums of all sorts. They all have documents they want to keep and that need to be organized. They will have some book collections as well. I once cataloged a library for the use of the docents at a local house museum.
- If you have the necessary skills and patience, there is a big demand for book repair. Ask your local libraries to keep your name on file to offer when people call for help—and they do call libraries frequently. For this you usually charge by the book. I had one friend who repaired the spines on the hymnals for her church.
- There are places other than libraries where you can seek employment. A librarian background is obviously an advantage if you would like to work part-time in a bookstore. You also get discounts on books. If you want to do something completely different, go ahead, but you might as well take advantage of the skills you have.
- I have saved the fun part for last: travel librarianship! If you know libraries and you like to travel, you can combine the two. There are libraries all over the world that might be interested in hiring a consultant for one reason or another. Strengths in technological applications can be very valuable. Knowing the language of the country where you would like to work can be helpful, but it is not always a requirement. I have a friend who spent three months in Japan as a consultant. She had formerly been a government documents librarian and knew no Japanese. Consultants sometimes receive transportation and living expenses as well as a fee. Another friend and her husband went to Scotland for a year after both were retired, and she cataloged the library of a nobleman. They lived

in a cozy cottage rather than a drafty old castle. Weekends were free for travel. Opportunities of this type abound and are just a click away on the Internet.

- Do you realize that cruise ships have libraries and therefore must hire librarians? While still employed, I once investigated the possibility of working for a program where college students from wealthy families spent a semester cruising around the world while having classes on board. Of course they needed lots of books, all of which required a librarian to acquire, catalog, and circulate.

If you are not interested in working for pay, there are many volunteer opportunities in which to utilize your librarian skills. Following are a few:

- Before I found my current part-time job, I volunteered every other Saturday morning at a nature center where I could draw upon my reference skills to answer questions.
- More tedious was the volunteer job I had in helping to create an image database for another museum.
- Are you interested in history? Librarians are good at gathering and organizing oral histories. I live in an old section of my city and think that it would be great to interview some of the old-timers before their stories are lost. Recently, a young librarian at the academic library where I was formerly employed organized a project to gather videotaped interviews of retired and long-time employees. It turned out to be fascinating.
- Start your own book club in your church or neighborhood. You know how to find the best books for your group to read.

Now aren't you glad that you got that MLS? You never need to worry about being unemployed. On the other hand, you may never find time to read all of those wonderful books on your own shelves! In three more years I will be 78, and that seems like a good age at which to retire again. Or maybe not?

PART V

VOLUNTEERING AFTER RETIREMENT

15

"I THOUGHT YOU RETIRED!"
VOLUNTEERING IN YOUR LIBRARY

Mary Redmond

FORMER PRESIDENT JIMMY Carter and his wife Rosalynn donate a week of their time and construction skills to Habitat for Humanity® every year "to build homes and raise awareness of the critical need for affordable housing."[1]

Retired U.S. Supreme Court Justice Sandra Day O'Connor (in addition to writing, lecturing, and hearing cases at the appellate level around the country) is working with universities, schools, and the Internet community on her goal "to educate an entire generation of young Americans about how our government works."[2]

TV's *Maverick* and *Rockford Files* actor James Garner has done public awareness work about lupus, a disease that affects an estimated 1.5 million Americans.[3]

These celebrities are representative of retirees continuing or returning to work as volunteers beyond the conventional retirement age. They are not alone. In 1950, a 65-year-old could expect 13.9 more years of life.[4] By 2007, that figure had risen by almost five years, to 18.6 years.[5] And with more healthful lifestyles and better medical care, a retiree can get a lot out of that "extra" time, including donating at least some of it to volunteer activities.

WHO VOLUNTEERS?

The Corporation for National and Community Service reports that 63.4 million people age 16 and over volunteered in 2009.[6] And the value of that donated time is estimated at almost $169 billion.[7] Among people 65 and over, the 2009 figures are 9.1 million people, or 23.9 percent of that age range, donating 1.6 billion hours of service.[8]

WHY VOLUNTEER?

Of course the main reason for volunteering is to contribute your time and talents, both to help in emergencies and to make a long-term commitment to projects. But there are advantages for volunteers in addition to the satisfaction of contributing to worthy causes and the building/maintaining of social ties among fellow volunteers.

A March 2010 United Healthcare/VolunteerMatch online survey of 4,582 people (both volunteers and nonvolunteers) on the benefits of volunteering found that seniors who volunteer "maintain more positive feelings about getting older (55) . . . are more inclined to feel control over their health (57) . . . are more likely to express contentment with their emotional well-being (59) . . . and . . . are significantly more likely to have an optimistic look on life." (61)[9]

VOLUNTEER OPPORTUNITIES FOR LIBRARIANS

Opportunities for librarians are legion! The Peace Corps, VolunteerMatch, the Senior Corps RSVP network, and similar organizations are good places to start a general search for volunteer opportunities. More specifically for librarians, the Canada-based Librarians without Borders and professional organizations, including the American Library Association and state/local library groups, can be the first step in identifying possibilities. And there are vast numbers of other groups (religious organizations, schools, community organizations, and similar entities) sponsoring many valuable projects. These can range all the way from fundraising for buying materials for donation to a library, to volunteering to set up a library, training other volunteers to take over the day to day running of a library, and many other variations, both in the United States and all over the world.

Anyone with a desire to volunteer should be able to find many options from which to choose. But in the excitement of looking through all these possible choices, don't forget that the place you have been working might also be an option. For those considering this possibility, there are a number of things to sort out (both for you and for the organization) before and during volunteer work there.

TALK TO YOURSELF FIRST

Why are you considering this step? It should go without saying that you are a dedicated person who wants to contribute to the organization that is so important to you and the community it serves. But what other factors come into play for you?

- To do something that you (and the library) know should be done but that nobody has had the time to do
- To concentrate on a specific, manageable workload—maybe even be able to get something finished without interruptions
- To keep up the friendships and social interactions that you enjoyed with your coworkers
- To keep busy (not a bad thing as long as you aren't wasting other people's time)
- To have fun

OTHER CONSIDERATIONS

If you're still interested, following are more things that you (and the library) need to consider before signing on:

- This is probably stating the obvious, but be sure that the library wants or can use your services. Don't assume that because you've been there many years or have experience working on many assignments that what you are proposing will be helpful to the library or will fit in with what the library currently needs to have done.
- Take a two-year hiatus between your retirement and returning as a volunteer. This will give time to put a little space between your work experience and returning to volunteer and offer a fresh look and a new face, at least to some staff.

- Talk to the director and/or volunteer coordinator to see what they want you to do, which might not necessarily be what you want to do. You might have noticed opportunities while you were working there, but are they what the library wants/needs to have done?
- Be sure to investigate the library's policies on volunteering in general, including any potential concerns of unions and/or staff attitudes toward volunteers. Most libraries structure their volunteer programs so that they don't overlap with responsibilities of paid staff.

YOU'RE "HIRED": WORKING OUT THE DETAILS

If these things aren't addressed in a volunteer manual (or if there isn't such a volume in your library), it's good to get an understanding of these matters so that you and the institution have the same expectations. Following are some things to consider:

- Be sure that you and the library have a clear agreement regarding your assignments and details on starting/leaving times, plans to be away, and so on. A commitment for unpaid work is a responsibility and should be taken as seriously as for a paid job.
- It's a good idea to inquire about the library's volunteer or general liability insurance "just in case." Be sure to keep your emergency contact and related information up-to-date.
- If neither you nor the library is ready to make an open-ended commitment, it might be a good idea to agree on a specific project with a beginning and ending time line. If things work out well for both of you, the agreement can be renewed. If it's not what either of you hoped for, completion of the project can offer the opportunity for an amicable parting.
- Find out what kinds of statistics or reports you might be expected to maintain and how often they would be submitted.
- What kind of support can you expect? An office, desk, phone, Internet access, use of photocopy/fax machines, or staff assistance? These things are often at a premium so don't assume that you will automatically have access to things you had as an employee.
- Along the same lines, can you use staff facilities like lockers and break rooms or kitchens? Will you be able to sit in on staff training sessions?
- What will the supervisory arrangements be? If you used to head up a unit and are now coming back as a volunteer, you might be reporting to the

person you formerly supervised. How comfortable will both of you be with this arrangement? And will others on staff or the patrons still look to you with questions that should be going to your successor? How will you deal with these situations?

- You might be surprised at how complicated some of the procedures in other units are, even if you were at the library for a long time. Be sure that you understand and follow the procedures of the unit where you are volunteering. If there isn't an up-to-date written guide, take good notes and clarify any questions that you might have.

A FEW CAVEATS

Being a volunteer is not the same as being an employee. Even if you are in the same building and working with the same people, procedures and relationships may be different. You and the library staff will both have to negotiate these changes as you settle into your new role.

- You're not on the staff any longer, so don't expect access to nonpublic areas, after-hours access, and other "staff only" privileges. Even if you know a collection better than anyone on the staff, you will need to be aware of and comply with security procedures.
- If your responsibilities include publicity and/or newsletter production and dissemination, make sure that you check with library staff on all the details about the articles you are writing. The most up-to-date information about the library resources, policies, and other details should be included in any external communications. And, of course, never presume to speak for the library unless you have specifically been empowered to do so by library management.
- You might have worked in the library for thirty or more years, but new staff probably won't know that. Don't be insulted by explanations of policies that you instituted or requests for identification from people who don't know you.
- If you have access to a library e-mail account, be sure you understand and follow the rules for appropriate use. If it's a personal message, it's better to go to a public Internet station and sign in there. Similarly, find out about limits of telephone usage and library materials.

- Remember that others are there to work, not to socialize (unless it's during break, lunch, and other designated times). Volunteers, including former staff members, must respect the rules of conduct for all.

NOW I'M *REALLY* LEAVING!

All good things come to an end. Perhaps you want to move on to a paid job or another volunteer opportunity, relocate out of the area, or just relax and not be on a schedule. For whatever reason, at some time you'll be leaving for good. Ideally, this separation should be treated like any other.

- Give as much advance notice as possible.
- Turn in any identification badges, keys, and so on, to the appropriate office.
- Make sure your reports, statistics, and other records are up-to-date and submitted.
- Offer to document procedures for what you have been doing to make things easier for your supervisor and any successor volunteer.
- If it's not part of the usual process, consider asking for an exit interview with the director or volunteer coordinator to share your experiences and make suggestions. Now enjoy the next stage of your life!

TWO EXPERIENCES AT THE NEW YORK STATE LIBRARY

After a 30-year career with the New York State Library, Marilyn Douglas now volunteers with the New Netherland Institute, a support group for the state library's New Netherland Project Dutch translation work. Mary Redmond worked at the New York State Library for twenty-five years and is now the volunteer Special Liaison for the New York State Library.

WHAT DID YOU DO AS A NEW YORK STATE LIBRARY EMPLOYEE?

Douglas: I worked in the Technical Services unit and then moved to the Local History, Manuscripts, and Special Collections unit. Following this stint, I worked in the Planning unit to organize and facilitate the move of furniture and equipment to the then new Cultural Education Center (CEC) building, which now houses the state library's collection and staff. I served as coordinator of library services to state agency libraries and state agency personnel, and then became a library consultant to public, school, and academic libraries in the Rochester region; established the Electronic Doorway Library Recognition program; worked with the Gates Foundation to upgrade computer capabilities in public libraries; and administered several New York State grant programs.

Redmond: My official title was Head of Reference Services, but my responsibilities changed a lot over the twenty-five years on the job.

WHAT MADE YOU DECIDE TO VOLUNTEER FOR YOUR POST-RETIREMENT WORK AT THE LIBRARY?

Douglas: When I retired, I knew I needed to do something to reinvent myself. I also knew I didn't want to do library work per se and that I wanted to get involved with something where I felt I could make a difference without making a full-time commitment. As one of the founding trustees of the New Netherland Institute when it began as the Friends of the New Netherland Project in 1986, it seemed the logical step to take. Contrary to what one should do, I announced to the director of the project that I was planning to volunteer when I retired. Luckily, he accepted my offer quite willingly, though I'm sure at the time he had no idea what I would do. Since 1986, I had been a member and officer of the board of trustees and was confident that there were things I could do that would suit my skill set.

Redmond: During my years working in the library, I didn't have time to do much more for the Friends of the State Library than just be a member. But I wanted to be more active and thought that my experience as a staff member might be valuable both to the library and to the Friends.

DESCRIBE WHAT YOU DO AS A VOLUNTEER.

Douglas: I began as a volunteer with the New Netherland Institute in 2004. It was just about that time that the board was beginning to plan for the 2009 Quadricentennial of Henry Hudson's voyage up the Hudson River to Albany, so there were many things to think about, plan, and organize. One of my primary volunteer activities was organizing and publicizing our annual meeting and the New Netherland Dinner, in conjunction with the New Netherland Seminar. In addition, I established an information list, NEWMARC-L, to publicize events throughout the world that would be of interest to people who are interested in the Dutch role in colonial history in the Atlantic World and provide copy for *de Nieu Nederlanse Marcurius,* our quarterly newsletter. With the attention gained with the 2009 celebrations, we received a large matching grant that with other established grants allows us to bring in researchers to spend time with us doing research in the world's largest collection of New Netherland material housed in the state library and the state archives. I handle the arrangements for these internships, fellowships, and so on. We also give two annual awards, and I facilitate that process as well. I handle general reference questions about the library and archives collections and their use, and I often refer people to an expert in a Dutch-related field who may be able to help them. I supervise the data entry for our bibliographic citation database. We now have almost 1,000 articles, essays, and lectures in the database. It is my hope that someday all these items will be scanned so that the full text will be available online.

Redmond: I'm treasurer of the Friends of the New York State Library. I've worked with the Friends on coordinating some special projects such as raising matching funds for a Save America's Treasures grant for the state library to begin conservation work on a fragile collection of seventeenth century manuscripts (the Van Rensselaer Manor Collection). The Friends have also received a legislative member item to purchase African American and African Caribbean family history/research materials for the New York State Library's collection. I worked with staff of the state library to identify appropriate materials, and then coordinated the ordering and payment by the Friends from the vendors.

I'm also liaison to the editor of the *New York State Library News,* the quarterly newsletter of the Friends. I work with the state library to provide items for the newsletter, secure appropriate graphics from the library's collection, and try to make sure that the readers are kept up-to-date about the New York State Library.

The Friends financially support and staff exhibit tables about the state library at conferences and special events. We are also working to expand our sponsorship of speakers for state library programs.

WHAT ARE THE TIME AND TRAVEL COMMITMENTS FOR YOUR VOLUNTEER WORK?

Douglas: Generally, I work two full days a week, though during busy times around events I may spend more time in the office. Of course, e-mail is 24/7, so I often find myself following up on NNI-related activities in my off time. I live about a ten-minute drive or a two-mile walk from the CEC, which houses the NNI offices, the state library, and the state archives.

Redmond: I am here pretty much every day, although as a retiree I have the luxury of setting my own hours. The travel commitment is just the usual half-hour bus ride that I used to take during my working years.

ANY UNEXPECTED JOYS OR DRAWBACKS, AND ANY FINAL THOUGHTS?

Douglas: Though not a historian by training, I do know how to find information. I often help the director and assistant director in their search for specific items. I enjoy helping people, facilitating communication among experts, and constantly learning about a period of history with which I was unfamiliar. Being in the building where I used to work means that many of the people are known to me as I am to them. This helps when trying to get things done. It also helps that we are not part of the bureaucracy and have much more freedom in making things happen. Probably the biggest drawback, if one can call it that, is volunteering in the same building where you worked. I count it as a lucky day when I don't meet someone on the elevator who says "I thought you retired." If you do decide to volunteer— know what you're getting yourself into, keep it in perspective, and do it because it's something you enjoy.

Redmond: The work is even more fulfilling than I imagined. It's an adjustment to go from being on the staff to being a liaison without the authority that I used to have by virtue of the positions I held. But after four years of volunteering, things have smoothed out and each day is a new adventure.

NOTES

1. Habitat for Humanity, "Jimmy & Rosalynn Carter Work Project," http://www.habitat.org/how/default_jcwp.aspx (accessed February 3, 2011).
2. Susannah A. Nesmith, "Where Are They Now? Sandra Day O'Connor," *AARP Bulletin,* July 1, 2010, http://www.aarp.org/politics-society/newsmakers/info-06–2010/where_are _they_now_sandra_day_oconnor.html (accessed February 3, 2011).
3. Lupus Research Institute, "New Public Service Advertising Campaign Alerts Young Women to Dangers of Lupus," http://lupusresearchinstitute.org/news/discoveries/050406 (accessed February 3, 2011).

4. Centers for Disease Control and Prevention, "Table 24. Life Expectancy at Birth, at 65 Years of Age, and at 75 Years of Age, by Race and Sex: United States, Selected Years 1900–2007," *Health, United States 2009 Web Update,* http://www.cdc.gov/nchs/data/hus/hus 2009tables/Table024.pdf (accessed February 3, 2011).

5. Ibid.

6. Corporation for National & Community Service, "Volunteering in America 2010 Fact Sheet," http://www.volunteeringinamerica.gov/assets/resources/FactSheetFinal.pdf (accessed February 3, 2011).

7. Ibid.

8. Corporation for National & Community Service, "Volunteering of Older Adults (age 65 and over)," http://www.volunteeringinamerica.gov/special/Older-Adults-(age-65-and-over) (accessed February 3, 2011).

9. UnitedHealth Group, "United Healthcare/Volunteer Match Do Good Live Well Study; reviewing the benefits of volunteering, March 2010," http://www.dogoodlivewell.org/UnitedHealthcare_VolunteerMatch_DoGoodLiveWell_Survey.pdf (accessed February 4, 2011).

16

VOLUNTEERING IN RETIREMENT

Renee B. Bush

WHY VOLUNTEER?

You are finally going to have more free time, time for which you may have been longing for years, or perhaps secretly dreading. Most retirees will still need to tend to family demands and their home as well as other continuing personal commitments. However, many do find (sometimes to their great surprise) that the transition from decades of heavily scheduled days with many commitments to days with little structure and few constraints can be difficult. For those people, and even for others who move into retirement with ease, there are some very good reasons to give serious thought to volunteering. If any of the following resonate or just pique your curiosity, consider giving this option a closer look:

- Exploring new territory, developing new skills, and discovering talents you never knew you had, all while performing a service
- Developing a sense of satisfaction in helping to address the needs of others and the social or environmental problems that have meaning for you
- Forming new connections in your community
- Moderating a sense of loss associated with lack of contact with colleagues and the social opportunities afforded by the workplace

- Finding you can be appreciated and respected by others working in new contexts, thus enhancing your sense of purpose
- Investigating possibilities and building a resume for a new career

Volunteerism has been on the rise in the United States and is a research subject of considerable interest to psychologists and sociologists. It is clear that doing for others can help people feel a greater sense of purpose, and that a retiree may find a well-chosen volunteer position restores much of what was beneficial in his or her work life. Just the process of exploring the possibilities can be surprisingly stimulating, and the notions you had regarding what volunteer work looks like may be significantly altered. It is quite possible there are opportunities out there—or ones you could create—that you never imagined.

BEGIN BY TAKING STOCK

What activities, familiar as well as unexplored, and volunteer environments seem attractive to you?

- Have you wished for an opportunity to spend more time outdoors or would something in a quiet office space sound just right?
- Would you prefer interacting with many different people or being more on your own?
- Have you been hoping for more contact with children, animals, the homeless, and so on?
- Do you long to travel?
- Would you like to experience more theater and musical performances or more contact with artists and artisans?

What skills and talents do you have or would you like to develop?

- Would you happily transfer what you know to another situation in which you find and organize information, design websites, teach, or write?
- Is there anything you've been wishing you could do better or try for the first time that has nothing at all to do with the work world you are leaving? For example, perhaps you want to learn how to rehabilitate injured

wildlife, become more self-sufficient with home repairs, or brush up your foreign language skills.

- Do you know your patient nature and listening abilities could be put to use working with the elderly, or as an advocate or arbitrator? Might those "A type" traits your family and friends tease you about be well-applied to help organize offices or plan events? Can you imagine settings where that terrific eye for color and design could be of value?

What is it you know you do not want to do? What activities would physical constraints not permit you to do?

- Are you certain you no longer want the responsibility of managing people or large budgets? Burned out dealing with the public? Glad you'll never have to make another presentation?
- Is manual labor such as painting, gardening, moving, or unpacking boxes out of the question?

To what extent is location a limiting factor?

- Do you need to stay local? Would you want and be able to travel to volunteer?
- Will a need to rely on public transportation be a factor?
- Would the cost of fuel and parking be a constraint?

How are you able and how do you wish to allocate your free time?

- What are the existing demands on your time and energy?
- Do you believe you can easily and happily make a regular commitment of a few hours or a few days per week? A couple of days per month?
- Do you have health problems or other limiting factors that would make a regular commitment difficult but still wish to contribute when you are able? Could you commit to working on a particular day or a specific number of days agreed upon in advance? How about agreeing to be on a call list and then participating when you can?
- Would you prefer to take on tasks you could do at home?

WHAT MIGHT YOU DO AND WHERE?

You have taken stock and now want a sense of where you could find a role that would meet your criteria. If you have a clear idea about the sort of (or which specific) organization and type of work you are intent upon, you may be able to zero in on something great with little effort. But most people do not know what the realm of possibilities encompasses and would like to explore their options. There are three primary areas you will want to keep in focus as you begin your search—although you may well find these changing as you learn more about what is being done and what might be done in service to others:

- The population or cause served (e.g., the elderly, orphaned animals, historic architecture preservation, literacy)
- The setting in which you see yourself (e.g., nursing homes, animal shelters, private foundations, educational centers)
- The actual work you would like to do (e.g., telephoning, animal care, grant writing, tutoring)

You will find selected resources at the end of this chapter that will help you get started. Consider also the following:

- Most issues of any newspaper, national or local, large or small, will have articles that at least mention not-for-profit organizations and often report on specific projects for volunteers. Magazines of all sorts cover organizations of interest and volunteer efforts from many different angles.
- Monitor various local media for the area in which you would wish to volunteer, such as network and cable television websites and community weeklies. Even if you are not interested in business per se, you will find that many organizations and community projects are mentioned in publications aimed at the business community.
- Start networking. Contact people you know who do volunteer work and find out how they found their positions and ask for suggestions or contacts they can provide. Find out why they chose what they are doing and what they find satisfying about it. If you have been participating in online social networks (e.g., Facebook, LinkedIn), this is a great way to make use of them.

- Check with any organization with which you are or have been affiliated or that has always sounded interesting. National not-for-profits, local community organizations, and religious groups are all logical places to make inquiries about the work they do and whether there might be a place for you. Your alumni association or the human resources department of your former employer may also provide opportunities for volunteering.
- Watch for calls for volunteers for specific local events. Fundraisers such as races or walks or wrapping holiday gifts in stores are the most common, but there are many other projects that require only a short-term commitment. These can be a great way to test your notions about what you would enjoy and what you would want to avoid. It can also afford a closer look at a particular organization.

Note: You should be aware there may be instances for which volunteering in the organization that interests you is not possible. Some of the places you believe would be suitable may have collective bargaining agreements with unions. This can include not-for-profit organizations such as state universities or federal parks or nature preserves. In these cases, there may be very strict regulations about what volunteers may or may not do. Often, friends groups exist within organizations to help raise money and coordinate volunteers in support of some facets of their mission.

TRAVELING TO VOLUNTEER

If making your contribution away from home, perhaps very far from home, sounds appealing, you will be delighted to find that opportunities abound:

- If you are already interested in some national or international organizations, you might check out their websites first.
- Many opportunities will require expenditures on your part; depending on the organization and the location, it may be a considerable amount.
- Be sure you determine in advance whether difficult or dangerous conditions and sensitive cultural situations might be encountered.
- Here are some pertinent search terms to use: volunteer travel; volunteer vacations; volunteer abroad; voluntourism; long-distance volunteering; working vacations; eco-voluntourism; agritourism; edu-voluntourism.

WORKING FROM HOME

Opportunities for virtual volunteering, that is, performing volunteer service using the Internet, are increasing and not all require advanced technical skills. Should your software expertise extend beyond the usual Microsoft Office suite, however, you may find some exciting opportunities in service organizations to apply those skills. If you value Wikipedia, consider supporting it by applying your librarian's expertise there.

If spending more time at a computer is not what you are looking for, but you are unable to commit to projects away from home, take heart! There are still needs for people to perform all sorts of tasks that need not be done somewhere else, such as telephoning shut-ins, knitting for preemie hospital units, mailing letters to armed forces personnel abroad, or being a penpal to a person learning English in another country.

CREATING YOUR OWN SERVICE PROJECTS

Perhaps you would most like to create your own projects rather than become part of an existing organization. There are countless exciting possibilities, but it is very important to know where the service you wish to provide will fit into the larger scheme of things and how best to maximize the benefits you can generate without having a negative impact on the efforts of others. The very best place to begin is the National Services Resources' Resource Center, which provides a wealth of information on volunteer self-organizing to get you moving in the right direction from the start. See the resources at the end of the chapter for other relevant websites.

TIME BANKING

Strictly speaking, this is not volunteer work in that the rewards gained by your efforts are somewhat more tangible. You spend an hour doing something for someone in your community, you earn a Time Dollar, which you use to pay someone to do something for you. It is, actually, an alternative economic system that is also about doing something for someone else and ultimately building stronger communities. Time Banks, also known as Service Exchanges or Time Trades, provide incentives for work that is often done by volunteers. For links to more information about the philosophical underpinnings and history, as well as information about how to locate or start a Time Bank in your community, refer to the resources section at the end of this chapter.

NOT RETIRED YET? ALL THE BETTER!

Take stock before you retire so that you have a better idea of what you believe would best suit you. Many people find the transition from full-time employment to retirement much easier to navigate if there are some regular activities that lend structure to their days and prevent them from feeling the loss of contact with colleagues or others in the workplace. Knowing ahead of time that volunteer work might be a good fit will enable you to take advantage of opportunities to get a head start on preparing for a volunteer position you could really love. Following are a few ways to do just that:

- Enroll in continuing education courses available to you at your place of employment or in your community (some are helpful at work in addition to being useful after you leave), such as time management, supervisory skills, software applications.
- Employers often partner with local charities and provide time off for employees' participation, so keep an eye on what they have lined up and talk with coworkers who have some experience with the program.
- If your employer has not formed such relationships in the community, consider being the one to introduce the idea or even volunteer to organize a suitable partnership or sponsorship.
- As mentioned above, consider volunteering for single events or projects that do not require a long-term commitment. Such experiences can help you sort out your preferences and identify constraints.

HOW TO BE A GREAT VOLUNTEER

Have you ever had volunteers do work for you? Chaired a committee in your workplace or professional organization? Trained and supervised student assistants? In any of these situations, you may have come across the difficulties of trying to coordinate the efforts of people who do not have a strong commitment to the task or organization, consider what they are doing with you a lower priority, or are simply ill-suited to tasks that they have gladly taken on. The results can be frustration, disruption, and delays.

Do not be surprised to find that organizations may take great care in selecting volunteers and do not just accept anyone who shows some interest in "free help."

Training and supervising volunteers certainly does cost the organization something. They want to avoid frustration, disruption, and delays, too! Another serious concern can be that volunteers are often the face of that organization to the public. Clearly, it is in the organization's best interest to make sure a volunteer is a good fit.

For your sake and for that of any organization with which you might wish to volunteer, give serious thought to the position under consideration and try to have realistic expectations.

- Find out where the work you would be doing fits into the bigger scheme of things. Who would be relying on you for what? Are you willing to commit to doing what the organization needs you to do?
- Just as not every boss you've ever had was the best supervisor, not every volunteer coordinator will be outstanding either. Be willing to give it some time and work with the coordinator to find the best way to work together. Remember that the volunteer coordinator will have other demands on his or her time.
- It is quite possible that you will be coming to a volunteer position after years of being the boss. The transition from giving direction to taking direction might be challenging, but if you are mentally prepared for it, you may ultimately find making that adjustment more enlightening than jarring.
- Treat everyone with respect, understand that there may be reasons for things not being done the way you believe they should be, and remember that even the most well-motivated "constructive criticism" may not be well-received.

See the websites at the end of the chapter for some excellent guidelines available that provide many more aspects to consider.

ONE LAST WORD: BURNOUT

Volunteer burnout is not uncommon. It is better for everyone involved if you make your commitment knowing this is a possibility and make a conscious effort to avoid it, rather than end up leaving later, exhausted and unhappy. Decide how much time you can devote to the position and communicate that clearly. If you are unsure, it's better to underestimate and perhaps add more time later than to have to scale back or quit. If you have tendencies to take on more than you can comfortably handle or find it difficult to refuse requests for your time, you will need to be vigilant about how your position is affecting you and your family and communicate any problems as soon as they become evident. Volunteers' personality traits may not be the only factors in burnout situations, however. Poor management, unrealistic expectations, or lack of support on the part of the organization may contribute as well. It may be possible to address these situations to everyone's satisfaction, but it is important to do so as soon as you realize there is a problem.

If you have decided to organize your own service project, you may also be in danger of ending up overwhelmed and unsatisfied with your efforts. If you have never done a project similar to what you intend to take on, try to find others who have; you may discover that some aspects could require more time and effort than you had thought. Pace yourself, delegate when you can, and be flexible about parameters or deadlines you have set that can be changed without creating problems for you or for others.

Start with something you feel sure you can do. Enjoy the sense of accomplishment and happiness that comes from making a contribution, and look forward to more interesting opportunities to generate those feelings again.

RESOURCES

In your search for information, don't ignore resources written for those who are organizing and managing service organizations or projects. A great deal of useful information is available for those seeking to volunteer.

ABOUT VOLUNTEERISM

www.volunteeringinamerica.gov/. The Volunteering in America website contains information on volunteering and civic engagement, and data galore about who is volunteering where in America and what they are doing with links to current research.

Altruism and Health: Perspectives from Empirical Research. Edited by Stephen G. Post. New York: Oxford University Press, 2007. This book is a compilation of research from multiple disciplines.

www.nationalservice.gov/pdf/07_0506_hbr.pdf. *The Health Benefits of Volunteering: A Review of Recent Research.* By Robert Grimm, Jr., Kimberly Spring, and Nathan Dietz. Washington: Corporation for National & Community Service, 2007.

www.serviceleader.org/volunteers. The website has some excellent tips for those considering volunteering and even for those already so engaged, including guidance for finding volunteer opportunities.

INFORMATION ON WHAT TO DO AND WHERE

www.aarp.org/giving-back/volunteering/. AARP's "Create the Good" service allows you to identify projects in your area by zip code. There are also how-to guides and a blog for sharing ideas and stories. (See also the resources for creating your own service projects below.)

http://nationalserviceresources.org/. "Resource Center: Tools and training for volunteer and service programs" appears to have been compiled for service providers, but don't let that stop you. There is a wealth of information here for anyone considering doing volunteer work.

http://nationalserviceresources.org/corporation-national-community-service. This web page provides links to resources developed by grantees of the Corporation for National & Community Service: Senior Corps, AmeriCorps, AmeriCorps VISTA, Learn and Serve America, Tribal Program and State Commission.

www.craigslist.org/about/sites. Pick your area and go to "Volunteers" in the "Community" section.

www.serviceleader.org/volunteers/parks. "Guide to Volunteering Outdoors in Parks and Wilderness Areas."

TRAVELING TO VOLUNTEER

Volunteer: A Traveler's Guide to Making a Difference around the World. By Charlotte Hindle et al. Oakland, CA: Lonely Planet, 2010. This is an outstanding resource covering just about every aspect you have imagined and many you might not have.

www.voluntourism.org/index.html. VolunTourism.org claims to be "THE Resource on All Things VolunTourism!" It offers detailed guidance through self-assessment, trip selection, trip assessment, and processing experiences and includes blogs, podcasts, and newsletters.

www.volunteerinternational.org/whoweare.html. IVPA is "an association of nongovernmental organizations involved in international volunteer work and internship exchanges." You'll find plenty of valuable information about finding the program that is right for you.

www.idealist.org/info/IntlVolunteer. International Volunteerism Resource Center. From Idealist.org, a project of Action without Borders, this link provides broad and in-depth content plus discussion forums.

CREATING YOUR OWN SERVICE PROJECTS

www.serve.gov/toolkits.asp. This website provides detailed instructions on how to get started on projects addressing problems in several areas, such as education, health, community renewal, energy, and environment.

www.serve.gov/recruit.asp. Follow the links to websites where you can register your own projects and solicit volunteers.

http://createthegood.org/how-to-guides. AARP provides detailed information about services you could perform on your own or in conjunction with other individuals or groups.

Librarians as Community Partners: An Outreach Handbook. Edited by Carol Smallwood. Chicago: American Library Association, 2010. Although compiled for practicing librarians, this book provides information about populations to be served and ideas for possible approaches to employ.

TIME BANKS

http://en.wikipedia.org/wiki/Time_Banking. This website is good for a quick introduction to Time Banks.

www.timebanks.org/. This is the source of detailed information about Time Banks and where and how you can participate.

BEING A GOOD VOLUNTEER

www.voluntaryworker.co.uk/Whatorganisationslookforinagoodvolunteer.html. This web page provides an excellent summary of what it means to be a good volunteer.

www.serviceleader.org/volunteers/10points. Ten Points of Advice for Volunteers from the Hiroshima Volunteer Network in Japan. This is excellent advice coming from an interesting perspective.

17

MY EXPERIENCE VOLUNTEERING WITH VSO IN ETHIOPIA

Shirley Lewis

RETIREMENT CAN BE a big challenge for some seniors and may be less so for others. Studies have shown that individuals who have a lot of outside interests find retirement easier to adjust to than those who focused mainly on their careers. Whether or not the adjustment to retirement is easy, every retiree has to fill in eight hours or more a day that formerly was allotted to a job. After I retired I surprised myself by volunteering in a third world country, and I liked it so much that I now recommend this option as a real possibility for others.

My career was a checkered one: I was a children's librarian, a chief librarian, then a librarian in a university library specializing in nursing, a school librarian, a cataloger, and finally a book wholesaler. I was used to change. Indeed, when I prepared for my retirement, the challenge for me seemed to be the sudden regularity of my life, pleasant as it seemed at first. Exercise class three days a week, interesting university courses at a reduced senior's rate, book club regular meetings, and neighborhood volunteer work. But while waiting in a post office line my pulse quickened as I read a magazine ad for Volunteer Service Overseas (VSO). It was a brief ad suggesting that volunteering in another country combines adventure with doing good.

The motto of VSO is "Sharing Skills—Changing Lives." I clipped the ad, which listed a website, and the minute I got home I made inquiries. Still, I didn't really expect much. After all, I was turning 65, had suffered a heart attack in the past, and although fit and healthy now, I really didn't think that I would be a viable candidate.

So it was with gratifying surprise when I received a call from VSO expressing great interest in my library expertise, and I was invited to come to Ottawa to VSO's Canadian headquarters to attend a workshop for potential volunteers. This was an excellent eye-opener, a weekend with forty other professionals from all walks of life who were entertaining thoughts of volunteering overseas. We were oriented in the basics of what is involved in being a volunteer—what kinds of cultural adjustments would be required, what kind of challenges and conditions we might face, and other elements involved in volunteering to share our expertise in a foreign land. This program combined numerous group "games" and simulations that exposed us to puzzling and seemingly pointless objectives. For example, one game involved putting colored balls into variously colored baskets and changing the colors at the blow of a whistle. We didn't know that observers were watching our reactions to the inexplicable rules of the game as a guide to how we would handle unexplained bureaucratic decisions in a very different setting in a foreign country. Indeed, almost every game we played provided a hidden insight into our individual abilities to cope with organizational adjustment. I found the weekend fascinating, and I also found that I really enjoyed the company of all the people attending the sessions. I never saw any of them again as those of us selected went to over seventy different countries. I was the only one invited to serve in Ethiopia.

Ethiopia! I barely knew where it was, although Emperor Haile Selassie was one personality that popped up in my head, followed by a recollection of Band-Aid's Bob Geldorf, who raised millions for the starving people of Ethiopia. However, using my library reference skills, I soon learned enough about Ethiopia to eagerly accept a two-year assignment as a volunteer librarian in Jimma, a coffee-growing area in southwestern Ethiopia. I was quickly able to discover that Jimma had a very pleasing climate in the Ethiopian highlands—hot by day, cool at night. Jimma's population was around 250,000, and it had a teacher's college, a university, and an agricultural college. Unaware that most people think long and hard about taking such a step, I jumped in with both feet and joyfully set about renting my condo, telling the family, and informing my friends. My grown-up children were fascinated and supportive, but my older relatives and most of my friends were aghast. Had I lost my mind? One of my friends asked me why I hadn't just lain down until the feeling passed. I dismissed their reservations and proceeded to pack with the utmost care, because I could only take twenty-five kilograms (fifty-five pounds) of luggage with me.

I shamelessly raised money to cover my plane trip and the cost of a laptop and digital camera. My puzzled friends gave freely, fearful that I would never be seen again. Actually, their emotional fears were quite unfounded, since volunteer organizations such as VSO take very good care of their volunteers, covering their health insurance during the volunteer period, placing each volunteer in a suitable position, and providing counseling for returnees who may need to find employment. Out of our group of thirty-five Canadian volunteers, there were only two retired people; the rest were taking a leave of absence or had resigned their jobs and would be seeking employment at the end of their service.

Even so, at the last moment as I headed to the airport with my children I suddenly thought, "What the heck was I THINKING?" But it was too late to change my mind, and off I flew, first to Rome and then to Addis Ababa, the teeming capital city of Ethiopia.

Culture shock? Yes, indeed. As the plane landed on a dusty, quite ugly landing field and we filed into customs in a crowded, rather dingy old building I could see Ethiopian women in their cotton garb, clothed head to toe with white *netellas*, head scarves draped over their hair. Most of them seemed bent, looking down rather than up, somehow projecting servility. It was not killingly hot, but definitely warmer than home, dusty, and as it turned out, very bureaucratic. Our passports were closely inspected with suspicion on the faces of the customs clerks. Slowly we emerged and were handed over to the tender care of the VSO staff in Ethiopia, who shepherded us past crowds of Ethiopians—vendors, taxi drivers, beggars—and into the battered VSO Land Rover that whisked us off to the Jerusalem Hotel. There I discovered that VSO had virtually taken over the hotel for the three-week in-service training of their naïve and newly arrived trainees.

We ate together, trained together, and partied together. VSO staff covered most of the cultural issues that we needed to know—customs of dress, religions, language, and behavior—we even learned the basics of Amharic, Ethiopia's "official" language, although there are in fact over ninety regional languages. Heedless of the necessity of knowing these basics, we were all anxious to go to our assignments. Although the majority of the volunteers were teachers, there were architects, engineers, computer experts, even a doctor, and we were assigned all over Ethiopia.

Three weeks' training seemed excessive, so keen were we to get started. But once we were in place, we were more than grateful for that orientation, as we bumped along, encountering resistance to our enthusiastic ideas for improvement in a culture that is fundamentally resistant to change. We in the West are quite unaware of how deeply traditional people are and how cautiously they proceed when changes are proposed. We can seem rambunctious, insensitive, and abrupt in many of the more traditional cultures. Although we know this intellectually, it is quite a different thing to adjust to it in practice, and resistance does not come openly but is shrouded in excuses that at first seem reasonable. For example, one enthusiastic programmer had an ambitious plan for the computers in his workplace but was not given the password for the network. He was promised the password, but with one thing and another he never seemed to get it. Mind you, he unwisely had not shared his plan, nor got his superiors on board before he outlined his plans, but it's easy to see how plans can be foiled if a volunteer cannot find a way to proceed effectively.

In my particular case, the Teacher's College Library was more than open to improvement, and the staff librarian, Abiti, was delighted with every idea that I had. We set out to apply a new spine label for every library book in the collection, and then followed this up with a digital catalog, using the new computers that had been donated to the library. Next we planned to introduce Internet facilities to the staff with a long-range objective of providing access to the Web to students as well as staff. Time and space do not permit me to give a step-by-step outline of how we proceeded, but by the time I left, all the books were arranged on the shelves in Dewey order, and there was a catalog that was printed out for the use of students. A far cry from the OPAC facilities we are used to at home, but a vast improvement nevertheless, and the digitization of the catalog meant that the library staff could export the fields into an automated program when they were ready.

In the meanwhile, word spread that a *real* librarian was living in Jimma, and I was soon inundated by requests for my services. Although it is true that most Ethiopians adjust slowly to change, it is also true that word spreads quickly when someone new comes along, and I had barely settled before I met the local high school principal, Tadesse, who was determined to get my help organizing his large but severely dated school library. Concurrently, the University of Jimma librarian, Ato Getachew, helped me with my research by letting me use the university's busy Internet facilities after hours. He also was working on the improvement of the university library facilities, so I joined his deliberations committee. Then the Jimma Community School jumped on the bandwagon, and next thing I knew I was teaching English classes three times a week.

My fellow VSO volunteers were assigned to interesting educational institutions across Ethiopia, which invariably had libraries in dilapidated disarray, and they petitioned to have me come visit and bring my library expertise. So I was invited to Bonga, a very rural community in the middle of nowhere, and Adi Abbi, another town with a library that needed resuscitation. I was delighted to be invited to these far-flung places, which I wouldn't even have known about otherwise.

When I wasn't working, I spent my time trying to fit into the community where the culture was so very different from my own. It was difficult to get to know other women, because there were few educated women to meet. Ethiopia has neglected the education of women, and the society is so deeply traditional that the role of women, by and large, still remains that of housewife and mother to large broods of children. There was only one professional woman at the Jimma Teacher's College, and we became friends, but the neighborhood women were far too shy to speak to me. Eventually, it was the bolder teenage boys in the neighborhood who knocked on my door and inquisitively visited me, delighted to open my books, inspect my ukulele, and eventually to nose through all my belongings. I insisted on meeting their mothers and fathers, and gradually the world of Ethiopian women opened to me. I attended weddings, funerals, and religious holidays such as Eid celebrations (Muslim) and Timkat (Christian). I didn't learn the local language (Oromo) very well because everyone was so keen to practice their English and improve their English vocabulary and syntax. My son Dave was so intrigued by my letters home that he decided to spend his summer holidays in Ethiopia and visited Jimma to the total delight of the community. He was wined and dined by my very hospitable neighbors and friends. Hospitality is an Ethiopian specialty, especially their elaborate coffee ceremony that features coffee being made fresh for each sitting from bean to brew, including an hour roasting the beans on a small metal plate over a bed of coals. Dave was struck by the crippling poverty, to which I had adjusted somewhat. When he heard that the local soccer team had no uniforms, he coughed up enough money for shirts, soccer ball, and all the paraphernalia that a team needs, so they named the team "SuperDave." Needless to say, Dave became famous in the town of Jimma.

Two years passed in the blink of an eye, and when it came time to go home, I had enjoyed myself so thoroughly and done so many productive things that it struck me that this was a life-altering experience for me. Indeed, my perspective about retirement has changed. I sold my car, moved downtown, took environment change seriously, and started a charity that helps girls to continue their education rather than drop out because their parents can't afford to keep them in school. I believe Ethiopia changed me more than I changed Ethiopia, because in spite of all the things I did, I was impressed by the simple dignity of Ethiopians who have almost nothing but strive for a better life in spite of economic obstacles and crippling bureaucracy. Most of the people I met were educated but were also the children of illiterate farmers. I have nothing but high praise for my Ethiopian friends who struggle to improve the educational opportunities for their students. I ended up staying in Ethiopia for another three years, taking on an automation project at Gondar University.

My tips for retirement are geared to those of you who would consider taking on an unpaid job after retirement in order to help out in a country that can't afford the expertise it so desperately needs. Start by asking yourself some tough questions:

- What skills do you have that you would be lucky to share with others less fortunate?
- Do you have the necessary flexibility to live for a while outside your usual comfort zone? I'm not talking about living in a mud hut—but I only had a cold water tap in the front yard, and the electricity failed so often that a fridge was of little or no use. I learned to make an "oven" out of a large tin pot lined with sand, but out of this makeshift little oven came some very tasty cakes, and once or twice even a cheese soufflé—which no Ethiopian in Jimma had ever seen before.
- Can you adjust to a slower, more leisurely lifestyle—but still encourage people to come to work on time and follow some productivity standards that improve their workplace?

If you think that you could handle this, let me assure you that you would have such a rewarding experience that you would never regret your decision to volunteer.

There are many agencies looking for volunteers, and not all of them are as sophisticated as VSO. Some simply invite you to come at your own expense and offer no screening to ensure that your skills will be put to good use. There are even scams for goodhearted volunteers who make Internet enquiries, so be sure you thoroughly investigate any volunteer opportunities. Start with reputable agencies such as the following:

- Peace Corps, CUSO-VSO, the Canadian arm of Canadian University Service Overseas–Volunteer Service Overseas. U.S. citizens are accepted by application to the Ottawa office.
- Oxfam International. Its U.S. office is located in New York City.
- IFESH (International Foundation for Education and Self Help). Its offices are in Scottsdale, Arizona.

All of these agencies have websites, and if you visit them you will be on the road to working your way to an agency that suits your abilities. There is a website that clearly outlines what agencies are looking for these days and gives sterling advice to potential volunteers: www.coyotecommunications.com/volunteer/international .html.

Also consider that there are volunteer opportunities closer to home—indeed you can volunteer in so many capacities that the possibilities are endless. But there's something special about pulling up stakes and immersing yourself in a whole new world where your skills are not only appreciated but also eagerly accepted and put right to work and passed on to staff members whose future you have enhanced immeasurably. I can think of no greater way to enhance your retirement years.

PART VI

HEALTH

18

SEVEN LESSONS FOR ADJUSTING TO RETIREMENT

Janet Husband

Many people actually fear retirement because, like librarians, they are dedicated to a profession they love. Retirement is one of the big life changes, and to some extent any change can be frightening. In planning for retirement, pensions and health care are usually at the top of the list; however, I suspect that most librarians are prudent enough to attend to these matters well in advance.

But what about the psychological aspects of retirement? In our culture, our identity is closely tied to our work. Psychologists tell us that retirement involves an "identity shift." They also tell us that retirement is a transitional process, that there are stages of retirement, and that the *first* step is recognizing and exploring the emotional issues surrounding retirement.

I know a woman, a type-A professional, who asked every one of her retired friends and acquaintances how they adjusted to retirement. She was terrified that she wouldn't know what to do with herself. She was working well over forty hours a week, with frequent breakfast meetings and evening events, so it's not surprising that she equated not being employed with having nothing to do. Before her actual retirement date, she had already arranged for her first volunteer job. Upon retirement, she kept her alarm set to its usual early bird chirping, got dressed, and went to her local deli for coffee and the newspaper, then followed the rest of the day's schedule that she had carefully written out. This included four hours a week volunteering as a teacher at a local high school. By the end of the semester of teaching, which hadn't been as successful or as satisfying as she had hoped, she had relaxed enough to enjoy the slower tempo of her life. She began to enjoy retirement. She stopped setting the alarm.

Dominique Browning's (2010) article "Losing It" is an instructive and humorous description of how she reacted when the magazine she edited, *House & Garden*, folded and she found herself forcibly retired. She writes that her "addled brain interpreted the white noise of unemployment to mean that I was going into hibernation." Her main activities became sleeping and eating; she saw "no reason to get out of my pajamas."

LESSON 1: YOU CAN'T READ ALL DAY

Many librarians see retirement as an opportunity to read all day. We finally have a chance to read all the books on that long list of must-read titles that we didn't have time to read while we were working. I admit that for the first couple weeks of my retirement, I read most of the day, sometimes still in my nightgown. I roused myself to get up and feed the dog and the husband at the appropriate times. I was always dressed before dinner—cooking in a nightgown is hazardous. My little dog loved having me as a pillow, especially as my muscles started to atrophy. But before long, I got restless. I began to notice the potato chips between the sofa cushions and the paint chips missing from the nearby windowsill. The lampshades were dusty and a strip of wallpaper next to the mantle was drooping. I did my best to ignore these things, but when the dishwasher broke down, it was the last straw. I got up and vacuumed, then I went to the library to check dishwasher ratings in *Consumer Reports*. The hardware store was my next stop: I bought sandpaper and paint and browsed through wallpaper books. And so began my "House Beautiful stage" that lasted for four months, ending with the near collapse of our checking account.

Of course, my retirement wasn't sudden like that of Dominique Browning. At 62, retirement had been on my horizon for a few years. My husband was already retired, but I didn't envy his status. I loved my job as library director in Cohasset (MA), an affluent coastal town. I had a great staff, supportive trustees, and appreciative patrons. And we had just constructed a beautiful new library building.

But six months earlier, I had had an epiphany of sorts. I'd had laparoscopic surgery to remove my gallbladder, which is normally a routine procedure requiring two days in the hospital at most. I was told that there would be only tiny incisions that would heal quickly. I'd be back to work in less than a week. However, it turned out that I was in that unlucky 1 percent of patients who get complications—pain, nausea, fever, and peritonitis. Mortality rates for postoperative peritonitis can be as high as 60 percent, depending on the source. Believe me, I was sick. After eighteen days in the hospital, I was released, cured but terribly weak and shaky, both physically and emotionally. I was still alive, so apparently I was going to have a future. Enjoying that future seemed very important to me. What did I really want to do with the rest of my life? Did I want to spend the next eight years (or five years or even one year) preparing level-funded budgets, unsnarling tangled work schedules, struggling to learn new library technology? Not really. Somebody else could do that, after all. What I wanted to do was spend more time with my family and friends, travel, read, and listen to beautiful music. Even just sitting and breathing and petting my little dog seemed immensely more appealing.

Luckily for me, four months after I went back to work the Commonwealth of Massachusetts decided to offer an early retirement incentive package to state and local employees. (In Massachusetts, most city and town employees are in the statewide pension system.) It took me only a week to decide. I signed the papers and gave the library trustees my two-month notice. After helping the board hire a new director, I said my tearful farewells, and I was free. I took a deep breath and let my shoulders relax. Then I took out my reading list.

LESSON 2: NOBODY WANTS TO MAKE ME HAPPY

My "House Beautiful stage," redecorating and modestly remodeling my home, claimed a lot of my time for a while and I was very pleased with the results. But it made me realize something basic about retirement. Along the way I noticed a peculiar thing: nobody was really interested in pleasing me. Not Home Depot when they sent the wrong wallpaper, not the carpenter who went way overbudget, and certainly not the cable guy who installed my new wireless computer. They didn't notice or care that I was a fair and benevolent employer. To them I wasn't "The Boss": I was just the lady whose wallpaper was wrong and whose network didn't work right. They didn't have their eye on the next performance review. They just presented their bills (without apology and *with* a restocking fee for the wallpaper). Most of them didn't even say good-bye.

I had always worked with wonderful staff. When they got something wrong, they fixed it. They learned how to reset the public access computers, how to unjam the printers, and how to jiggle the ink cartridge in the copy machine to make it last longer. They were prompt, they explained problems to me, they coordinated their breaks and lunches to fit circulation desk coverage. They showed initiative and creativity because they wanted me to value and reward their work—long term.

I'd grown accustomed to this treatment and was dismayed to realize that I was no longer regarded as someone who must be pleased. I'd lost a power that I hadn't even fully recognized I'd had. I had returned to being just a regular person. That was my first identity shift, and it was more comic than painful.

LESSON 3: VOLUNTEERING

"Volunteer. It will keep you busy and do some good." That's the first suggestion people make to newly retired people. And it is especially relevant for librarians who know how understaffed most libraries are. Volunteering at a library will put your skills to good use, and many librarians are able to find the right match between their skills and the needs of the library. I know a librarian who happily volunteers twenty hours a week doing the same job in the same library that she worked in before she retired. Most of the patrons don't even realize that she is no longer employed there.

But I know other retired librarians whose volunteer experience isn't so felicitous. One friend volunteered to weed nonfiction for three hours every week at her local public library. She knew from experience that weeding is universally a low priority in public libraries. The volunteer coordinator was delighted.

Now my friend is a crack weeder, having done it in small and medium-sized public libraries for many years. She told me that her favorite way to end a long day at her desk was to go find a book truck and head for the stacks to do some weeding. She regarded weeding as mental therapy as well as aerobically beneficial and essential for the collection.

But weeding as a volunteer was a different matter. After the first few weeks she noticed that many of the books she had weeded out were slipping back onto the shelves, and it became clear that the staff person charged with reviewing her weeding decisions was a timid soul. As a director, she had blithely overruled staff who tried to save a ratty old piece of nostalgia. But volunteers don't overrule paid staff—it's simply not *comme il faut*. She had met another kind of loss, a loss in status (another identity shift). In the end, doing the work without the authority seemed foolish, and she begged off.

LESSON 4: FIND NEW WAYS TO USE YOUR SKILLS

People who have hobbies look forward to retirement so they can spend more time doing what they enjoy. Readers can read more, cooks can cook more, travelers can travel more. I've always enjoyed gardening, and at the first sign of spring I was out there planning and planting. Neighboring gardeners began to stop by when they saw me up to my elbows in mud and manure, and before I knew it I was a member of the local garden club. At committee sign-up time the president made a plea for more member participation, so I agreed to help out with the bylaws. Later, when nobody else was willing to investigate starting a website, I volunteered and had fun learning the simple Yahoo! program that makes it easy for any small organization to create a website. Then the nominating committee asked if I would run for club secretary, and so it went. Now I'm vice president, and next year I'll be president.

Along the way I learned that garden club members are not "little old ladies." They are retired professors, nurses, teachers, and bankers—some of the sharpest women I've ever met. But more relevant, all the skills I'd mastered as a library manager were useful in a new capacity. Committee work, research, technical writing, decision making, delegation, and budgeting are essential for running an effective organization. I have those skills and I enjoy using them. And yes, I am enjoying the positive regard of my colleagues. Like so many other organizations a retired librarian might join and help lead, our garden club makes a modest contribution to the community—we tend gardens in the town's public parks, give scholarships, and advocate for environmental issues. Plus, I enjoy working with all the new friends I've made. Many of the retired librarians I know have become active members of some organization—their condo association, their church group, or their local food pantry. It seems to fill a need characteristic to many librarians: the need to be of service, to be doing something useful and worthwhile.

LESSON 5: TRY SOMETHING NEW AND DIFFERENT

A newly retired friend of mine decided to take up woodworking as a hobby when she saw a free class offered by her local adult education agency. She started the course with great enthusiasm, which slowly waned over time. When I asked her how it was going, she told me that she enjoyed learning and using the power saws and drills in the shop, but to continue on her own would require a significant investment in equipment and she had neither the funds nor the space to set up a home shop. She didn't regret taking the class, and she was very proud of the wooden box she made, even though the lid was a little crooked. But it was a learning experience—she learned that woodworking is a lot harder than it looks on those TV shows.

Retirement is a great time to try new things, and each new challenge helps keep your brain limber. Many universities offer a wide range of classes for seniors at a modest cost. I have friends who love UMass's OLLI (Osher Lifelong Learning Institute) Center. They offer an amazing array of classes from Greco-Roman mythology to Ocean Planning. My friends took a number of classes about China, and then joined a tour of China with their instructor as the guide.

I used my new free time to surf the Net, something I never had the time to do when I was working. I discovered eBay, craigslist, and banking online. I hooked up my digital camera, learned to edit my snapshots, and discovered I loved working with photos. And no surprise, I discovered hundreds of interesting book and library websites like librarygarden.net, libraryhistorybuff.com, and stopyourekillingme.com. Sad to say, I had missed ALA's Book Cart Drill Team competitions, but there they were, just waiting for me on YouTube with hundreds of other wonderful library videos. Some were instructive—earnest or flip or hip (check out the Dewey Decimal Rap) and some deconstructive—impromptu opera and flash mob dancing in libraries.

When our local cable TV public access studio advertised a free class in video production, I signed up and learned how to run a video camera in the field and in the studio. I also learned that editing raw video into something useful took a lot of time and patience. While I haven't made any award-winning videos yet, I did get involved in the local video scene. I became a regular cameraperson for a local talk show. And I was asked to join the town's cable TV advisory committee on the eve of contract negotiations with a national cable company. As a result, a new local five-town cooperative will soon have a beautiful new public access video studio. Not that I was personally responsible, but as a member of the team I am proud of the outcome.

LESSON 6: MAKE NEW FRIENDS AND KEEP THE OLD

Remember the song from Girl Scout days? I've found that making new friends follows naturally from the new activities you might pursue in retirement. But keeping the old is not as easy as you might think. For one thing, staff turnover in your former workplace seems to speed up. While you've been enjoying your leisure, your colleagues have been climbing their various career ladders, so it is easy to lose track of friends. One successful solution is to join or start an alumni group. Friends of mine who worked for a large city library attend quarterly group luncheons for retired employees. They are not sure who founded the group, but there are usually a couple of willing volunteers to communicate and organize meetings. I also know of an informal group of retired library directors who meet for lunch on a regular basis. They all worked in small town public libraries but got to know each other as members of their automation network. Meeting regularly allows them to keep up with each other and with network library news and changes. Of course if you've been active in ALA, you will want to keep attending meetings after your retirement.

LESSON 7: THINGS NOT TO DO

One thing you should definitely not do is haunt your old library. Visit once or twice at most. Answer any questions your successor may have—if he or she initiates the contact. Wave to any trustees you may see socially on the sidewalk or at a restaurant. Somebody else is in charge of the library now. Let it go. How would you have liked it if your predecessor had been forever looking over *your* shoulder?

Another thing not to do is sell your house and move to another state in the first year after retirement. From what I hear, Florida is full of people who wish they had not moved there. They miss their home and family and friends. Some even pack up and move back.

In fact, you should put off making big decisions of any kind during your first year of retirement. Give yourself time to settle and assess your new status.

SUMMARY

In the past, when I asked retired friends how they liked retirement, they often told me that they were busier than ever. I was always puzzled by that response. Busy doing what? But now I know, and I say the same thing when asked. I'm busy doing the things I want to do. Now I am the one who defines what is worth doing. For me retirement is a wonderful stage of life—my reward for many years of hard work. I am still healthy and solvent, so my identity shifts have been minor so far.

REFERENCE

Browning, Dominique. 2010. Losing it. *The New York Times,* March 25, 2010. http://www.nytimes.com/2010/03/28/magazine/28fasttrack-t.html.

19

WHAT ABOUT HEALTH INSURANCE IN RETIREMENT?

Sandra Cortese

PASSAGE OF THE 2010 Affordable Care Act has changed the playing field for health insurance in America. Implementing all the changes will take several years. Consequently, some of the following advice may become outdated over time, so remember that it is important for you as a retiree to keep informed. You need to be active in seeking data that may impact your own health insurance coverage. You can receive e-mail updates on Medicare coverage by signing up at www.medicarerights.org and www.kff.org.

The entire topic of health care and insurance has always seemed vastly complicated and confusing. A wrong choice at the beginning of the process can become very costly over time, and the days of choosing a health plan and sticking to it are gone. Each year you will need to make new decisions as plans change and more options become available. The good news is that there is help in this process, and you should use it.

SHIP (State Health Insurance Assistance Program) counselors are available in each state to provide free, confidential, unbiased advice on health insurance options for seniors. To find your SHIP office, go to Medicare.gov, or call your state office dealing with senior concerns.

THREE QUESTIONS YOU NEED TO ASK

When you begin to think about what your health insurance coverage will be in retirement, you need to first answer these questions.

WHAT IS YOUR CURRENT HEALTH INSURANCE PLAN?

Employer Coverage

Will your employer coverage continue after you retire? If so, will you also need Medicare? If you opt out of employer coverage, will you be able to re-enroll later? If you are under the Consolidated Omnibus Budget Reconciliation Act (COBRA), you must enroll in Medicare when you turn 65. Failure to enroll in Medicare will result in a premium penalty when you do enroll. Your employee benefits administrator will help you answer questions about coverage options.

Coverage under Spouse's Plan

Is your spouse actively employed? All people are required to enroll in Medicare at age 65, unless they are covered by an equivalent employer plan carried by an actively employed person. Will your coverage continue when your spouse retires? If so, will it be the same coverage, or will you also need Medicare? If you opt out of this coverage, will you be able to opt in at a future time? Will your coverage continue if your spouse dies or you get divorced? Your spouse's benefits administrator will help you answer these questions.

VA Health Insurance Plan

VA health insurance is available to honorably discharged veterans of all military branches. You may use VA health insurance alone or with another health insurance, or you may use it only for drug coverage. However, it is not available to spouses. You may continue your VA health insurance when you turn 65, or you may add Medicare to it. Contact your local veterans agent or go online to myhealthyvet.va .gov for more information.

Tricare

For most career military personnel, Tricare converts to Tricare for Life at age 65 and acts as a Medigap plan when the retiree enrolls in Medicare. There is no premium for Tricare for Life, and the retiree's spouse and eligible dependents will always be covered. For more information, go to www.military.com/benefits/tricare.

Private Plan

If you have a private health insurance plan, when you turn 65 you must enroll in Medicare. Otherwise, you will incur a premium penalty for life. The current penalty is 10 percent for each year of nonenrollment.

Medicare

If you have Medicare prior to your retirement, contact Social Security to determine whether your coverage is adequate to avoid a future premium penalty. At age 65 you must be enrolled in either Medicare A and B or Medicare C to avoid a premium penalty. Call Social Security at 800-772-1213 to ask your questions or make an appointment at your local Social Security office.

Medicaid

If your health care coverage is Medicaid, your retirement (and consequent reduction in income) should increase your Medicaid benefits and further reduce your costs. If you are 65, you will also need to enroll in Medicare.

No Health Insurance Plan

If you have no health insurance coverage due to its cost, the new health care law will assist you in finding affordable coverage. If you are 65, your coverage will be Medicare. Go online to HealthCare.gov to learn about your health insurance options under the Affordable Care Act.

WHAT WILL YOUR RETIREE HEALTH INSURANCE PLAN COVER?

Employer health insurance plans and private plans vary widely in the specific benefits they provide, and in the costs of those benefits. Often an insurer will offer an array of health plans from which to choose, each with a varying cost and benefit package. Consider the following benefits when you are evaluating potential health insurance plans:

- Inpatient hospital services
- Outpatient provider visits
- Mental health and behavioral health services
- Laboratory tests
- X-rays
- Medical procedures (colonoscopy, MRI, etc.)

- Ambulance transport
- Hearing, vision, dental, and podiatry services
- Out-of-country medical services (including cruise ships)
- Home health care
- Durable medical goods (bandages, wheelchairs, nebulizers, etc,)
- Inpatient rehabilitation services
- Physical, occupational, and speech therapy
- Prescription drugs

WHAT WILL YOUR RETIREE HEALTH INSURANCE PLAN COST?

Do not automatically choose what appears to be the least expensive plan available to you. Along with the monthly premiums, carefully consider the copayments for each benefit, the deductibles, and the types of benefits that are not covered at all. If you visit doctors, therapists, or other providers often, copayments can add up rapidly, and you must estimate your health care costs on an annual rather than a monthly basis. Costs to consider will include:

- Premiums
- Premium penalties
- Deductibles
- Copayments
- Noncovered medical expenses

You need to know the answers to such questions in order to make informed decisions about your health insurance choices in retirement. Once you know the answers, you can compare the costs and benefits among each of your available choices.

MEDICARE

The most common retirement health insurance plan involves Medicare alone or supplemented by either an employer plan or a private Medicare Supplement Insurance policy (Medigap). Medigap policies fill in some of the gaps in Medicare coverage. Medicare is a federal health insurance plan that covers approximately 80 percent of many medical expenses. If you have not paid into the Medicare system over time, you may purchase Medicare coverage at a higher premium rate. Go online to Medicare.gov, or call 800-633-4227 for any questions about Medicare coverage, eligibility, and costs.

You become eligible for Medicare when one of the following events occurs:

- You turn 65.
- You reach the twenty-fourth month of SSDI (Social Security Disability Insurance) benefits.
- You are diagnosed with ESRD (end-stage renal disease) or ALS (amyotrophic lateral sclerosis).

There are four Medicare programs you need to evaluate (Medicare A, B, C, and D), but you will never need all of them at the same time. Medigap plans are also important to consider because they can complete the coverage, paying any Medicare deductibles and copayments. Finally, I will cover three additional programs that may help eligible persons with health care costs.

ORIGINAL MEDICARE (A AND B)

Original Medicare is the first kind of Medicare coverage offered beginning in 1965. Since then, other forms of Medicare coverage have been created and will be presented in order.

Medicare A is called hospital insurance. For most people there is no premium for Medicare A. It covers you when you are an inpatient in a Medicare-participating facility, such as a hospital or skilled nursing facility (SNF). An annual deductible applies in the hospital, and there is a time limit of twenty days for Medicare to pay for care in an SNF. Medigap plans are available to pay the deductible and extend the available SNF time.

Medicare B is called medical insurance. There is a monthly premium for Medicare B. It covers your outpatient provider visits, lab tests, x-rays, and home health services. There is also a small annual deductible, and some services have copayments, while others are completely covered. Medigap plans are available to pay the deductible and copayments. With Medicare A and B you may go to any Medicare-participating provider in the United States without a referral. Over 90 percent of American doctors and health care facilities participate in Medicare.

Although Medicare A and B provide excellent coverage for most health care services, there are some services it does not cover all the time. During the first six months you are a Medicare beneficiary, Medicare will cover one baseline physical examination. If that exam does not reveal medical conditions that require follow-up medical attention, further routine physical exams will not be covered. Medicare also does not cover routine vision, hearing, dental, or podiatry services. If any of these health care needs are the result of a medical condition, such as glaucoma or diabetes, Medicare will cover them, however.

QUICK TIP

Since Medicare will not pay for routine physical exams, always be sure your exam is not routine. You may be short of breath or have specific pain that requires a medical examination. Tell your provider what has brought you to see him or her for the physical exam so your visit can be coded for billing properly.

MEDIGAP

Medigap plans are offered by private insurance companies. The plans are standardized by Medicare to pay the deductibles and copayments Medicare does not cover. There are fourteen specific plans, labeled A to M, structured to provide coverage for various combinations of Medicare deductibles and copayments. In addition, there are two benefits in some plans that are not covered by Medicare at all: the first three pints of blood transfused and out-of-country medical expenses. In each state, these plans may be offered by many different insurers, resulting in a bewildering array of choices. Some states (Massachusetts, Minnesota, and Wisconsin) have limited the choices available, making the Medigap plan decision process significantly less challenging. Some Medigap plans have an open enrollment period, which means you may enroll in them at any time, with an effective date of the first of the month following the time of enrollment. Other Medigap plans have closed enrollment periods, limiting the window for enrollment. To learn which Medigap plans are available in your state, go to Medicare.gov, or consult your State Health Insurance Assistance Program (SHIP) counselor.

MEDICAID BUY-IN PROGRAMS

Medicaid buy-in programs are plans for income-eligible persons who can benefit from financial assistance in paying for their Medicare premiums, deductibles, and

> **QUICK TIP**
>
> If you do not have a Medigap policy and are scheduled for inpatient and rehab procedures, try to find a Medigap plan with an open enrollment period. Enroll in the Medigap in order to be covered by the time of your procedure, have your procedure, and disenroll after you are well again. The approximately $200/month premium for the Medigap plan will save you the Medicare A hospital deductible (over $1,000) and the SNF copayments after twenty days (over $130/day).

copayments. Both assets and income are considered in determining financial eligibility. In some cases, a buy-in program can replace a Medigap plan, thereby saving thousands of dollars in premium payments annually.

MEDICARE D

Medicare D (I'll get to Medicare C below) is a prescription drug program created in 2005. It helps to pay for most prescription medications, but it does so within a very complicated and confusing structure. The Medicare Affordability Act will begin to reduce the confusion, but until then you really need to consult your SHIP counselor to determine which of the dozens of available plans is the best one for you. Just because a particular Medicare D plan works well for your best friend does not mean it will work as well for you. If you do not have creditable prescription coverage from another source (such as a limited employer plan), you are required to enroll in a Medicare D plan or face a premium penalty when you finally do enroll. The current penalty is 1 percent per month of nonenrollment, or 12 percent per year. This is a lifetime penalty that is added each month to your premium. To see the Medicare D prescription drug plans available in your county, go to Medicare .gov or consult your SHIP counselor.

Explaining the Medicare D program is beyond the scope of this chapter, but here is a simple example: You enroll in a Medicare D prescription drug plan and pay your first month's premium and continue to pay premiums each month. If there is a deductible, you buy your covered prescription drugs and pay out-of-pocket until you have met the deductible. Then the plan usually pays for 75 percent of your covered prescription drug costs and you pay 25 percent.

When the retail cost (your 25% and the plan's 75%) of the covered prescription drugs reaches the "initial coverage limit," the plan stops paying anything for a

---

QUICK TIP

If you have access to a big-box pharmacy such as Wal-Mart that charges only $4 or less for a wide range of common prescription drugs, you do not need to use your Medicare D plan to purchase them. Keeping those prescription drugs out of your Medicare D account can slow your progress toward the donut hole.

---

while. The dollar amount of the initial coverage limit changes each year, but let's use $2,500 for our example. This period when the plan provides no benefits but you must still pay your premiums is known as the coverage gap or the donut hole.

You remain in the donut hole until you reach the next coverage limit after you have spent a total of, for example, $5,500 out-of-pocket (not counting premiums!). Then you enter "catastrophic coverage" where you pay 5 percent of the cost of the covered prescription drugs and the plan pays 95 percent. All these limits must be reached within a calendar year (ending December 31) because the entire process begins again on January 1.

Low-income subsidy (LIS) is a Medicare program to assist people with low incomes by helping to pay for their Medicare D plan associated costs. Consult

---

QUICK TIP

You need to reassess your Medicare D plan each year because everything about the plan can change. The prescription drugs that the company covers (known as the formulary) and the premiums, deductibles, and copayments can all change from one year to the next. Make an appointment with your SHIP counselor in the fall in order to be ready for the new Medicare D plan year starting in January.

---

with advisors at your local Social Security office or with your SHIP counselor to determine your eligibility and level of benefits under this program.

State Pharmaceutical Assistance Programs (SPAPs) have been created by some states (about twenty-five) to further help with the high costs of prescription drugs. The SPAP works with your Medicare D plan, and it may help to pay for the premiums, deductibles, and copayments of the plan. Some SPAPs will pay for specific medications (such as benzodiazepines) not allowed by Medicare D plans. The

QUICK TIP

When you are applying for LIS at the Social Security office, ask to also be considered for the Medicaid buy-in programs offered in your state.

eligibility requirements and benefits of SPAPs vary by state. Consult your SHIP counselor for your state's offering. Many private organizations help people to pay for needed prescription drugs. Go online to www.benefitscheckuprx.org to learn more. The National Council on Aging provides this site.

SUMMARY OF ORIGINAL MEDICARE

If you choose Original Medicare as your retirement health insurance option, enroll in Medicare A, Medicare B, and Medicare D. For more complete coverage, you will also need a Medigap plan. To help reduce costs, also determine whether you are financially eligible for LIS, a Medicare buy-in program, and your state's SPAP.

MEDICARE C

Medicare C or Medicare Advantage plans are alternative Medicare plans. If you choose Original Medicare, you will not have a Medicare C plan. Medicare C plans are offered by private companies that contract with Medicare to provide your health care needs. In return, Medicare pays the company hundreds of dollars (varies by region) each month per member to care for each enrollee. There are three forms of Medicare Advantage plans, and each offers some benefits that Original Medicare does not while imposing some constraints that Original Medicare does not have. The types of Medicare Advantage plans are as follows:

- Medicare HMO (health maintenance organization) is the most constraining form of Medicare in that you are required to receive you health care from a restricted group of providers within a prescribed geographical area. Also, you need a referral from your primary care physician to be covered for visits to specialists. In return, you may receive some limited routine physical exam, vision, hearing, and dental services not available from Original Medicare. Some HMOs provide prescription drug coverage and some do not. If you choose one with no prescription drug coverage and you do not have other drug coverage, you will face a premium penalty in the future. HMOs have premiums, copayments for almost every service, and sometimes hefty deductibles. When comparing HMO costs with Original Medicare, look at your estimated HMO costs on an annual basis, rather than just the monthly premium.

- Medicare PPO (preferred provider organization) offers more choice in providers than the HMO does, allowing you to seek health care outside of the established provider group. The copayments for doing so are higher than using the restricted group. There are premiums, deductibles, and copayments.

- PFFS (private fee-for-service) plans are the newest form of Medicare. There are no provider groups or geographical restrictions. However, the PFFS enrollee (you) must negotiate with each provider as to whether she or he will accept payment from this plan. Once a provider agrees to accept the plan, the decision may be rescinded at any time. As with each Medicare Advantage plan, you must be enrolled in Medicare B to become a member.

Other limited Medicare options are available in specific areas. You can consult the publication *Medicare and You*, available at your local Social Security office, or go online to Medicare.gov for more information.

THINKING ABOUT THE UNTHINKABLE

Two health care topics are difficult to consider: nursing homes and hospice care. Insurers try to scare us into buying long-term care insurance; however, most retir-

---

QUICK TIP

If you were an HMO or PPO member before going on Medicare, do not assume that your health care providers will accept the Medicare versions. Medicare HMOs and PPOs are different from their non-Medicare counterparts. Before you enroll in a Medicare Advantage plan, always check to see whether your providers participate in the new plan and make your enrollment decision accordingly.

ees would never get to use it. Before you succumb to the sales pitch, answer these questions:

- Can I afford it now?
- Will it protect my house from a Medicaid lien?
- How much will it pay daily?
- How much will I need to pay in addition?
- Is there a waiting period before it begins to pay?
- How long will the policy pay?

There are many other questions to ask about this kind of insurance; however, if you do not like the answers to this list, do not buy the policy.

Hospice is not a place; it is a way of taking care of people. The Medicare hospice benefit is excellent, sometimes resulting in no charges at all. Care can occur in the home or in a dedicated hospice facility, at the option of the family and loved one.

DECISIONS, DECISIONS

As we have seen, the health insurance decisions the retiring librarian must make are varied and complex:

- Should I take my employer plan?
- Will my health care providers accept it?
- Is Medicare a better option for me?
- Should it be Original Medicare or Medicare Advantage?
- Should I buy a Medigap plan? Which one?
- Am I eligible for any assistance programs?
- Does my state have an SPAP?
- Do I really need long-term care insurance?

Librarians are expert researchers. With the information provided here, the listed sources, and consultation with your local SHIP counselor, you will be able to make the best decision for you. And don't forget that you can reconsider your choices next year!

PART VII

FINANCIAL PLANNING

20

THE LOGISTICS OF DOWNSIZING

Patricia H. Atwood

TEN DUMPSTERS

One family story involved months of family discussions, sorting, storage, and a truck to auction. "What should we do with the postcard album? Does anyone want the settee? Will you take the steamer trunk? Maybe Amy's daughter can use it? No, it's too beaten up and much too heavy." Others have had similar experiences.

Often it goes something like this: "My mother always said that this chest is very valuable, but no one in the family wants it. We gave away her books and clothing, but what should we do with the silver (or is it silver plate?), the Limoges dinner service, the paintings, the pottery, and the clocks? Is that huge Oriental rug from Persia? How old is the Canadian Red Ensign flag in the attic?" After the family has selected a few mementos and a desk or lamp and maybe a painting or two, then the discussion begins. "Do you think it's fair if I take the painting? What should we do with the rest of this stuff? How do we know if it's worth anything?" Then someone says, "I'll find out; I'll call an appraiser."

I've been the appraiser on the other end of the phone for countless of these conversations. Most of the people calling to ask for an appraisal do not need an appraisal; they just need answers to questions about the logistics of downsizing. Each case is different both because of the type of property and the varying needs of the family.

When I receive a call, I am often asked for an appraisal because it seems logical to find out first what a property is worth before determining how best to begin downsizing. The problem, as I frequently explain, is that an appraiser is not able to offer "ballpark" estimates over the phone for items he or she has neither seen nor researched. Any appraiser who complies with the Uniform Standards of Professional Appraisal Practice (USPAP) must also issue a signed certification and keep meticulous records for each and every opinion of value. These requirements help hold appraisers accountable and contribute to maintaining public trust in appraisers who comply with these standards. But this can make the process difficult for people seeking quick answers over the phone.

So, how do I answer? By listening I try to ascertain the general type and quality of the personal property and then to figure out what the family wants to achieve. If I sense that there is a unanimous family decision to sell relatively common items of personal property, then I can sometimes recommend several specific sale options.

I explain that I have no connection to any of the sale venues and clarify that I have no "dog in the hunt," that is, absolutely nothing to gain by mentioning this or that business. If I can, I will offer the names of a few specific companies that seem to me to be appropriate venues in which to sell the property. I also recommend that the caller do "business due diligence" and ask lots of questions before consigning the property to be sold. These seem to me to be straightforward cases in which an appraisal is probably not worth the expense.

FOUR KEY QUESTIONS

If money were no object, then it would indeed make sense to obtain an appraisal before taking any decisions about disposing of personal property. However, before you spend money on an appraisal, it is a good idea to think through the answers to these four key questions: (1) What is the principal goal? For example, do you wish to give property away to family members or to a charity? Or do you want to sell personal property? Once the principal objective is determined, then it is important to consider whether the chosen method of disposition is (2) legal and (3) fair. By this point, it makes sense to ask (4) whether or not an appraisal is warranted. Whether you are clearing out the home of an elderly aunt or beginning to sort out your own personal property, you will avoid many problems if you do some advance planning.

1. GIVE AWAY OR SELL? WHAT IS YOUR MAIN OBJECTIVE?

Defining the main objective is not always easy. If you plan to give away some of your property, that is only the first decision. If it is to your family, then you may need to consider issues of legality, fairness, and appraisal documentation. If your primary objective is to make a charitable donation, then there may be tax considerations that require special timing and paperwork. In addition, it often takes research to find an appropriate charity.

HOW TO MAKE CHARITABLE CONTRIBUTIONS HELPFUL AND WELCOME

Have you noticed that Salvation Army and Goodwill have large dumpsters outside their drop-off centers? You are well aware that libraries also receive outdated, damaged, or otherwise unusable donated materials. Librarians are all too familiar with the problems of unwanted items that are donated in very poor condition. You know better than to assume that every charity will accept every donation.

If your main goal is to make a donation, then you will want to do your homework. The IRS rules about charitable donations can be complicated. I recommend beginning by verifying the 501(c)(3) status of the organization and consulting your accountant or attorney before making a commitment.

If you can take the time to work on the details, it can be rewarding to find an organization seeking the very items that you no longer need. For example, you may discover that a stack of tiles or other building materials from an old renovation project will be gratefully accepted by Habitat for Humanity. Sometimes your local hardware store accepts this type of item for charities. Some municipalities collect unused medication, hearing aids, and glasses for donation. It is not always easy to find this information, though, and many families underestimate the amount of time it will take to accomplish.

> **FOUR KEY QUESTIONS**
>
> 1. Give away or sell? What is your main objective?
> 2. Is it legal?
> 3. Is it fair?
> 4. Do you need an appraisal?

IS MAXIMUM PRICE, SPEED, OR DISCRETION THE PRIORITY?

If your main objective is to sell, then what is the highest priority? Is it maximum price, speed, or discretion? Depending on your priorities, it may be worthwhile to go far afield to find the most appropriate market for special items. If time is short, you may need to do a quick estate sale to liquidate all of the property. These considerations will help you answer the question of where to sell. While a garage sale may be the simplest option, it is not always wise if maximum price is your main goal. Note that many sensational news stories begin with an inexpensive item purchased at a garage sale. No one likes to be the one who sold the $20 steamer trunk that was later sold at auction for over $5,000, but sometimes time is the driving factor. [1]

Fortunately, librarians are very good at research. If you think an item should not go to a garage sale, then you can look around for other venues. Go to antique shops or art galleries and see what is being offered. Look online and see if you can find similar items. Read books to see if you can verify the identification. Compare condition. Call up resale shops and auction galleries and ask for their terms and conditions. Ask if they have sold similar items.

TIPS ON MAKING A DONATION

1. Do not donate items that are dirty or in poor condition.
2. Donate appropriately; that is, bring books to the library and blankets to the homeless shelter.
3. Allow plenty of time and be patient, especially if you need to schedule a pickup.
4. If you plan to take a tax deduction, be sure that you know all of the rules.

If the priority is maximum price, then you must study the market on your own or enlist professional help. Many appraisers will accept consulting assignments to research the benefits of alternative market choices. One appraiser I know advised a client to ship a sculpture to England, where it realized ten times the amount it was estimated to have brought at a U.S. auction.

Sometimes the primary objective of a family is simply to clear out a home expeditiously. Speed and efficiency are often the primary goals after a family has removed the items they wish to retain. One approach is to call a local or regional auction company, which will come remove all saleable property from a home. Another approach is to hire an estate seller, who will either organize a sale on-site or make an offer to buy the entire contents and leave the home broom clean when everything has been removed. This service helps families who do not have the time or expertise to do this on their own. It's hard to generalize about what's best because it often depends on both the local or regional market and the type of objects that will be sold.

When discretion is the highest priority, then you may want to contact an art or antique dealer. These individuals can often come to a quick and private agreement to purchase and remove art or antiques. Since the dealer will need to resell the items for more than he or she paid in order to stay in business, this is not for those seeking the highest price. Another option is to bring the property to a larger metropolitan auction where it will be combined with many other similar items.

2. IS IT LEGAL?

In the case of charitable donations, there are many regulations. Some donations require an appraisal and also require that the appraisal be written within a short time prior to the actual donation. To be safe rather than sorry, you can read the current IRS regulations, which are available online.[2]

When you are selling items to a dealer for resale, there is generally no sales tax to be paid. However, when you sell to individuals, even in a private transaction, you may be required to collect sales tax. Consider the following example from the state of New York:

> Mr. and Mrs. A are retiring and moving into a smaller home. They decide to sell their dining room set, which includes a table, chairs, and hutch, for $800. They list the furniture in their local newspaper for sale. The furniture is taxable, but this sale does not require registration for sales tax purposes because it is an isolated one-time sale. However, it does not meet the special rules for garage sales (because the selling price of the items exceeds $600; see rules below). Mr. and Mrs. A are required to collect sales tax on the selling price of the items and send it to New York State with Form ST-131, Seller's Report of Sales Tax Due on a Casual Sale.[3]

Many people are unaware of these regulations, and they vary from state to state. Therefore, it is wise to consult your attorney or tax accountant.

Here are some other important questions. Are you the legal owner? If the property was stolen at any point in its history (even if this was a long time ago and even if you have no knowledge of this), you may not have good legal title. Another question is, Can this type of property legally be sold? Some states have special regulations related to historical documents, and there are federal injunctions against selling items such as eagle feathers or ivory. Yet another consideration is, Are there any dangerous contaminants in the property? If so, how do you dispose of these properly? Sometimes your city will publish information or your fire department may know. And finally, bear in mind that substantial gifts of personal property may be taxable. If an item or group of items has a fair market value of $13,000 or more (the 2010 threshold), then you may owe gift tax if you transfer ownership to a single individual.

3. IS IT FAIR?

This question applies to personal property given to family members. Generous good intentions sometimes create problems that could have been avoided with better communication and planning. For example, when one family member is given a set of furniture and another family member receives an oriental rug, there is often an unspoken but lingering question about whether the distribution was equitable. Sometimes a recipient will sell an item ten years later and discover that the value was higher or lower than he or she thought. This may be the result of a change in the marketability of the item or a lack of knowledge at the time of the original gift.

There are also questions about ownership rights. You can't take it with you, but is it yours to sell? If not, many family woes can be avoided if the donor makes his or her wishes clear to all concerned at the time of the gift. For example, what if the recipient decides later to sell the family heirloom and there is an unspoken assumption that it should be given (or sold) to someone in the family?

Depending on the quality of these items, there may also be a question about whether or not gift tax should be assessed. Some of these questions can be answered and some avoided by getting an appraisal.

4. DO YOU NEED AN APPRAISAL?

Most of the telephone calls I receive are from people who do not need an appraisal. Generally, they are calling about common items of modest value that they are intending to sell. Their primary objective is to sell for the maximum price, but they lack knowledge of the most appropriate market for their type of property. My sense is that many people turn first to an appraiser because they have an expectation that an appraiser will be impartial and trustworthy.

If I think that it does not make sense for a caller to pay for an appraisal, I try to offer a few words of friendly advice related to the logistics of downsizing. This is usually what a caller really needs, rather than an answer to the question that prompted the call, How much is it worth? After thinking it over, most callers realize that no one can do more than guess at the value of their items after merely listening to a description over the phone.

WHAT SHOULD YOU EXPECT IN AN APPRAISAL?

A reasonable appraisal will be based on correct identification of the objects (that the appraiser has personally inspected) and on factual evidence of the results of recent sales of closely comparable objects in similar condition and in an appropriate venue. The result is an authoritative document focused on the designated objects at a particular point in time. It is written to answer a specific question posed by the client. The type of questions answered by an appraisal might be, for example, "What is the net amount after expenses that I am likely to receive for these items if I sell them today?" or "What is the *fair market value* that I could claim as a tax deduction if I were to donate these items to a qualified charity?" Many are amazed to discover that the intricacies of the tax code sometimes require a different value for the same item.

If you do not need an appraisal but nevertheless are curious and just wish to have a quick and general idea of what an item might sell for, you can do your own research. I recommend reading reference books in order to correctly identify the object, and then searching antique shows and auctions to get a general idea of asking and selling prices. You can also turn to some of the online appraisal sites that offer a quick and inexpensive service sufficient for a ballpark value.[4] An appraisal based solely on a photograph is unlikely to hold up in an insurance claim or in a court of law. However, these online services fill a real need for those who only have a few items about which they are curious.

WHEN IS AN APPRAISAL WARRANTED?

Sometimes it is a good idea to get an appraisal regardless of the actual value of the items of personal property. In some cases, I have been hired to appraise the contents of modest homes because a trustee finds that it is worth paying for an appraisal in order to prove to beneficiaries that the contents were, in fact, modest. In other cases, it is helpful to have an appraisal when one friend wishes to buy out another friend's share of a collection. Some families commission appraisals of all of the significant personal property in their home many years before their retirement. On the basis of this appraisal, they are able to ensure equitable distribution among their children, whether by giving annual gifts or by designating the bequest of specific items. Another scenario in which a formal appraisal is a good idea is if there is a potential that the value of specified objects might be relevant to a legal matter, whether it be an insurance claim, a tax matter, or the dissolution of a marriage. Thus, it doesn't matter whether the items are Hummel figurines or Gilbert Rhode clocks because the goal of a three-party appraisal is to provide legal protection or to ensure fairness.

However, if a family simply wishes to sell unwanted items, then it is less clear why an appraisal is needed first. Even inexpensive online appraisals take time. The key question in these cases usually seems to be, Where would be a logical venue or most appropriate market at which to sell the items? An appraiser is a good source for this information and is usually happy to share it if it's just a quick telephone call.

CONCLUSION: TRASH OR TREASURE?

One librarian's Internet posting suggests that many people forfeit substantial financial gain by donating or throwing away valuable items by mistake.[5] Ironically, this comment appears in a blog written by librarians describing the nuisance of items of zero value in dreadful condition being donated to libraries. It is true that some items are more valuable than people think, but in my experience the reverse is more likely to be true.

In the same way that patient librarians respond politely to donation offers of boxes of moldy *National Geographic* magazines, many personal property appraisers find themselves seeking tactful ways to dampen their callers' inflated hopes that often have been piqued by television auction shows. The upholstered furniture or twentieth century Hakata dolls will probably have far more sentimental than financial value. However, appraisers cannot simply tell callers this over the phone, because they cannot ethically make pronouncements about values in the absence of inspection, record keeping, and research.

The logistics of downsizing are not the same for everyone. However, good sense, planning, communication, and a little homework can help ease the process. My best advice: First figure out what you want to achieve, then research how best to do it. Think about fairness, and be sure that you know the law.

If you cannot do this on your own, there are many honest and helpful people available. Check the credentials of any appraiser that you hire. Is the appraiser listed a current member of a major professional society? Ask people you trust for recommendations for an accountant or lawyer. Take a look at the websites of auctioneers or antique dealers and see if they have experience with the type of property that you wish to sell. Go to one of their auctions or visit their shop. Talk to a charity about the items that you wish to donate.

If you select the right people, then you can relax and enjoy the process of passing personal property to others. Many people take the opportunity of downsizing to enjoy learning about the history of their items. It is enriching to be able to make new discoveries about when and where an object was made and to communicate this history. Far better to do this yourself in a gradual and pleasant process than to leave everything for your family to sort through and perhaps discard unappreciated in ten dumpsters!

NOTES

1. Auction House PR, "Trunk bought for $20 at garage sale nets $5,600+ at Clars sale," *Auction Central News* (August 16, 2010), http://acn.liveauctioneers.com/index.php/auctions/auction-results/2970-trunk-bought-for-20-at-garage-sale-nets-5600-at-clars-sale.
2. See IRS Publication 526 (2010), *Charitable Publications,* http://www.irs.gov/pub/irs-pdf/p526.pdf.
3. New York State Department of Taxation and Finance, *Tax Bulletin ST-807 (TB-ST-807)* (March 26, 2010), http://www.tax.state.ny.us/pubs_and_bulls/tg_bulletins/st/sales_from_your_home.htm.
4. Alina Dizik, "Services Spot Hidden Gems among the Junk," *The Wall Street Journal*, August 26, 2010, http://online.wsj.com/article/SB10001424052748703447004575450170902767324.html.
5. Mary Kelly, "Donations gone wrong," *Awful Library Books*, http://awfullibrarybooks.net/?p=3714.

21

MEDIATION AS A TOOL IN LEGACIES AND FINANCIAL PLANNING

A PLAY IN THREE ACTS

Carolyn J. Rodis and Steven Henick

PLANNING IS SMART. But what happens when family members don't want to discuss and make plans around the transitions that may accompany aging, such as retirement, downsizing, moving, caregiving, end-of-life decision making, or writing a will? Or when complicated family dynamics play out that prevent implementation of those plans? Or when people simply disagree?

ACT I. THE PROBLEM
SCENE 1. THE PLAYERS

You are planning to retire or you have already retired. You are thinking about what you want to do with the rest of your life and how to make your available resources last long enough to fulfill your dream. You may have a spouse. He or she may have already retired or may still be working. You may have several adult children. Your family may be close or some members may be estranged.

SCENE 2. THE PLAN

You have thought about your retirement goals, when to retire, and what you want to do in retirement. Financial planners and attorneys are available to assist in planning and implementing your decisions. You have consulted these experts and together you have figured out timing and how to maximize your income over the rest of your life. You have implemented an investment plan and have drafted a will and durable health care power of attorney. You are pleased that you have taken charge of these crucial matters.

SCENE 3. YOUR LEGACY

How do you want to be remembered? What are the values you want to pass on to your loved ones? How do you want to be treated if you are unable to care for yourself? Who do you want to take charge if you are unable to do so? The answers to these questions will shape an important part of your legacy. Legacy also involves traditions, family and personal history, assessing your own contributions, making sense of what has gone before, and communicating those values to the next generation. A 2005 survey by Allianz Life Insurance Company, called The Allianz American Legacies Study (www.allianz.com), asked 2,627 people—boomers and elders—to identify how they define leaving a legacy and whether families are communicating about these issues. The respondents said they were having in-depth conversations about legacy and inheritance. Yet they also revealed that the communication was not productive or meaningful.

Why are these conversations so difficult? Both parents and children may not want to think about the parent's aging and death. Parents may not want to fan the flames of long-simmering disputes among their children by raising controversial subjects or even bringing them together. Or parents may assume their children will know what to do and how to act without giving them the gift of guidance.

SCENE 4. FINANCIAL AND ESTATE PLANNING

You have given careful thought to your financial future. You have consulted an expert to help you determine whether and when you can afford to retire full-time or part-time and have estimated how long your savings will last while you pursue your dreams. Do your children know what you intend? Does your daughter, pregnant with her first child, expect you to be available five days a week for child care while you have visions of world travel while you are still healthy? Is your son counting on an inheritance from you to send his children to college while you plan to spend your resources?

In surveys retired people often say they want to leave an inheritance to their loved ones. The recent downturn in the financial markets may have adversely impacted those intentions. Discussions about money bring up values and emotions in addition to expectations. Failure to be open about those matters can lead to strife.

You have also been to see an attorney who specializes in elder law and/or estate planning. You have provided information about your assets and to whom you want to leave them. You have decided to leave your home to your son and daughter. You have thought about end-of-life issues, and you have decided what you want doctors to do or refrain from doing if you are unable to communicate. You have signed the advance health care directive, naming your oldest daughter as your health care agent. You have signed the will your lawyer prepared according to your instructions. So far, so good.

ACT II. THINGS FALL APART

The best plans may not be followed if you don't communicate your wishes and plans to all your children, your spouse, and other close relatives—your beneficiaries and the people who will be asked to carry out your wishes. The lack of communication among families can have disastrous consequences for legacy, retirement, and estate planning. If these matters aren't discussed and understandings reached in advance, family members may be hurt, disagree, and argue.

You haven't called your children together so you can explain how and where you want to be cared for if you are unable to take care of yourself. You then have a stroke that leaves you impaired, and your children argue over whether you should be cared for at home or in a long-term care facility.

You haven't discussed with your health care agent what you want her to communicate to your doctors if you are unable to do so. She may not understand your wishes or may have very different ideas and fail to follow your instructions. Your son, who knows what you would have said if you could, disagrees with what she decides and tells the doctors to do something else. The doctor may have to call in the hospital ethics committee or the facility may file a guardianship action in court in order to get the guidance the doctor needs. This is exactly what you didn't want to happen when you signed the advance health care directive.

Children who cannot come to agreement may resort to litigation. Hiring attorneys and going to court is expensive and destructive to relationships. If children do not clearly understand a parent's wishes or cannot agree on how to carry them out, one or more may file a guardianship action, which will deplete your estate and derail your plans.

Guardianship should be a last resort. While it is a safety net for vulnerable people who cannot care for themselves or make their own financial decisions, have not made plans, and do not have agents to take care of them, guardianship abrogates civil rights. It is the antithesis of planning and communication and undermines self-determination.

If your children are surprised by the terms of your will, feeling that provisions are unfair to them or not as much as they felt they deserved, they may file a court action to contest the will. Litigation is time-consuming, expensive, and divisive, often creating rifts that never heal. Defending your will against those who contest it uses the money you planned to leave as inheritances, leaving less for everyone and defeating your careful plans.

Talking about future changes, especially where money is involved or death or illness is contemplated, is frequently fraught with tension. You may want to discuss these topics and the children may resist. Or your adult children may not get along, and you are reluctant to stir up past resentments and hear their arguments. Even in close relationships, adult children often know very little about their parents' financial affairs, and even less about their parents' wishes. Especially when they are close to you, they may not want to talk about your death or disability.

The emotional attachments children have to certain of their parents' possessions may far outweigh the object's monetary value. How will you know about those attachments unless you provide the space to talk about them? If you do find out their preferences and attachments, you might make provisions accordingly in your will, or make gifts to particular persons while you are living, perhaps as you downsize.

You've decided to leave your home jointly to your two children. The one who lives in-state is pleased; she's been in an apartment and would be happy to move in. However, your daughter, who lives out-of-state and already owns a home, would rather sell the house and take her half of the proceeds to use to send her children to college. The in-state daughter doesn't agree, but the out-of-state child can force a sale since she is half owner. They may never speak to each other again.

More than one child may value the same object among your possessions. The vase that was placed on the dining room table for special occasions may evoke memories of warm, family dinners for one child. That same vase may be a reminder of the bouquet another child bought you with her first paycheck. Absent these meaningful conversations, your children may argue over the vase and end up estranged and bitter.

You may own a vacation home in the mountains and plan to leave it to your four children. Without a family meeting, you might not know that two of your children wouldn't be able to work together to figure out a plan for how to share the home. Or one of them may prefer the beach to the mountains. Alternatively, you might decide to sell that vacation home because it's too much trouble to maintain. Or you might direct in your will that after your death it be sold and the proceeds divided among your children. You may not know that your children are counting on being able to go there, just as they have been doing for the past forty years, and will feel betrayed when they find out you have directed that it be sold.

ACT III. AN ALTERNATIVE SCENARIO
SCENE 1. THE MEDIATION PROCESS

Mediation, or facilitated conversation, can help retirees and those considering retirement and their family members and loved ones have these difficult conversations in a safe, confidential environment. When you convene such a meeting, you are giving your family a gift.

Mediation is voluntary, meaning that everyone has to agree to participate. Who attends the family meeting may be the first issues to be resolved. Should spouses and grandchildren, nieces and nephews be present? Does anyone need a support person in order to access the process or to feel comfortable? Are separate meetings needed before everyone in the family gets together? The mediator or facilitator helps you and your family members sort this out.

The mediator is bound by his or her code of ethics to maintain confidentiality of the substance of what is discussed and documents presented in mediation. Depending on the circumstances, the mediator may be required to keep confidential conversations about whether to mediate. If family members want to keep the substance of their conversations confidential, that is a matter they can discuss and decide upon for themselves.

Either to make decisions as part of planning or to resolve conflicts that have arisen, the impartial mediator is there to guide the process. This person does not take sides or represent anyone's interests over anyone else's and does not judge or make decisions. The mediator listens, asks clarifying questions, and reflects and reframes what he or she hears in a way that validates the speaker, lets the speaker know he or she has been heard, and enables the others to hear, perhaps for the first time.

Family conversations in the presence of an impartial mediator or facilitator can provide an effective basis of empowerment. If there are decisions to be made, the mediator empowers you and your loved ones to creatively make plans that work for you. Generally, relationships are strengthened in the process because new understandings are reached.

The mediator does not replace the financial planner or attorney. Rather, the mediator complements their work, enabling the family members to figure out what they need and want. The planner or attorney can then draft the documents or take the actions to effectuate those plans.

Facilitated conversations or mediations generally follow a process that allows everyone's voice to be heard. Unlike court where an attorney or judge directs the questioning, in mediation participants are free to share information about whatever they want and need to discuss. The mediator makes notes of the issues raised and checks with those participating to identify those and other issues they wish to resolve and decisions they wish to reach.

You may learn for the first time that your daughter wants and expects you to take care of her baby. You may find out that your grandson is hoping to have the watch that belonged to the great-grandfather he hardly remembers.

The mediator then facilitates the family to brainstorm possible solutions. Brainstorming is a process that allows the family members to look at the issues creatively with fresh perspectives. Participants are encouraged to think outside the box, to propose alternatives, no matter how wild or unrealistic, that might resolve the issue or effectuate the decision. Ideas offered in brainstorming frequently stimulate even more creative ideas from the others.

After all ideas have been expressed on all the issues, the mediator or facilitator asks clarifying questions to help the family pick and choose among the options. They may combine those ideas with other ideas or parts of ideas, or the brainstormed concepts may lead them to other options. With the mediator's help, the group is empowered to agree on options that work for them, that may resolve some or all of their conflicts.

A decision may be made to delay your travel plans for two years until the toddler can enter preschool. You may agree to leave your home to the in-state daughter and make monetary bequests to the out-of-state child.

SCENE 2. THE RESOLUTION

If family members come up with solutions that are agreeable to everyone, with the mediator's help they can draft a memorandum of understanding that embodies their agreement. That document might be submitted for review by lawyers or others. Or the document may be a blueprint of which loved one wants which possessions that you can then take to your lawyer to incorporate into your will. The family members may decide a written document is not necessary.

Mediated agreements have a high rate of compliance because the participants have come up with their own solution. They have figured out for themselves what they need rather than having a decision imposed by a court or an arbitrator, or by the dominant family member.

In the unfortunate circumstance where guardianship or a contest of will or other litigation has been undertaken, mediation may still be possible. If a court makes a decision, someone wins and someone loses every time. In mediation, everyone has the chance to win because each can contribute to the solution and ultimately make the decisions together beyond the scope of a judge's authority under the law.

Even if the family is not able to resolve all the conflicts or is unable to make decisions that work for everyone, the family relationships usually have been strengthened as a result of going through the mediation process. Frequently, family members have learned different ways of communicating. Your family members may reach greater understanding of each other. You have learned valuable information to guide you as you make financial and legacy plans.

In our society, we tend to avoid talking about death and money, which are challenging subjects, fraught with emotions and denial. You are giving your loved ones a gift by convening a family meeting to communicate your legacy and your plans, and to find out your children's wishes to help you in your decision making. The information you learn may lead you to change your will or the agent you have designated, or not to move out of state until your grandchildren start school.

It is never too early—and frequently may be too late if a crisis has occurred—to communicate deeply about these issues. You and your loved ones will be glad you did.

EPILOGUE
FINDING A MEDIATOR

To find a mediator or facilitator, you can seek guidance from professional organizations of mediators and facilitators, such as the Association for Conflict Resolution (ACR). You can do web searches including your state, and then look for expertise in the subject area you will be discussing, such as elder mediation or estate planning. Ask for referrals from friends and professionals in the field. Your attorney or financial planner may have a suggestion. Ask your county department of aging also.

You will want to research the mediator's or facilitator's credentials and experience. How much training has he or she received and in what areas? Is the training in the areas you need? Does he or she teach or conduct trainings? How many mediations or facilitations has he or she conducted? To what professional organizations does he or she belong? Ask for references. If your state has credentialing or licensing, does the mediator/facilitator meet those requirements? Does he or she mediate for the courts in your state?

There may also be a community mediation program in your area. The website of the National Association for Community Mediation is a resource to help you find a program (www.nafcm.org).

22

THE SINGLE BIGGEST MONEY MISTAKE RETIREES MAKE

Brian Fricke, CFP

THE ROLE OF A FINANCIAL PLANNER IN PREPARING FOR RETIREMENT

Recently, I met with Joe, who was thinking about hiring my firm as his trusted financial advisor. Joe had pretty much decided that he could handle everything himself. Quite frankly, he had done a really good job on his own, and I told him that. I could understand why he was having trouble justifying hiring us. "That's great, Joe, but what about Helen?" I asked. My point was that if something happened to Joe, his wife and children needed to be in a position to deal with the estate. Wouldn't it make more sense for Joe to work with us to make decisions now so that his wife and children wouldn't have to be making them later on during a stressful time without him?

In fact, this situation is quite common. Many spouses assume certain roles so that one tends to make more of the financial decisions, excluding the other spouse from the process and, unfortunately, sometimes keeping important information from their family.

Here's another example. Mary, a very wise and knowledgeable investor, would come and visit with me about every year or so but would never hire my firm. She was managing her money pretty well and I suspect she just wasn't comfortable paying me or anyone else for financial advice. Her husband Mark had absolutely no interest in money or finances. He was a retired military man and was happy knowing that he always had his monthly "allowance" in his pocket and that all their bills were being paid. The couple owed no one. They didn't have a mortgage. Mark was very proud of Mary and the excellent job she had done, not only raising their children and managing the household but also in taking responsibility for all their financial affairs.

Then one day, Mark called me and I immediately knew something wasn't right. Since Mark would always delegate any money issues to Mary, he would never call a financial advisor. Mark was very distressed and told me that Mary had passed away two weeks earlier. On her deathbed, Mary had told Mark not to worry about anything and to call me. She had said that I would take care of him. Well, the couple had two grown children—a daughter who had been estranged from the family for many years and a son with bipolar disorder that was managed with medication but who would always require a certain level of supervision.

When Mark came in to meet with me for the first time, he brought in a stack of thirty-seven envelopes, one on top of the other. This stack—exactly five and three-quarters inches high—consisted of empty envelopes from thirty-seven different mutual fund and investment companies. Mark was pretty sure they had money invested with all of these companies, but he had no idea where the monthly statements were or how much was in any of the accounts. Needless to say, he had no idea what the statements looked like or how to even read one.

This is where we started. One of my colleagues spent two and a half days at Mark's home going through all his legal and financial papers. Fortunately, the couple did have a little over $1 million in addition to their home. Along with Mark's military pension and Social Security, there would be more than enough money to take care of Mark and his special needs son.

This is not an isolated situation. Just recently, my wife ran into a family friend at the grocery store. The two women caught each other up on the latest family news. Diana was telling my wife about a medical scare with her husband Rob. As he was being prepared for serious back surgery, he told Diana that she should call me if he didn't make it through the operation! In fact, while I had met the couple six or seven years before, I was not familiar with their finances. Like other couples, Diana let Rob handle all the financial matters for the family.

What do Mary and Rob have in common? They each have spouses who have little or no knowledge or the desire to learn about their financial matters. As a result, Mary and Rob made the financial decisions without consulting their spouses. The real problem comes when the uninterested spouse—as with Mark—suddenly has to take charge of the family finances when the other person gets ill or dies. The absolute worst type of client a financial advisor could ever have is a newly widowed spouse who has never taken any interest in the household investments and is now left alone to make investing decisions. It's good that they're seeking the advice of a financial advisor, but even finding the right advisor can be a scary decision. They're just not comfortable handling any type of financial decision, especially if they have just lost their trusted spouse.

If you love your spouse, do them a favor—start working with a financial advisor now! You should find an advisor whom you both like and trust. That way, when your spouse is left alone, he or she will already have a trusted financial advisor in place. This will reduce the stress the surviving spouse feels. This is one of the best legacies you can ever give your spouse, and one they will always be grateful for.

THE NEW DEFINITION OF RETIREMENT

Not too many years ago, the word *retirement* was associated with people spending hours on the golf course or traveling leisurely around the world. Today, the images of retirement aren't so promising. Increasing health care costs, recent declines in the stock market, and the subprime mortgage crisis have all added to the concerns people have about their retirement, especially from a financial view. Fortunately, there are some reasons to be optimistic. People are living longer and in many cases are healthier, thanks to lifestyle changes and advances in medical care. Also, the notion that at age 65 you must stop working and move to a retirement community is out-of-date. There is no universal definition of retirement that meets everyone's needs.

What's important is that you take charge of planning for your retirement so that you can enjoy it to the fullest. Some things, such as an unexpected health crisis, are not in your control, but planning for travel, a new career, volunteer work, and so on, are all within your power! I tell my clients to strive for a worry-free retirement. This means that you will be able to do what you want, when you want, and where you want. An increasing number of people are choosing to continue working beyond their full retirement age, not because they *have to* but because they *want to*. Some will even trade in one career for new employment opportunities.

I consider myself retired because I'm in the position of being able to do what I want, when I want, and where I want. I'm still working because my business brings me purpose and passion. If you're fortunate enough to have a position that also brings you great satisfaction, consider yourself lucky and don't think about giving it up. If you're living and leading a balanced life, keep doing so.

Following are some examples of how our clients handled their retirement plans.

Several years ago John accepted an early retirement package. About six months into retirement, he called me in a panic. His former employer had contacted him to see if he would be willing to work on a project as an independent contractor. John thought it would take three to four months to complete. His primary concern was how this extra income might affect his Social Security benefits.

Before answering his question, I asked him if doing this work would bring joy and satisfaction into his life. John told me that he had finished all his retirement projects and was starting to get a little bored. While the opportunity seemed interesting, he was concerned for his wife, Wanda, as it would require him living overseas for three or four months. I asked John whether his wife might want to visit and spend time with him overseas. He was sure that she would like this opportunity, but he wasn't convinced that the company would pay the additional expense.

I recommended that he let his former employer know that he would be willing to accept the assignment if the company was willing to accept his terms. I told John to be ready for either an initial rejection or possibly a delayed response. John asked the company to fly him and his wife first class and provide them with a Marriott-type quality hotel suite. I also advised him to ask for a daily fee that was 30 percent higher than his previous salary, if calculated on a daily basis. My reasoning was that the firm was still saving money because John was no longer an employee and also was saving this 30 percent because the company wouldn't be paying Social Security and Medicare taxes as well as other employee benefits.

Sure enough, John's initial request was turned down. However, a week later his contact called back to see if he was still interested at his original terms. As it turned out his immediate supervisor only had financial authority up to a certain level. So he had to get permission "from above," which he had hoped to avoid.

That was nearly ten years ago and John is still doing project work for his former employer and has no plans to quit. He occasionally turns down projects that conflict with his personal travel plans or if he doesn't like the project. The last time we spoke John commented that he's having more fun now than ever. I'm not surprised. People are generally happier when they feel that they're in control of their time.

When the company Kathy worked for went public, the stock shot up like a rocket. Her stock options and retirement plan were now worth several million dollars. This was more than enough money for her and her husband David to enjoy life as they had always envisioned. Although the couple were relatively young, not quite age 50, they didn't want to work at all. Instead, they bought a brand new forty-eight-foot sport fishing boat. David even got his captain's license. They've cruised all over the Bahamas, the Caribbean, and Florida Keys, sometimes by themselves and other times with friends and family. That was nearly a decade ago, and recently they've put the boat up for sale. They are looking forward to the next chapter in their lives, though they're not certain what it will be. Fortunately, they've made smart investment decisions and will never have to return to work for financial reasons.

Nine years ago Danny accepted an early retirement offer and since has been spending most of his time in a national leadership role with his church. When he's not involved with his voluntary, unpaid church business, Danny and his wife Carolyn spend time traveling or visiting their children and grandchildren. More important, they are living their lives with a sense of purpose and passion.

Over the years, I've observed that my retired clients who stay active and involved, whether working part-time, volunteering for their church or other charity they care about, traveling, or pursuing hobbies, all end up having a happier and more fulfilling life. Also, their lives are a lot less stressful than when they worked full-time. As a group, their health is significantly better compared to other people who have retired but don't remain active.

No matter how you choose to define your worry-free retirement, including your financial planner in your financial decisions and staying active and involved will guarantee you the freedom of a life filled with purpose and passion!

LOCATION AFTER RETIREMENT

23

ON THE MOVE
RELOCATING WHEN YOU RETIRE

Susan Montgomery

THE IDEA OF relocating when they retire appeals to many prospective retirees. It provides a reason to retire *to* something, rather than retiring *from* something, as one retired librarian told me. It contains an element of adventure, making us feel that we are just starting out again. It may be the opportunity to realize a long-held dream: "I've always dreamed of living in Buenos Aires."

Not everyone may be looking for an adventure but may have other compelling reasons to relocate. Our reasons could be anything from living where it doesn't snow all winter, being closer to the grandchildren, living more economically, or you fill in the blank with your reason. In any case, we sense that now's our chance—maybe the first chance we've had since we started working.

DECIDING WHETHER TO RELOCATE

A surprising number of retirees who relocate return to their original hometown or state. Precise figures are hard to come by; however, Charles F. Longino Jr., a former gerontologist at Wake Forest University, estimated (based on U.S. Census data) that about 10 percent of retirees who have moved to another state eventually return (Brock 2004, 80).

Others, known as "halfback retirees," who originally headed for Sunbelt states move back to locations with more moderate climates. They may realize that they want to be closer to relatives or may have found that the climate—either environmentally or socially—of their first choice location did not live up to their expectations.

One retired librarian told me, "I relocated for all the right reasons; they just didn't meet my expectations." Even if it is for the best of reasons, will relocating be the right decision for you? Following are some questions to ask yourself when you are making a decision about relocating:

- How strong are your family ties where you are currently living? How will you keep those ties strong?
- If you are relocating to be closer to family, can you reasonably expect that your family will not move away?
- How strong and longstanding are your close friendships? How will you replace those ties?
- How easily do you make new friends and acquaintances?
- What about your doctors? Do you have medical reasons for continuing with professionals who are aware of your medical needs?
- What do you like about where you live now? What do you want to find in your new location?
- What do you dislike where you live now? How will moving make a positive difference?
- Will you find venues to fit your spiritual path?

The New Retirement: The Ultimate Guide to the Rest of Your Life by Jan Cullinane and Cathy Fitzgerald (2004) also has a questionnaire that will help you decide whether relocating is a good idea for you.

DECIDING WHERE TO RELOCATE

The beauty of relocating when you retire is that unless you are relocating to be near family you get to decide where you want to go. It's a decision that can take several years to make. It will probably require some travel to visit the places on your prospective list, including if possible extended stays to really get the feel of the place. It will require some money as well—after all, this is an investment in the rest of your life. Even if you have been summering in Maine or wintering in Florida for years, have you ever *experienced* winter in Maine or summer in Florida?

According to the *2010 Del Webb Baby Boomer Survey* (Del Webb 2010), cost of living and access to preferred health care programs are the two most important factors that retirees consider when deciding where to move. Other highly desirable factors include favorable climate, cultural and recreational amenities, and community and networking opportunities. Curiously enough, being close to children, grandchildren, or parents ranks lowest in the list.

Ratings and rankings of the best places to retire are a dime a dozen. *AARP The Magazine* publishes articles on subjects such as "Top Places for Boomers to Retire," as do *U.S. News & World Report, Money Magazine,* and other publications. On the *U.S. News & World Report* website you can enter criteria, including median house prices, crime rates, and weather, to find locations that might be right for you. Similarly, *Kiplinger's Personal Finance* magazine publishes an annual best cities report. The website allows you to take an eight-question questionnaire to find cities that meet your criteria.

What does quality of life mean to you? The cost of living might be great, the climate ideal, but if the location doesn't satisfy your needs for the intangibles of life such as mental stimulation, relationships, and fulfilling activities, you probably will be disappointed. It is important to consider the availability of activities that you enjoy, and organizations and people that you can connect with. Especially for boomers, places that have a "youthful vibe" and amenities like ethnic restaurants may be more important than low taxes or golf courses.

Now is the time to be honest with yourself and think about what really makes you happy. A good example of decision making that incorporates the "happiness factor" was reported in the *New York Times* (Rosenbloom 2010). Ed Diener, a former president of the International Positive Psychology Association, and his wife, both avid hikers, were house-hunting. Diener wrote, "I argued that [proximity to] the

---

TEN FACTORS TO CONSIDER

Ted Wetzel of RetirementLiving.com lists these factors to consider when looking for a retirement place to live (Brock 2004, 92–93):

- Cost of living (including taxes)
- Climate
- Medical care
- Culture
- Distance from family and friends
- Crime
- Recreational opportunities
- Part-time employment opportunities
- Nearest airport
- Quality of restaurants

hiking trails could be a factor contributing to our happiness, and we should worry less about things like how pretty the kitchen floor is or whether the sinks are fancy. We bought a home near the hiking trail and it has been great, and we haven't tired of this feature because we take a walk four or five days a week." Instead of focusing on the material elements of the house, they focused on the intangible benefits and the result has been continuing satisfaction.

Following are questions to ask yourself:

- Like the Dieners, what gives you lasting pleasure in life? What does the area you are considering have to offer?
- How friendly is the community? As one person put it, "Where a place is, is not nearly as important as what the people are like." (This is tough to evaluate from a distance and another good reason to spend some extended time in the areas you are considering before making your decision.)
- Are there organizations for people who share your interests whether they are bird watching, salsa dancing, politics, or poker?
- Are there the kinds of restaurants, shops, sports, or cultural activities that you love?
- What continuing education facilities are available?
- What does the area offer for part-time work, entrepreneurial opportunities, or community service (keep in mind that full-time leisure will accelerate your aging process)?

KEEP IN MIND THAT THERE ARE ALTERNATIVES

When I moved to London from the suburbs of New Jersey, I put my belongings in storage and rented my house for a year. That was my safety net. In case it didn't work out, I still had a place to come home to. Another option would be to arrange a home exchange for several months with someone in the area that you are considering. There are numerous organizations that facilitate home exchanges: HomeExchange (www.homeexchange.com) and HomeLink International (www .homelink.org) are two.

A popular alternative, finances permitting, is to relocate for part of the year. For example, buy an RV and travel part of the year, or become a snowbird and spend part of the year in a warmer climate. One retired librarian told me that she should have more seriously considered the option of keeping her home in the city where she had lived for many years, living in it for part of the year and renting a place near her family for the rest of the year.

PLANNING FOR GROWING OLDER
HEALTH CARE

Let's face it, we're not getting any younger. Although relocating after retirement does not have to be a permanent move, moving is costly both financially and emotionally. It would be smart to look ahead now at what the location you plan to move to has to offer the aging. Following are questions to ask:

- What is the quality of medical care, especially if you have a condition that requires specialist treatment?
- What about the availability and costs of assisted living, adult day care programs, or nursing home care?
- Are there convenient public transportation options?
- Are there public amenities like parks, recreation centers, and lifetime learning programs?
- If you are not moving near your children or other family, how easy is it for them to come to see you?

When it comes to medical care, we're only going to need more of it. Relocating means starting over with new doctors, dentists, and health care services. In addition to doing an Internet search for hospital ratings or rankings (see figure 23.1), check out the local paper for any reports about the quality and costs of medical services. If you can, make appointments with doctors that you are considering using to interview them and see for yourself how their offices are run. (This may not be practicable in some cases. Some doctors will not see you unless you have had your medical records transferred first.)

TRANSPORTATION

Transportation is another factor that can affect your quality of life in a big way as you age. There are at least three points to consider here:

- Access to good, convenient public transport can make a real difference to your ability to get around town as you get older. Some cities provide

---

FIGURE 23.1 **HOSPITAL RATINGS**

U.S. News & World Report Best Hospitals http://health.usnews.com/best-hospitals/ rankings	• Rates hospitals based on death rates, patient safety, and reputation with more than 9,000 specialists • Allows searches by location, medical specialty, or special services
HealthGrades www.healthgrades.com/	• Rates doctors, hospitals, and nursing homes
Hospital Compare www.hospitalcompare.hhs.gov/hospital -search.aspx?loc=80247&lat=39.697455 18lng=-&stype=SURGICAL&bpid=CAT_ 68spid=GRP_348AspxAutoDetectCooki eSupport=1	• Provided by Medicare • Search by location and type of treatment • Compare patients' reports on quality of care
Consumer Reports www.consumerreports.org/health/doc tors-hospitals/hospital-ratings.htm	• Ratings based on the federal government's survey of millions of patients regarding their experiences during a recent hospital stay • Requires subscription to *Consumer Reports*

senior ride services in addition to regular public transport. Driving might not be a problem right now, but will you always want to drive at night or on superhighways? For that matter, do you want to be driving narrow country roads with poor road markings? One popular retirement relocation destination that I considered was in a region that had twisting, poorly maintained mountain roads.

- Likewise, do you want to be in a location where you have to rely on a car for everything? Proximity to local shopping and entertainment can make a big difference in quality of life. Cities like New York, Cleveland, and Fayetteville, Georgia, are already taking steps to become more "age-friendly" (Ruffenach 2009; Hartocollis 2010). As the boomer generation ages, we can expect more improvements geared to the needs of city-dwelling seniors. Before heading for the hills, think about options that might free you from dependency on the automobile.

- Choose a location that has direct flights to the places where you want to go. One popular retirement destination that I considered is a beautiful location but requires taking a small commuter plane to a larger airport. The older we get, the more we want hassle-free travel and the less we want to have to change planes or deal with delays.

Many of us will be adjusting to a lower level of income than when we were working. Good public amenities like parks, recreation centers, and libraries, therefore, can add a great deal to your quality of life. Good public facilities offer not only activities but also the opportunity to meet people and, in some cases, to volunteer. In a book whose target audience is librarians, it seems obvious that we would investigate the public library system in any community to which we are thinking of moving.

BE PREPARED

You should get to know as much as you can about any location that you are thinking of moving to before you actually make the move. There are plenty of resources to help you, including of course your local public library. In addition to the many books and magazines available, there are any number of websites that will help you in your decision making.

Contact the local chamber of commerce and request information about the community and expected growth plans. Before buying property, make sure you find a knowledgeable Realtor. We all know that real estate is all about "location, location, location," and it is hard to judge locations when you are new to an area. The City-Data Forum has lots of good insights both on specific areas and on buying property. One couple said, "I wish we would have waited at

RELOCATION WEBSITES

- **www.55places.com**
  Provides information about active adult communities (55 and over) around the United States.
- **www.bestplaces.net**
  Enables you to compare costs of living.
- **www.retirementliving.com**
  Ranks states by the total tax burden.
- **www.city-data.com**
  Provides statistics and data about U.S. cities and has discussion groups that you can join.
- **www.zillow.com**
  Enables you to compare housing prices.
- **www.taxfoundation.org**
  Also has information on property taxes.

least a few months to get to know the area better. We could have *probably* found a house and neighborhood that we liked even better. . . ." Another said, "We retired to Jacksonville, Florida, ten years ago. . . . About the same time the developers were turned loose resulting in many thousands of new homes and much more traffic. We are looking to move and this time we will pay attention to future developments and zoning."

One retired librarian that I spoke to moved back to her hometown when she retired. Even though she was familiar with the town, she took out an online subscription to the local newspaper to keep her abreast of what was going on in town. Although we might tend to overlook them, the small things such as "Is there a Kiwanis Club and when does it meet?" make a difference in helping you to feel like you really know the place.

MAKING FRIENDS

Over the years, I have developed "Montgomery's law," a rule of thumb about making friends when I move. It takes me three months just to know in which aisle to find the cereal in the grocery store. It takes six months to find new doctors and dentists. It takes a year before I can go to the grocery store and expect that maybe I'll see someone I know. When that happens, I know that I am now a part of the community.

Making friends in a new place takes effort, no matter how "friendly" the community that you've chosen. As one acquaintance who has recently relocated says, "In the beginning, people will invite the newcomer over for drinks or dinner. Then you return the invitation. Now you are acquainted, but it's not until you roll up your sleeves—volunteer at the hospital or take part in the political campaign or head up a committee for the garden club—that you develop real friendships."

RETIRING ABROAD

Retiring abroad is a popular fantasy. It conjures up images of beachfront homes bought for a song and a cost of living that would make even Scrooge rejoice, or perhaps living in an old world European city and having your own table in the café on the park. Having relocated to London and lived there for fifteen years before returning to the United States, I can vouch for the fact that living abroad can be a wonderful experience. It also requires careful research and planning. I spent about two years planning to relocate abroad.

In addition to the considerations that this article has already addressed, retiring abroad means looking at the following:

- Residency requirements. What are the residency requirements regarding foreign residents of the country you want to move to?
- Employment restrictions. In addition to residency requirements, some countries place restrictions on whether you are allowed to work. If you are thinking that it would be nice to pick up some extra income, this is something you need to investigate beforehand.
- Taxes. You need to understand your tax obligations both in the country you plan to move to and in the United States. U.S. citizens who live abroad still must file U.S. returns and report foreign income.
- Banking. It is advisable to maintain your bank account(s) in the United States for pension income, Social Security, and so on. Open a local account for day-to-day checking and bank transactions.
- Real estate. If you plan to purchase a home, you may find that real estate practices are very different to those in the United States.
- Medical care. What is available and what are you eligible for? Medicare does not cover the cost of treatment outside the United States. In addition to health insurance, you may need to consider purchasing medical evacuation insurance.
- Travel costs. Don't forget to factor in how often you expect to come back to the states and how much it will cost you.
- Expatriate status Is there an expatriate community where you are planning to move? Do you want to be an expatriate, or do you want to become part of the local community? Even though London has a large and active American expatriate community, I knew when I moved there that I wanted to live a British life and I worked hard to form friendships with Brits.

Barry Golson (2010) suggests seven questions to ask yourself if you are thinking of moving abroad:

- Have you thoroughly researched your target country and traveled there at least two or three times? I did extensive research on life in the UK and had traveled there at least five times. As a result, there were not too many surprises once I arrived.

- Have you examined what it will mean to be away from family? I found that much of my holiday time and money was spent coming home to visit family. I traveled less in Europe than I thought I would when I moved to London.
- Are you patient? Do things roll off your back? Life in the rest of the world tends not to move at the pace Americans are accustomed to. In Latin countries, the "mañana effect" can be aggravating to Americans.
- Are you willing to learn a new language? Unless you can speak the language reasonably well, you will find it difficult to make friends.
- Are you willing to be in a minority? You will, after all, be the foreigner.
- Have you asked yourself what you are willing to do without? My home in London was quite small by U.S. standards, and I did not have a car. From my perspective, my standard of living was perhaps a bit lower but my quality of life was higher than in the United States.
- Are you really cut out for a life-changing adventure? Because living abroad almost certainly will be.

CONCLUSION

Relocating can open new doors in retirement. You can improve your quality of life, make new friends, and explore places you have never been. In my experience, it takes time to settle in after any move, and you may have second thoughts or doubts. But if you have done your research carefully and looked honestly at what is right for you, relocating can help to make retirement your best years yet.

REFERENCES

Best places to retire. 2010. *U.S. News & World Report.* http://money.usnews.com/money/retirement/best-places-to-retire (accessed September 20, 2010).

Brandon, Emily. 2009. 8 tips for an affordable retirement abroad. *U.S. News & World Report*, April 6. http://money.usnews.com/money/retirement/articles/2009/04/06/8-tips-for-an-affordable-retirement-abroad.html (accessed September 20, 2010).

Brock, Fred. 2004. *Retire on less than you think: The New York Times guide to planning your financial future.* New York: Times Books, 80, 92–93.

Creative Retirement Exploration Weekend (CREW). North Carolina Center for Creative Retirement. http://www2.unca.edu/ncccr/programs/crew/index .html (accessed September 20, 2010).

Cullinane, Jan, and Cathy Fitzgerald. 2004. *The new retirement: The ultimate guide to the rest of your life.* Emmaus, PA: Rodale Books.

Del Webb. 2010. 2010 Del Webb baby boomer survey. Bloomfield Hills, MI: PulteGroup. http://dwboomersurvey.com/ (accessed September 20, 2010).

Golson, Barry. 2010. Paradise found: Five fun affordable, stunningly beautiful places to retire abroad." *AARP The Magazine,* August, 55.

Golson, Barry, and Thia Golson. 2008. *Retirement without borders: How to retire abroad—In Mexico, France, Italy, Spain, Costa Rica, Panama, and other sunny, foreign places (and the secret to making it happen without stress).* New York: Scribner.

Hartocollis, Anemona. 2010. A fast-paced city tries to be a gentler place to grow old. *The New York Times,* July 18, 2010. http://www.nytimes.com/2010/07/19/ nyregion/19aging.html?_r=1&ref=anemona_hartocollis (accessed September 20, 2010).

Kiplinger Washington Editors. Best cities 2009: It's all about jobs. *Kiplinger.com.* http://www.kiplinger.com/reports/best-cities/ (accessed September 20, 2010).

Peddicord, Kathleen. 2010. *How to retire overseas: Everything you need to know to live well (for less) abroad.* New York: Hudson Street Press.

Quilty, Susan. Halfback retirees: Why relocated retirees return halfway home. *Retirement communities—55 plus active adult community guide.* http:// www.55places.com (accessed September 20, 2010).

Retirement relocation reflections (weather, moving, community, states). City-Data Forum. http://www.city-data.com/forum/retirement/157833-retirement -relocation-reflections.html (accessed September 20. 2010).

Rosenbloom, Stephanie. 2010. But will it make you happy. *The New York Times,* August 7, 2010. http://www.nytimes.com/2010/08/08/business/08consume .html?ref=stephanie_rosenbloom (accessed September 20, 2010).

Ruffenach, Glenn. 2009. Making suburbia more livable. *The Wall Street Journal,* September 19, 2009. http://online.wsj.com/article/SB100014240529702036 74704574330801650897252.html (accessed August 9, 2010).

Smith, Ralph. 2005. When you retire, should you move? *FedSmith.com,* April 21. http://www.fedsmith.com/articles/articles.printformat.db .php?intArticleID=544 (accessed September 8, 2010).

Stone, Marika, and Howard Stone. 2004. *Too young to retire—101 ways to start the rest of your life.* New York: Plume.

24

FINDING THE PERFECT PLACE TO RETIRE

Jeanne Munn Bracken

MY HUSBAND HAS already retired twice: once from a twenty-year career in the Coast Guard and then from another twenty years of working for a local business. By the time this reaches print, I will also be retired after more than forty years working as a librarian. We have enjoyed some travel and have often played the what-if game when visiting an especially appealing place.

We have lived in Massachusetts for decades, although we were both raised elsewhere: my husband in Colorado and me in upstate New York and New Hampshire. We have lived in the same house since 1972. Obviously, we like being settled and don't do change well (as elementary school teachers always told us about our daughters).

Economically we thought it would be difficult, if not impossible, to stay in our home, and frankly we weren't sure we wanted the upkeep hassles. Also, the flights of stairs up to the bedrooms and down to the laundry become more daunting as we age.

So we looked around. Our first glimmer was Cape Cod, where we have vacationed many times. The slightly milder climate and lower housing prices appealed to us, and the Cape is often listed in books as a retirees' mecca. On further thought, we realized we were judging the Cape from mostly an off-season perspective, and for the warmer months of the year the popular vacation destination has horrendous traffic both to the region and on the streets and byways of the charming villages.

Over the years, too, we saw a big jump in growth leading to urban-type sprawl throughout much of the area.

Our next what-if destination was Martha's Vineyard. By then we were thinking more about the retirement experience. Living on an island sounded romantic and intriguing, and Martha's Vineyard has a thriving literary community that appealed to my inner writer. Housing costs for moderate residences sounded within reach, but the summer traffic was even worse than that on Cape Cod. We were also concerned about health care, since we both have medical concerns and would be dependent on a ferry schedule (not to mention weather) for services beyond basic medicine.

Then the real pie-in-the-sky idea hit us: the Kenai Peninsula of Alaska. We had visited a couple of times and loved it for its beauty, its laid-back atmosphere, and its off-the-beaten-path location. That idea was short-lived, though, when we considered the winters. The cold didn't daunt us, since the proximity to saltwater gentles the frigid temperatures of, say, Fairbanks, but the long, dark hours of December and January did give us pause. Too, we felt that the frontier life was a poor match for our semi-sedentary lifestyle.

Since we have vacationed in Maine many times over the past decades and have explored its coast and interior from Kittery (outlet malls) to Eastport and the Lewiston-Auburn area, we thought the Pine Tree State would be a good, new home for us. It was relatively close to family and good friends, housing costs were more affordable for us, and we reasoned that we could handle the harsh winter (no worse than what we've been used to in Metro-West Boston) by using our travel funds to spend a few weeks in Florida during the worst of the winter. And failing that, as retirees we would not have to deal with the bad weather on a daily basis; we could just sit tight until the roads were clear.

We drove around southwestern Maine looking at towns and decided on an area, began our research, and were about to contact a Realtor when I realized the economic implications: Maine would tax our pensions, where many other states would not. Reluctantly, we crossed the Pine Tree State off our list.

Time to get real. In the icy February of 2006, we visited close friends who have a winter home on the Space Coast of Florida. Leaving behind treacherous driveways and streets, we luxuriated in warm weather and really understood for the first time the concept of snowbirds. We spent part of our visit studying real estate ads, meeting a Realtor, and visiting open houses. We were hooked. Since summers can be oppressive in Florida, we reasoned that the cheaper housing and other costs would allow us to continue with our seasonal visits to Maine—the best of both worlds!

We came home and announced that I would be retiring in 2010 and that our daughters had four years to make plans for their independence. They rallied beautifully and now are well-established adults, living in an adjacent town. Meanwhile, we researched communities on Florida's east coast and narrowed our choices to a few towns just outside the bigger cities. Thinking about what we wanted, we discovered excellent libraries, cultural events, spring training baseball, health care services, and even a promising church. We had good friends in the area. Our concern about hurricanes was trumped by our loathing of snow, ice, sleet, and freezing temperatures. The plan seemed like a keeper.

No epiphany occurred to alter our Florida strategy. Rather, we began to think about retirement in more depth, taking into consideration the stories we had heard about snowbirds who moved "back home" when faced with serious illness or the loss of a partner. A national newspaper article about one of our targeted condominium complexes also gave us pause, reporting that the snowbirds from the Midwest and from the Northeast, for example, kept to themselves and didn't mix very much. Too, the rapid growth of the state concerned us, with potential for water shortages in the near future. Florida, we ultimately decided, was off our list.

Still thinking to leave the New England winter behind, we settled on North Carolina. For the better part of a year, we read up on different regions in the state, studied real estate listings, signed up for daily news feeds from a major area newspaper, and pored over maps of the Tarheel State. We figured we could avoid the hot and humid summers by spending time in Maine. We discovered good bookstores and libraries, favorite chain restaurants and retail stores, and some towns with attractive amenities. We liked the real change of seasons that Florida lacks.

Again, no major revelation negated the North Carolina plan. We just realized that the state is a long way from our family and friends. My husband isn't very gregarious, so I would have to form new relationships and develop a support system. I was bemused to discover that the locals call Cary, a Raleigh-Durham area town, the "containment area for retired Yankees." The rapid growth of the state also concerned us a little, but it was really the isolation from our loved (and liked) ones that put paid to the notion.

Since our family and friends are primarily in New England, we sought an alternative location in the Northeast that would fit our needs. As a graduate of the University of New Hampshire at Durham, I was somewhat familiar with the seacoast region of the Granite State. Shifting focus, we started to research the cities and towns in that area. Portsmouth has a thriving historic and cultural scene, our unusual health care system (active only in four areas of the country) was available there, the variety in housing was attractive, we would be an hour's drive from the towns where we have lived and worked for decades, and we had close friends in the area.

We chose Exeter, a lovely small town with a private school, lots of cultural and social possibilities, an excellent health club, varied affordable housing opportunities, access to our health care system, and a location central to friends in three states. We drove around Exeter, talked with real estate professionals, and studied housing opportunities online. Then, just a few months before we planned to put our house on the market, we discovered the perfect condominium: a restored historic house with one-floor living, a garage, a deck, a small yard, pet friendly atmosphere, and walking distance to downtown and the health club.

The next step was to contact our Realtor friend, who stopped by to evaluate our current home, suggest simple upgrades and steps to make it more attractive for sale, and get some idea of our financial situation. Although prices and demand for houses in our area had fallen, we were not overly concerned because a huge multinational corporation would be moving hundreds of employees into a new complex a couple of miles from our house.

It was therefore a shock for us to discover that houses similar to ours had gone into foreclosure, dropping the value of our home. And in this economic climate, those houses that sell are what our friend called "the bright shiny pennies" on the market—places without blemishes, perfect and ready for a new owner to move in and settle right down. We had expected to do some painting and other cosmetic upgrades, but there was a lot more than that required: landscaping, major decluttering, some utility upgrades, and more. Our reality check indicated we would not be able to comfortably do the work, sell the house, and move within the time frame, especially since I would still be working full-time and finishing up and promoting my new book. The final disappointment was that we could not afford the "perfect" Exeter condo either.

In 1972 when we bought the house, we had spent hour after hour doing the math. We could not really afford the house, but we were optimists, and we turned out to be right. All these years later, we were doing the math again. Could we afford to stay put at least until the market improved, taking our time to do the upgrades and fixes? We have decided to give it a try, and in the months since making that decision, we have watched similar houses in our neighborhood languish on the market without selling. We also weathered a nightmare street reconstruction project that would have sent potential buyers running—if they were able to get here in the first place. We have begun new landscaping and some home improvements, secure in the knowledge that we have time to do things well.

So for the foreseeable future, we are retiring in place. We realized that the home we've lived in and loved for so many years still is right for us for now. Some day, when the time comes to really sell the house, we will probably stay in this community that has been right for us all along.

Ironically, the North Carolina drawback—lack of a support system—has turned around. Among the influx of new North Carolinians are a high school friend, some of my cousins, and several close friends. Still, we're comfortable with our choice, especially staying close to our daughters.

Throughout the process of choosing our best place for retirement, I used all my reference librarian skills to mine information about our various potential locations. Of course, the Internet played a major role, since print sources are quickly outdated. All of the advice we give patrons to evaluate resources applies:

- Who put the data online?
- How current is it?
- How reliable is the source?
- How biased is the source?

Other things we thought about: In evaluating potential new home locations, don't forget to check out types of Internet access, cell phone service availability, utility costs, and other less-advertised but important services. Maps of coverage areas on the different cellular providers' websites seem to be accurate, judging by our experiences when traveling.

While the Internet is a useful tool, it warms the heart of this older librarian to report that books—real printed books!—were also important in our research. While there are probably hundreds of books on the topic of retirement and the best place to live, I found these most helpful.

The Basics

- *What Color Is Your Parachute? for Retirement,* 2nd ed., by John E. Nelson and Richard N. Bolles (Berkeley: Ten Speed Press, 2010). This guide to "the new retirement" carries on where Bolles's familiar job-hunting guide leaves off.
- The American Association of Retired Persons website: www.aarp.org. The AARP really does provide a wealth of interesting information in

their publications and online. Reprints of articles from their magazine are accessible online, for example, the annual "Best Places to Live" feature and tax information by state.

- www.bestplaces.com. This website has a lot of links to Internet information: Looking for the cheapest place to retire? A gay-friendly town? A new home outside the Unites States? Start here and click away. The websites are all commercial, but the content is interesting and varied.

- Another great source is www.bestplaces.net. Oh, the difference between the .com and the .net sites! The latter has excellent comparisons of locations in terms of climate, economy, cost of living, and other factors. I was able to compare the town where we now live with Exeter, New Hampshire, even though both are small towns. But beware: this website is addictive. The data is drawn from valid, up-to-date sources, both governmental and private. The "Find Your Best Place" quiz is fun and revealing; the top results I got included the area where I was born and raised, the area where I have lived for forty years, and Exeter!

Financial Sources

- *State Tax Handbook* (Chicago: Commerce Clearinghouse, 2010). This annual publication shows how the various states tax specific types of income and other assets, clearly laid out in table format with plenty of detail so you can compare those that tax Social Security benefits, pensions, and other forms of income.

- www.taxadmin.org. This is the website of the Federation of Tax Administrators, with some comparison tables of various state tax collections and links to other related web resources.

- *America's Best Low Tax Retirement Towns,* 3rd ed., by Eve Evans and Elizabeth Niven (Houston: Vacation Publications, 2008). This fact-packed book lists state-by-state the tax implications for different income levels and notes Tax Havens and Tax Hells for each, with a brief discussion of top retirement towns.

Relocation Sources

- *The Comparative Guide to American Suburbs,* 5th ed. (Millerton, NY: Grey House Publications, 2009–2010). This quadrennial publication is a quick and easy look at suburban areas around the United States.

- *America's Top-Rated Small Towns & Cities: A Statistical Handbook* (Armenia, NY: Grey House Publications, 2010). This title rates smaller locations with populations ranging from 3,000 to 25,000 for various quality-of-life factors,
- www.relocateamerica.com. This website is a commercial site with uneven listings and heavy advertising, but the basic real estate information might be a helpful place to compare interesting locations.
- *Retirement without Borders,* Barry Golson (New York: Simon and Schuster, 2008). Golson has lived in several foreign countries, so his book is a knowledgeable source of information for those thinking of moving outside the United States.
- www.internationalliving.com. The International Living website provides a lot of information on living abroad in all areas of the world. Some of the material carries a price, but a great deal of it is free. Sign up for regular (roughly, daily) "postcards" with tips and deals on living in different countries. International Living also has a Facebook presence.
- http://retirementliving.com. The Retirement Living Information Center calls itself "The Gateway to Resources for Senior Living." One link has an excellent explanation of taxation of senior citizens for each state. To access some information you must join and pay a fee, but other links are free.
- www.tripadvisor.com. Trip Adviser is a service of the online travel giant Expedia and was created so travelers could share good and bad experiences. That said, most locations have discussions that link locals or regular visitors with folks seeking information on a city or town. As with other online content, the site provides individual opinions, some of which might not agree with yours.

Local Information

- www.earth.google.com. One of the niftiest websites is downloadable for free. There is a bit of a learning curve, but the site is really fun and informative. Check out your potential new homes by neighborhood. See how close you really would be to the interstate, golf course, and so on, but beware: Google Earth is also addictive.
- Sign on for a daily news feed from a local or area newspaper.
- http://factfinder.census.gov. Get facts and figures from the U.S. Census Bureau website. Enter a zip code of interest and American Factfinder will

give you a snapshot of the demographics of the area, including population, social, economic, and housing characteristics. As of this writing, the data is still based on the 2000 census.

- Look at the town's website. Look for entertainment and educational opportunities and places of worship. See what services are provided for seniors: transportation to shopping and medical appointments, trips, exercise classes, lifelong learning opportunities, and social or game groups.
- www.publiclibraries.com. Check out the library link for a town you are investigating.
- http://hospitalcompare.hhs.gov. Get ratings of local health care services when you enter a zip code to generate a list of hospitals within twenty-four miles. Then compare the institutions for various factors from cleanliness to mortality rates for some conditions.
- http://data.medicare.gov. This health site is tricky to search but provides interesting data regarding the quality of services to Medicare patients.
- *Congressional Districts in the 2000s: A Portrait of America.* (Washington, DC: CQ Press, 2003). Since politics can make strange bedfellows, you might want to spend some time poking through publication. This stellar volume breaks down the different districts around the country, giving a great sense of how your potential new neighbors might have voted.

Entertainment

- *Leisureville; Adventures in America's Retirement Utopias,* by Andrew D. Blechman (New York: Atlantic Monthly Press, 2008). This somewhat sobering discussion of senior gated communities in the Sun Belt is interesting to read. While the lifestyle might not appeal to all retirees, I have a friend who lives in one of the places and loves it.
- *Early Bird,* by Rodney Rothman (New York: Simon and Schuster, 2005). Rothman found himself between jobs and decided at the age of 28 to move into a Florida retirement community and check out the lifestyle. His book is a lot of fun to read, very amusing, and occasionally touching.

Clearly all this research is time-consuming, but most of us will spend many years in our new homes, so the process of picking the right place is worth the effort. And for librarians it's also fun.

CONTRIBUTORS

CAROL SMALLWOOD, volume editor, received her MLS from Western Michigan University and her MA in History from Eastern Michigan University. She edited two ALA anthologies in 2010: *Writing and Publishing: The Librarian's Handbook* and *Librarians as Community Partners: An Outreach Handbook*. She also compiled and edited the 2011 ALA anthologies *The Frugal Librarian: Thriving in Tough Economic Times* and *Library Management Tips That Work*. Her magazine credits include *The Writer's Chronicle*, *English Journal*, and *American Libraries*. Ms. Smallwood's library experience has been in the areas of school, public, academic, and special libraries, and she has served as both administrator and consultant.

PATRICIA H. ATWOOD, ASA, helps people document the value of objects. An Accredited Senior Appraiser of the American Society of Appraisers, Atwood has degrees from Cornell and Princeton. She appraises antiques and decorative arts as well as clocks and furniture, and she also has experience with unusual collections. Working mostly in the Chicago area and southern Wisconsin, Atwood has been a featured speaker at national conferences and has appeared on the PBS show *History Detectives*. Contact www.timelyantiqueappraisals .com (or American Society of Appraisers www.appraisers.org).

LOUISE "LU" F. BENKE, former Lead Librarian for Children's Services at Poudre River Public Library District, Fort Collins, Colorado, obtained her MALS from the University of Chicago. Lu is a member of the American Library Association, Association of Library Services for Children, Public Library Association, Colorado Association of Libraries, and Colorado Libraries for Early Literacy. She has published in *Colorado Libraries* and presented at the Colorado Association of Libraries conferences. Lu is currently enrolled in the Master of Arts program in reading at the University of Northern Colorado.

JENNIFER BOXEN is the Senior Medical Librarian for the Florida Atlantic University Charles E. Schmidt College of Medicine, Boca Raton, Florida. After an earlier career in the lending industry, she received her MLS from Clarion University of Pennsylvania. Jennifer is a member of the American Library Association, the Association of College and Research Libraries, and the Medical Library Association. She has previously appeared in *The Reference Librarian* and has presented at both the Medical Library Association Annual Conference and the Conference on College Composition and Communication.

MARIA A. BRUNO, CFP®, is an investment analyst in Vanguard Investment Strategy Group. Ms. Bruno's areas of expertise include portfolio construction and financial planning, with concentrations in retirement income and wealth management. She is a featured expert for webcasts and podcasts and has authored several white papers on various aspects of retirement. Ms. Bruno has more than twenty years of experience in the financial services industry, including ten years in financial planning and advice. She holds the Certified Financial Planner™ designation and earned a BSBA from Villanova University.

RENEE B. BUSH, Head of Collection Management Services, Health Sciences Library, University at Buffalo, Buffalo, New York, obtained her MLS from the University at Buffalo. Her work has appeared in *Research Strategies, Science & Technology Libraries,* and research journals in the field of biomaterials. Renee received the SUNY Chancellor's Award for Excellence in Librarianship and is a Distinguished Member of Special Libraries Association's Biomedical and Life Sciences Division. She has volunteered with the Iroquois National Wildlife Refuge since 2002 and developed service projects that have been supporting local shelters for several years.

JAMES B. CASEY has been director of the Oak Lawn Public Library in the southwest suburban Chicago community since 1992. He holds a PhD in librarianship from Case Western Reserve University (1985), an MLS from SUNY Geneseo (1973), and an MA in history from Cleveland State University (1979). He has worked in public libraries since 1973. Dr. Casey has served four terms on ALA Council and received the Librarian of the Year award from Illinois Library Association in 2005. He is married to Diane Dates Casey, dean of the library at Governors State University, Illinois.

DOROTHEA J. COIFFE is assistant professor, media librarian and interlibrary loan librarian, and college archivist at the Borough of Manhattan Community College/CUNY, A. Philip Randolph Memorial Library in New York. She obtained her MSLIS from Pratt Institute and is a member of the ALA, Society of American Archivists, and the Library Association of CUNY. Coiffe wrote an entry in *The International Encyclopedia of Revolution & Protest,* and coauthored an article on online tutorials for *JLAMS.* Her current research focuses on the librarianship of online moving image sources for education.

SANDRA CORTESE, Circulation and Reference Librarian at Jonathan Bourne Public Library, Bourne, Massachusetts, since 1994 obtained her MBA, Health Care Administration, from Boston University and a Certificate of Librarianship from the Massachusetts Board of Library Commissioners. She is a certified SHIP (State Health Insurance Assistance Program) counselor and has received many honors from federal, state, and local officials for her work advising retirees. While she was an appointed delegate to the White House Conference on Aging, she helped to write the conference report on the Medicare drug plan.

SUSAN CAROL CURZON is the Dean Emeritus, University Library, at California State University, Northridge. Susan obtained her M.Libr. from the University of Washington and her PhD in Public Administration from the University of Southern California. She was *Library Journal's* 1993 Librarian of the Year. Susan is the author of *Managing Change* (Neal-Schuman, 2005) and *Managing the Interview* (Neal-Schuman, 1995) and coedited *Proven Strategies for Building an Information Literacy Program* (Neal-Schuman, 2007). She has written articles and given speeches extensively on library management, libraries of the future, disaster restoration, and information literacy.

DONALD G. FRANK is professor emeritus at Portland State University. He has participated in administrative positions in libraries at Texas Tech University, the University of Arizona, Harvard University, the Georgia Institute of Technology, and Portland State University. A member of the Association of College and Research Libraries (in ALA), he coauthored the 2001 Reference Service Press award-winning article published in *Reference & User Services Quarterly.* His current research interests include leadership, reference services, government information, the ACRL presidents, and baseball as social history.

BRIAN FRICKE, CFP®, is recognized as "America's Retirement Expert." He is the author of *Worry Free Retirement: Do What You Want, When You Want, Where You Want* (Advantage Media Group, 2008). Brian and his company have been named "Top Wealth Manager" by *Wealth Manager Magazine,* "Top Financial Planning Firm" by *Orlando Business Journal,* and "Top Financial Advisor" by *Financial Advisor Magazine.* Website: www.BrianFricke .com; phone: 1–800–393–1017; e-mail info@fmcretire.com; Financial Management Concepts, 1700 Town Plaza Court, Winter Springs, FL 32708.

BRETT HAMMOND is TIAA-CREF's ambassador on issues relating to the economy, financial markets, and long-term investing. His responsibilities include asset allocation modeling, economic and market commentary, and investment product research. While at TIAA-CREF, he has helped develop target-date portfolios, financial advice services, and a non-profit pension investment consortium. Mr. Hammond received BA degrees in economics and political science from the University of California at Santa Cruz and a PhD from the Massachusetts Institute of Technology. He has published over thirty articles and books about finance, higher education, and public policy.

STEVE HENICK, BA, MBA, of Rodis & Henick, LLC, is a seasoned businessman who has been recognized both for his business acumen and his ability to develop understanding and consensus among diverse groups. He is certified by the Maryland Council for Dispute Resolution and mediates for the Maryland Circuit and District Courts and the Commission on Human Relations. His mediation experience includes issues of the aging population, family and business disputes, torts, and discrimination complaints. Steve is an Adjunct Associate Professor at the University of Maryland University College.

JANET HUSBAND, retired director of Cohasset, Massachusetts Public Library, obtained her MLS from Rutgers, the State University of New Jersey. She is a member of ALA and the Massachusetts Library Association, having served as secretary and newsletter editor. Janet is the author of *Sequels: An Annotated Guide to Novels in Series* (ALA, 2009). She and her husband Jonathan created www.*eSequels.com,* the online version of *Sequels.* She contributed to *Writing and Publishing: The Librarian's Handbook* (ALA, 2010).

SHIRLEY LEWIS, past president of the Canadian School Library Association, obtained her BLS from the University of Toronto in 1958. She was employed in public libraries as chief librarian and director, and was a nursing science librarian at the University of Toronto. She coauthored *Nonbook Materials: Organization of Integrated Collections* (Canadian Library Association, 1969), and edited *Ten Terrific Titles* and *Current Canadiana.* Shirley owned and operated Shirley Lewis Information Services and MOD Publications until her retirement. She is currently the executive director of the Children of Ethiopia Education Fund.

DAHLMA LLANOS-FIGUEROA obtained her MLS from Queens College of the City University of New York after teaching English for many years, and served as a young adult librarian for the New York City Department of Education until her retirement in 2004. Dahlma was selected as one of two runner-ups for the *2009 PEN America Bingham Fellowship for Writers* for her first novel, *Daughters of the Stone* (St. Martin's Press, 2009). You can contact Dahlma through her website at www.llanosfigueroa.com.

RITA MARSALES, retired as Preservation Librarian from Fondren Library, Rice University in Houston Texas, after more than forty years. She currently works nineteen hours a week for the Library of the Menil Collection, a world-famous art museum. She obtained her MLS from the University of Texas in Austin and her Master of Art History from Rice University. She was active in ALA for many years and belonged to the Texas Library Association and Art Libraries Society of North America. Over the years she has had much experience at part-time library jobs.

SUSAN MONTGOMERY, recently retired Knowledge Manager at A.T. Kearney Inc., received her MLIS from Rutgers University. She is a member of the Special Libraries Association and the Institute for Supply Management. She won the H. W. Wilson Award for her article, "Writing an RFP for Information Products" (*Information Outlook,* June 2006). While working in London, Susan founded the ASLIB Information Resources Management Network (now NetIKX) and caught the English bug for gardening, which she plans to do more of in retirement.

JEANNE MUNN BRACKEN was a reference librarian for over forty years (MSLS Simmons 1971). She retired from the Lincoln (MA) Public Library, where she was honored in 2005 as a New York Times Librarian of the Year and is now a freelance writer. Her book, *Children with Cancer: A Comprehensive Reference Guide for Parents*, was published in 2010 by Oxford University Press. Jeanne has edited curriculum enrichment titles in American history, written a corporate history, and compiled a collection of columns from her local newspaper, where she was known as "Littleton's Erma Bombeck" for twenty-two years.

SHARON NOTTINGHAM retired from the Liverpool (NY) Public Library after working for both the Onondaga County (NY) Public Library and Liverpool (NY) Public Library. She has an MSLS from Syracuse University and experience in public relations and administration for public libraries. She has written articles, book reviews, and weekly columns that have been published in *AIIP Connections,* the magazine of the Association of Independent Information Professionals, *NYLA Bulletin,* and other local publications. She is currently the owner of Nottingham Information Services, a research and writing business based in Florida.

ROSE PARKMAN MARSHALL retired as Library Instruction Coordinator from the University of South Carolina–Aiken. She received her MLIS from the University of Alabama, and her poetry appears in *Go, Tell Michelle: African American Women Write to the New First* (SUNY Press, 2008) and *Out of the Rough: Women's Poems of Survival and Celebration* (Novello Festival Press, 2001). She has articles in *Mississippi Libraries* and the sixth edition of *Your College Experience: Strategies for Success* (Thompson, 2005).

MARY REDMOND, former Principal Librarian for Public Services at the New York State Library (NYSL), retired in 2007. During her twenty-five years at the NYSL, she headed units in legislative/governmental services, public and technical services, and library operations. She also served as interim director of the Research Library for four years. She is a member of the American Library Association and the New York Library Association. As the volunteer Special Liaison for the New York State Library, she serves on the Friends of the NYSL Board and assists with special projects.

CAROLYN J. RODIS, JD, MA, is certified by the Maryland Council on Dispute Resolution and mediates for the Maryland circuit and district courts. She is a cofounder of Senior Mediation and Decision-Making, Inc., a nonprofit providing training, education, and program development in the area of elder mediation. She has trained mediators and aging services providers since 2001. A former public interest lawyer, Carolyn was a chair of the Elder Section of the Association for Conflict Resolution and chairs its Training Standards Committee.

ROBERTA STEVENS has been on leave since August 2010 to serve as the 2010–2011 President of the American Library Association. Prior to her presidency, she managed the National Book Festival, which began in 2001 as a collaborative effort of the Library of Congress and then First Lady Laura Bush. The festival now includes President Barack Obama and First Lady Michelle Obama as its honorary cochairs. In addition to project management, Ms. Stevens has handled fundraising responsibilities for the Library of Congress.

JENNIFER TANG, Serials/Acquisitions Librarian at Hostos Community College Library, Bronx, New York, received her MLIS from Pratt Institute and MFA from Hunter College. Her background includes six years as a public relations writer. She is a member of the American Libraries Association and New York Technical Services Librarians Association. Her articles have appeared in library journals such as *Collection Building* as well as in periodicals such as *Newsweek*, the *Los Angeles Times*, *Fitness Magazine*, and on Popmatters.com.

LINDA BURKEY WADE obtained her MLIS from Dominican University in River Forest, Illinois, and earned an MS in Instructional Design from Western Illinois University (WIU). Wade has appeared in the *Journal of Interlibrary Loan, Document Delivery, & Electronic Reserve*. She is the Unit Coordinator of Digitization at the WIU Libraries in Macomb, Illinois, and was recently elected to the Brown County Library Board. She received the 2010 Distinguished Service Award for innovation, dedication, and service from President Goldfarb of WIU.

INDEX

You may also be interested in

WRITING AND PUBLISHING
THE LIBRARIAN'S HANDBOOK
Edited by Carol Smallwood

"For those who are just getting started and looking for resources in writing and publishing, as well as those who are experienced and looking for some creative ideas and directions, this book is an excellent resource."—*Public Services Quarterly*

ISBN: 978-0-8389-0996-6
199 PGS / 8.5" × 11"

ORDER TODAY!

Mail in this order form or visit
ALASTORE.ALA.ORG

ALA Member # (Must provide to receive your discount.)

☐ home   ☐ organization

_____

E-MAIL ADDRESS (REQUIRED in case we have questions about your order.)

Daytime Phone

_____

Ship to

_____
NAME

_____
TITLE

_____
ORGANIZATION

_____
ADDRESS

_____
CITY   STATE   ZIP

METHOD OF PAYMENT

☐ Check or money order enclosed $_____
(Make payable to ALA)

☐ Bill my library, school or organization. (Only orders of $50 or more from
established organizational accounts can be billed.)

☐ Purchase Order #_____ (Only for billed orders to libraries, schools
or other organizations. First-time customers, please provide organizational purchase order.)

☐ VISA   ☐ MasterCard   ☐ American Express

☐☐☐☐ ☐☐☐☐ ☐☐☐☐ ☐☐☐☐
Credit Card Number

☐☐ / ☐☐
Exp. Date

_____
SIGNATURE

FEDERAL TAX I.D. NUMBER

_____
(Library, Bookstore)

ISBN	Title	qty.	unit price	10% Member discount*	total (qty. × unit price − discount)

METHOD OF SHIPPING

All orders are sent UPS Ground Service unless otherwise
specified*. For the following alternate shipping options,
call 1-866-SHOP ALA for a shipping quote.

☐ UPS 2nd Day Air (Cost plus $20)

☐ UPS Next Day Air (Cost plus $10)

*AK, HI, Puerto Rico, U.S. Virgin Islands, and Guam orders
must select UPS 2nd Day.

Keycode 382010

SHIPPING & HANDLING CHARGES WILL BE ADDED TO ALL ORDERS

Within the U.S.:
Up to $49.99 . . . . $9
$50 to $99.99. . . . . $11
$100 to $149.99. . . . . $13
$150 to $199.99. . . . . $14
$200 to $299.99. . . . . $15
$300 to $999.99. . . . . $20
$1,000+ . . . . .Call 866-776-7252

For bulk rates, call 800-545-2433, ext. 2427

subtotal _____

sales tax ** _____

shipping and handling
(see chart above) _____

order total _____

American Library Association
50 East Huron Street
Chicago, IL 60611

PLACE
STAMP
HERE

ALA Store
PO Box 932501
Atlanta, GA 31193-2501

TAPE
HERE